TOTAL GOLF

Previous works by Dr. O'Brien include:

INDUSTRIAL BEHAVIOR MODIFICATION: A LEARNING BASED APPROACH
TO BUSINESS MANAGEMENT
R. M. O'Brien, A. M. Dickinson, M. Rosow (Eds.)

TOTAL GOLF

A Behavioral Approach to Lowering Your Score and Getting More Out of Your Game

Thomas C. Simek, M.A.
WESTERN KENTUCKY UNIVERSITY

&

Richard M. O'Brien, Ph.D.
HOFSTRA UNIVERSITY

Illustrated by Phillip Jones

Photographs by George R. Schenk

DOUBLEDAY & COMPANY, INC., Garden City, New York
1981

BOOK DESIGN BY SYLVIA DEMONTE-BAYARD

Library of Congress Cataloging in Publication Data

Simek, Thomas C.
Total golf.

Bibliography: p. 205
Includes index.
1. Golf—Psychological aspects.   I. O'Brien,
Richard M., joint author.   II. Title.
GV979.P75S57   796.352'01
ISBN: 0-385-15404-6
Library of Congress Catalog Card Number 79–6086

ACKNOWLEDGMENTS

A good many people and institutions provided us with invaluable assistance in the preparation of this work. Our early research in this area would have been impossible without the assistance of several golf courses and professional teaching staffs. In particular we would like to thank the Williamsport Country Club and its head pro Bernie Krick and Old Westbury Golf and Country Club and their pros Jim Andrews and Bob Murphy.

Since research is the foundation of this book, we owe our greatest debt to those poor hacking souls who acted as subjects for our endeavors. Without their willingness to try something new this book never could have been written.

Preparation of the manuscript was aided materially by Joe Lewis, Jr. and Pam Sargent who served as models and by our photographer George R. Schenk. Mr. Schenk's generosity with his time and skills considerably lightened the task of producing this book. We would also like to thank Robert Kohl who provided a number of out-of-print books that we used in reviewing earlier golf instruction. Throughout the production of this manuscript we received valuable, intangible support from the Psychology Departments at both Western Kentucky University and Hofstra University.

At the final stages of preparation the authors were helped considerably by Dave Rife, who kindly served as the manuscript reader. Our efforts were also aided by Joseph Gonzalez and the staff at Doubleday who solved all of the editorial "disasters" that we conjured up. It also seems appropriate to thank Jeff Nevid who initially directed us to Doubleday for this project.

Finally, we received immeasurable support from our families during the preparation of this manuscript. Mr. and Mrs. Charles Simek, the parents of the first author and both veteran players, provided emotional support, critical commentary, and financial backing throughout our work on this book in addition to financing the first author's education. Their efforts are most appreciated. The wife (Annette) and children (Elena and Janine) of the second author also provided emotional support while this manuscript was in preparation. In addition they endured the frequent absences of the male member of the household with understanding, and fed and nurtured the authors through many interminable writing sessions. It is very unlikely that this book would have been completed without the support of these important people and we are grateful for their patience.

T.C.S.
R.M.O'B.

CONTENTS

TOTAL GOLF

I

Behaviorally Based Golf: Learning from Green to Tee

TABLE 1

Complete Golf Chain and Mastery Criterion.

Step	Shot	Mastery Criterion
1	10-inch putt (between clubs optional)	4 putts consecutively holed
2	16-inch putt (between clubs optional)	4 putts consecutively holed
3	2-foot putt clubs removed	4 putts consecutively holed
4	3-foot putt	4 putts consecutively holed
5	4-foot putt some break	2 holed, 2 out of 4 within 6 inches
6	6-foot putt	4 consecutively within 6 inches
7	10-foot putt	4 consecutively within 12 inches
8	15-foot putt	4 consecutively within 15 inches
9	20-foot putt	4 consecutively within 18 inches
10	30-foot putt	4 consecutively within 24 inches
11	35-foot chip 5 feet off green 7-iron	4 out of 6 within 6 feet
12	35-foot chip 15 feet off green wedge	4 out of 6 within 6 feet
13	65-foot chip	4 out of 6 within 6 feet
14	25-yard pitch	4 out of 6 within 10 feet
15	35-yard pitch	4 out of 6 within 15 feet
16	50-yard pitch	4 out of 6 within 15 feet
17	75-yard shot	4 out of 6 within 30 feet
18	100-yard shot	4 out of 6 within 40 feet
19	125-yard shot	4 out of 6 within 45 feet
20	150-yard shot	4 out of 6 within 54 feet
21	175-yard shot	4 out of 6 within 66 feet
22	200-yard shot (if within your range)	4 out of 6 within 90 feet
23	Driver	See Chapter 5

1

An Introduction to the Mastery Chain

"The golf swing is muscle memory."
PATTY BERG

"The average golfer is capable of building a repeating swing and breaking 80 if he learns a small number of correct movements."

BEN HOGAN

The fact that you are reading this book suggests that you are interested either in learning golf or improving your current play. If you are just beginning you may consider yourself lucky. If you are already playing, it is our belief that the problems in your game probably stem from the fact that you were taught incorrectly. Whether you learned from your father, brother, spouse, college chum, or club pro, you undoubtedly began with a driver or five-iron and a bucket of balls on a practice tee of some kind. You then sliced, skied, or shanked that basket of balls in various directions, if you made contact at all. Throughout this ordeal, your friendly instructor would offer a variety of instructions amid mild but warm-hearted chuckles.

"Keep your head down!" "Keep your left arm straight!" "Take a full turn with your shoulders and a half-turn with your hips!" "Pause briefly at the top of your swing!" "Don't hurry!" "Slide your hips diagonally to the left to start your downswing!" "Now, swiftly slash your hands into the shot!" "No Peeking!" "Now remember: follow through in a high graceful finish!"

Whew! Is it any wonder that you couldn't learn to hit the ball straight? After that series of instructions you stood a better chance of throwing your back out than hitting the ball.

The full swing of a golf club has been measured at twenty-seven feet. You cannot hit consistently good shots if you are more than a fraction of an inch off line in any direction when you hit the ball. What are the odds that after swinging the club up over your head and back down you will make perfect contact with the ball? Pretty slim aren't they? Now figure that if you are an average golfer you are going to make that full backswing over thirty times during a round. It should come as no surprise to you that a large percentage of those shots fail to meet with your approval. In fact with the myriad instructions that you are asking your body to follow, it is amazing that anyone ever learns to hit the ball where he wants to with any consistency.

Although there have been many books on golf all advocating different techniques and appliances, the basic teaching method has not changed since the time of Old Tom Morris, in the early nineteenth century. Instruction has usually begun on the first tee or practice area with lectures on grip, stance, take away, backswing, downswing, and follow-through. Needless to say this highly complex series of responses was seldom quickly learned. When the novice begins to play, the typical result of this instruction is a series of whiffs ending in a topped or squibbed shot some forty yards down the fairway. At this point the novice is handed a long iron or fairway wood and asked to do what he has just proven himself incapable of doing with the ball teed up. Obviously the result is not likely to be any improvement on the tee shot. By the twelfth stroke, when the individual finally reaches the green, his instructor is likely to suggest that with a little practice the student will master the swing. This prediction is rarely borne out.

Thousands of swing theories have been developed over the years in an attempt to correct the inadequacies of previous theories. Unfortunately, each new theory of swing mechanics is taught in the same overly complex, unlearnable fashion. It is our contention that knowledge of the movements in the basic golf swing is as good as it needs to be. The failure has been in communicating this skill in a manner that can be easily learned. The way golf is currently taught, it is difficult to conceive of anyone learning to play the game competently. In fact, the percentage of people who do is quite small, since the average golfer shoots over 90 or one stroke a hole over par.

The premise of this book is that golf should be taught in the same manner as other complex skills. That is, the beginner should begin with the simplest actions and advance step by step to more intricate maneuvers as he masters the fundamentals. Scientists have found this the most efficient way of teaching any complex motor skill. More and more frequently people are turning to scientific techniques of behavior change, in business and industry (O'Brien, Dickinson, and Rosow, 1981) as well as in sports (Komaki and Barnett, 1977). In particular, the methods of behavioral psychology, as outlined by the renowned Harvard psychologist, B. F. Skinner (1953), seem to have wide application for mastering complex behavior. A behavioral psychologist looks at golf as a complex chain of responses from the long backswinged drive to the short putt. As in most other response chains, this should be taught by having the novice golfer begin with the simplest, and last, shot, the one closest to the reward of seeing the ball disappear into the cup. And that of course is the short putt.

The ten-inch putt is the shot on which you should begin to build your stroke. But the foundation must be firm. You must learn that putt to the point where your swing is perfectly grooved before you move on to a longer shot. That is the crux of the mastery-based instruction system presented in this book. In other words, you may not move on to the next step until you have demonstrated that you have mastered the previous skill. At the beginning, we require that an individual sink a specified number of consecutive "ten inchers" before he is allowed to try his luck at sixteen inches. From a behavioral perspective (Skinner, 1968) you learn what you do, so you must make the correct response over and over again until you master it and it becomes your normal way of swinging the club. This technique of not allowing the student to proceed until he has demonstrated competency on the previous, more fundamental step, is a primary component in much of modern educational technology. It has been exceptionally successful in programmed instruction, in industry (Nash, Muczyk, and Vettori, 1971) and the Personalized Systems Instruction approach to education (Keller, 1968; Johnson and Ruskin, 1977).

Doesn't it make sense to learn the simplest shot first? For instance when you teach your son to hit a baseball, you don't bring in Ron Guidry to blow his rising fastball by the child. When you took piano lessons you would have thought it absurd for the teacher to hand you a Chopin sonata for the first lesson. Similarly, in golf, it is unreasonable to begin by trying to hit two-hundred-fifty-yard drives. The full swing for a ten-inch putt is less than four inches long, whereas the full swing for a two-hundred-fifty-yard drive is some twenty-seven feet in length. What's more, you are likely to make some of those ten-inch putts and build your confidence. Trying to hit straight, two-hundred-fifty-yard drives is apt to result in failure and humiliation much more often than success and confidence. Our view is that the full swing can be attained if the golfer first masters the easier, short-backswinged, shots.

Traditional instruction handicaps the golfer from square one. Normally the student is shown or told how to hit a straight drive. Unfortunately, simply watching someone else perform a complex skill is not likely to help you learn how to do it. Just picture yourself learning to type by watching your secretary. Further, being told how to master the complex act of hitting a ball is of little benefit in getting your muscles to actually do it. As a baseball manager, Ted Williams told many ball players how to hit but no one has batted .400 since Ted Williams.

The golf swing is not an intellectual exercise. It is your muscles, not your mind, that must learn the correct action. The surest way to botch a stroke is to try to think your way through it. The correct action must be something that your muscles have learned to do automatically. Although they are often promoted,

5

demonstrations and verbal instructions can only help you identify what you are doing wrong. Your muscles will learn the correct response only by repeating the correct response many times. The reason it takes so long to learn to hit with the driver and long irons is that the correct muscular performance is so infrequent that it is not learned. Sinking ten-inch putts allows the muscles to repeat the same correct action over and over again. Thus, the basic unit of the stroke is correctly learned and you have the firm foundation on which to build the longer swing.

Suppose you slice your first drive one hundred twenty-five yards into the right rough. What did you do wrong? You don't know, do you? It could have been anything from tempo, to legwork, to hand-action. Learning requires knowledge of what was done right and what was done wrong. Even Sherlock Holmes would have difficulty discovering the interaction of things that went wrong on a bad drive. In fact, even the occasional good drive may just have been a fluke of different errors canceling each other out. By learning the less complex putt first it is easier to identify what was done correctly and what needs to be changed. Sinking the same putt over and over again allows you to stamp in the proper swing and tempo.

Now as a beginner picture yourself repeatedly sinking putts first from ten inches, then sixteen inches, and then two and three feet. Success feels good. It makes you want to continue playing. As you master each succeeding task your confidence grows. If you started on the tee, however, you are having a very different experience. The joy of watching that one good drive is rarely enough to make up for the humiliation and agony of the dribbles and hooks. As Bob Toski, currently golf's best-known teacher put it, "I'd like every beginner to start a foot from the cup. I'm convinced you'll get quicker results simply because everyone wants to see the ball go in the hole." (Toski, 1974)

There is one final reason for beginning with putting and mastering shots at increasing distance from the hole back to the tee. Putting involves learning a controlled, accurate stroke. The drive, on the other hand, must not only be accurate but powerful. It is a truism that the more you try for power the less accurate you are likely to be. In learning to drive you are at cross-purposes, fearing the loss of power for accuracy and vice versa. If you have learned backward from the green, your swing will be well established so that you can try for power while allowing your muscle memory to provide the accurate swing. You will have mastered that swing through putting, chipping, pitching, and ironwork before you try to drive for power. By learning putting first you put the emphasis on accuracy, where it belongs. In an interesting book, Nieporte and Sauers (1968) surveyed fifty top tournament pros on their views of the game. They found the pros considered putting accuracy and driving accuracy to be the most important skills a golfer could possess. Driving power finished well down in the rankings.

If the ten-inch, tap-in putt is the simplest shot in golf, it should be taught *and mastered* before trying the next easiest shot. This seems like simple common sense but a review of the golf literature suggests that such sense is anything but common. One person who seems to recognize the importance of putting is Gary Player. Player (1962) states that most tournament pros spend as much time on the practice putting green as they spend on the rest of their shots combined. Yet when golf professionals and teachers write books about golf, putting is usually given only a few pages after the rest of the game has been discussed. The typical table of contents reads: Grip, Stance, Backswing, Follow-through, Driver, Long Irons, Short Irons, Pitching, Chipping, Trouble Shots, and (finally) Putting. According to the late Tony Lema, putting accounts for 36 of the scratch player's 72 shots. Yet in his book, *Champagne Tony's Golf Tips* (Lema and Harvey, 1966) Lema devoted only 12 of 147 pages to putting. At the time of his death Lema was one of the best putters on the tour, but 50 percent of the score got less than 10 percent of his book. This represents the rule rather than the exception. Bobby Jones (1966), Ben Hogan (1948), Arnold Palmer (1967) and Chi Chi Rodriguez (1967) all relegate putting to less than 10 percent of their books' back pages. Things are even worse in women's golf. In a 200-page book, Sandra Haynie (1975) gives only 12 pages to putting but 15 pages to how to look and what to wear on the course. Books designed to teach golf to beginners also usually ignore the role of putting in developing a sound game. Perhaps the worst example in this category is *Sports Illustrated Book of Golf* (1970), a 73-page manual that introduces putting on page 73.

Even expert teachers often overlook the need to begin with the simplest stroke. Leslie King (1962), the noted English golf instructor, not only called putting "the most critical phase of the game" (p. 113), but also drew the connection between putting and all of the standard shots of golf. He also points out the role of putting in building confidence. With all this emphasis on putting, you might expect that he begins teaching swing, tempo, and form with the easy putt. He does not. He begins with the driver because "it is the longest and most difficult club to control" (p. 94). By that logic one would start a first-grader off reading Shakespeare or a description of nuclear fission.

Our method of mastering each shot as you proceed backward from the hole is new but it is not revolutionary. The role of putting in building confidence has long been recognized. Both Gary Player and Cary Middlecoff have argued that confidence in golf "occurs in a sort of reverse pattern from green to tee" (Editors of *Golf Digest,* 1973). Many of the game's greatest players have also recognized the role that putting plays in learning the tempo and feel of the swing. Billy Casper (Casper and Collett, 1961), the man that *Golf Magazine* picked as the All-American Putter for the first three years that it made such awards, begins his practice sessions by sinking several putts from two feet away. He then moves back to three feet and does the same thing. Casper believes that a player should spend twice as much time on short putts as on long ones. Even earlier than Casper, Tommy Armour, (1951), one of golf's great teachers, had outlined similar programs for practicing putting. Gary Player (1962) believes that "practicing full shots can destroy your touch, at least temporarily." He states that one should always start practice sessions with short shots in order to develop "rhythm in the swing" and "the feel of the club."

Casper and Player are talking about practice, and you may be wondering how that relates to learning the game. Essentially, practice is an attempt to remind your muscles to execute the correct action. It is a relearning of the proper swing. If starting with the short shots is the best way to relearn the proper swing, it is very likely to be the best way to learn it in the first place because muscle learning takes place through practice.

You may be convinced that our method is the best way to learn how to putt and still wonder how much putting is related to the rest of the game. In their book *All About Putting,* the Editors of *Golf Digest* state that ". . . experts agree . . . (that) the putting stroke is essentially a shortened version of the full swing" (p. 85). In the same book one of the tour's best-known putters, George Archer, takes a similar position: "Thus I see the putting stroke not as a variation of the basic golf stroke but as a miniature edition of it. The fundamentals of alignment, posture, and swing path that I apply with a driver or a 5-iron, I also apply on a smaller scale with the putter." Finally, listen to Jack Nicklaus describing his putting technique: "I try to putt through the ball the same as I try to hit through the ball on regular shots. If there is any one thing I concentrate on, it's contacting the ball with the solidest part of the putter, the sweetspot, just as I do with all the other clubs" (Nicklaus and Wind, 1969, p. 321).

Various experts see putting as involving all of the elements that make the longer swing successful. Perhaps the strongest statement comes from the strongest putter, the great putting hustler, George Low, who has been known to win putting matches using the instep of his foot instead of a club. In trying to correct one of the most common misconceptions in putting, Low stated: "A putt is a miniature golf swing. It starts back straight but then follows its natural tendency to come inside, just as the full swing with a driver comes inside" (Editors of *Golf Digest,* 1973).

The teacher of golf who comes closest to our teaching method is Bob Toski, who began putting when he was five years old. Twenty-five years ago when everyone was starting with the five-iron or the driver, Toski (1955) was advising beginners to start with chipping. Toski's sophistication about how people learn is impressive. Without formal psychological training, he has the skilled eye to discover principles, as he applies them. Like many others before him, he realized the importance of having his students experience correct shots so that they could duplicate the feel of the correct swing. In *The Touch System for Perfect Golf,* Toski (1971) assessed the question perfectly when he wrote:

> How does a 25-handicap player build a "success pattern" of solid driving when he only hits one or two solid drives in a whole month of play? The answer is that he can build "success patterns" in his computerlike mind only if he learns golf the way I teach it—*from the green to the tee.*

While Toski is not the first to suggest such an approach, he does deserve the credit for popularizing it with the adult golfer. Grant Bennett (1966) was starting children on the practice green as early as the mid-1950s, and somewhat later Lyle Wehrman (1965) reported taking a similar tack. Toski was one of the first to present a rationale for teaching backward from the green, but unfortunately he left something out. His approach lacks a systematic program to develop muscle memory at each step as we do with our mastery chain. Toski seems to have too much confidence in the golfer's mental ability to feel what is required. The system that he recommends proceeds too quickly and does not force the golfer to develop complete mastery before moving on to more difficult shots. If Toski had been given the opportunity to do controlled research comparing groups of golfers taught both from the tee and from the green, he would probably have reached the same conclusions that we have: that it is necessary to completely master a progression of behaviors in small steps back from the green in order to groove the swing.

Another great golfer who teaches backward from the green is Paul Runyan (1962). Runyan's system also lacks a mastery approach, but he has been very successful with it particularly with senior golfers. Almost anyone who has played golf for any length of time has probably had the experience of playing an elderly gentleman you could outdrive by one hundred yards but whose greenwork was outstanding. Of course, you knew that you were a better golfer than he was, although he "mistakenly" kept thinking that the winner was the person with the lowest score rather than the one who hit the ball farthest. Seniors can afford to begin with putting because they are less interested in how macho they look on the tee. Mastering the swing for accuracy remains the most important task of the golfer, male or female, in cut-offs or knickers.

The influence of teachers like Toski and Runyan, combined with the early reports of our findings, are probably some of the reasons that the Editors of *Golf Digest* (1979) have recently stated that the coming trend in golf teaching is an emphasis on the short game. The point should not be missed, however, that you are not just learning the short game to score better. You are learning the short game because that is the best way to improve the long game.

Starting at the hole is logical and defensible but does it work? The answer is yes! The first time this was tried in controlled research (O'Brien and Simek, 1978), Tom Simek gave eight lessons to two groups of six novice golfers. When these golfers played their first round, the group taught through our backward-chaining, mastery-based method averaged 10.67 strokes lower than the golfers who had been taught through a traditional tee to green procedure.

Using new groups of novices, a second study was attempted (O'Brien and Simek, 1978). After getting the kinks out of the program, the group average for the behavioral, chaining-mastery group was *17.33 strokes lower* than the group average for the traditionally trained subjects on their first eighteen-hole round. That is almost a stroke a hole superiority for the chaining-mastery group. Over a 6,100-yard, par 72 course, four of the six behaviorally trained beginners broke 100 on their first round. This includes one not particularly athletic young man who shot an 87 after losing six strokes in the sand. Unfortunately, in this second study, sand shots were not taught to the behavioral group because of time limitations. It is conceivable that given the full program, this novice could have broken 80.

At a second measurement session these same golfers were measured for accuracy by having them hit three balls at fourteen distances from three feet to two hundred yards away from the hole. At every distance the chaining-mastery group was closer to the hole than the traditional group. See Appendix 1.

Remembering Jack Nicklaus' observations, we held a final measurement session with these subjects in which we placed paper labels over their clubfaces. This enabled us to measure the distance from the sweetspot of the clubface to the impact point where they actually hit the ball. Each golfer hit three shots with each of six different clubs from wedge to driver. For every club, chaining-mastery golfers were closer to the sweetspot. See Appendix 2.

Our experiments consistently show a superiority for beginning golfers trained by behavioral methods over those who have been trained from the tee using traditional modeling and verbal instruction. But what about those players who 'already play and want to improve their game? When we began this chapter we said that if you were just beginning to play golf you were lucky. You hadn't learned the wrong things because you had not yet been taught the wrong way. If you are already playing and are dissatisfied with your game, we are going to tell you what almost every other golf instructor will tell you. *A bad swing must be relearned!* As Leslie King pointed out many years ago, a swing cannot be "patched" unless the problems are very minor. You see, you already have muscle memory for your old swing. To improve that swing, you must erase that muscle memory and, through practice, replace it with a memory of the proper stroke and timing. The advantages of using the mastery-based system that we propose are threefold. First, rather than promoting a patchwork quilt of temporary remedies, this method provides a clear, step-by-step process for attaining an integrated, repeatable, swing. Second, this method overcomes the inevitable awkwardness that one feels when changing an old, comfortable, but ineffective habit. Those of you long-time players who have attempted grip changes while practicing full swings will know what we are talking about. Finally, and perhaps most importantly, this mastery-based system gives you continuous feedback on how you are doing. It tells you what you have mastered and what still requires work. Research has shown time and again that this type of feedback is critical in changing behavior (Ammons, 1956).

Thus, for you veteran players, we suggest one of two plans of action. The first alternative is to STOP PLAYING and learn the proper swing from the beginning. Take five or six weeks, in April or September, and spend them practicing; grooving your swing, fine-tuning your tempo, and getting your muscles to the point where they naturally perform the correct action. Through informal observations of veteran golfers at The Old Westbury (N.Y.) Country Club early on in the development of this chaining-mastery-based system, we found that continued play and the pressure of competition caused our players to return to their previous bad habits before the newly taught skills were established. Hence our suggestion to stop playing temporarily. However, if this proves impossible we recommend plan two, whereby you work through the mastery-based strategies outlined in the following chapters, play as infrequently as possible, and keep a shot-by-shot behavior record of your rounds as delineated in Chapter 7. Our latest research (Simek and O'Brien, 1980) suggests that the immediate feedback technique of shot-by-shot behavior recording may be a powerful enough tool to overcome the difficulties of playing while developing new muscle habits.

One last note before we send you out to the putting green. The game of golf is more than just perfecting your swing. The role of the golfer's thoughts in either maximizing or sabotaging his game is at least as great as his form and finesse with his clubs. Headsteadiness is a necessary attribute for the golfer's thoughts as well as his actions. Learning to control anxiety, irrational thoughts, concentration lapses, and temper tantrums are at least as much a part of playing superior golf as putting, chipping, and driving.

If you follow the instructions in the first half of this book, you should finish with a sound mechanical game. The second half of this work is devoted to conquering the psychological demons of the links. From duffer to tournament pro, anxiety, sometimes called the "yips," has driven many a golfer off the course before his time. Young or old, no one is immune, not Ben Hogan, not Bobby Jones, not even Harry Vardon. In Part II you will see how proven principles of emotional control based on behavioral psychology can help you overcome the stress that golfers make for themselves on the course. If you find that your practice game is far better than your play, your emotional golf adjustment is suspect. For the player with good physical skills and a shoddy psychological approach, we suggest reading this book by beginning with the back nine, the section that deals with the psychological aspects of the game. Beginning with Chapter 8 you will discover various techniques for controlling the lapses on your emotional links.

2

Putting, or Beginning at the End

*". . . no part of golf is more important
than putting."*

JACK NICKLAUS

Pick up a putter. You are about to learn the single most important scoring aspect of the game as well as the foundation on which your full swing rests. We have found that there are a relatively small number of fundamentals that must be mastered in order to develop a sound, repeatable golf swing. Furthermore, through careful study we have determined that the best and easiest way to learn these fundamentals is not by starting out with the longest club and swing but rather with the shortest. It is here where the crucial skills of tempo, left-hand action through the ball (for right-handed golfers), headsteadiness, and address/ alignment are most easily learned and grooved. Thus, by the time you get to the longer shots, your basic swing will be second nature, freeing you to concentrate on generating power. So grab that putter and come with us.

Before we get into the important business of holding the club correctly, stand up and gently swing the putter back and forth in front of you. Keep the swing short—maybe twelve inches back away from an imaginary ball and then eighteen inches forward through that imaginary ball. While you are making these light and gentle swings, repeat to yourself, "Back and through." Make the putterhead flow with the rhythm of that phrase: "Back and through. Back and through. Back and through." The phrase has a count of three, one beat for each word. Say "Back" as the putterhead moves away from its starting position;

13

"and" as the clubhead changes direction; and "through" as it moves forward. This is the basic rhythm you will want to incorporate into *every* swing you make from now on. As we move you back progressively farther from the hole, this sense of rhythm will be mastered and ingrained.

How important and necessary is rhythm in a golf swing? Very important. Rhythm goes a long way toward making it easier for all the complex movements of a golf swing to blend smoothly together. The great professional golfers and teachers know the importance of rhythm and spend long hours grooving it. Listen to what they have to say about this aspect of the game.

According to Jack Nicklaus, winner of every major tournament in the game including the U.S. and British Opens, "The better the rhythm of the swing the better the swing is likely to work . . ." (Nicklaus and Bowden, 1974). Another great champion, Tommy Armour, author of three of the most enduring golf instruction books on the market, states, "It is rhythm that makes a golf swing beautiful and an expression of a true artist. There are some excellent golfers whose swings are smooth, and every detail is perfectly synchronized, yet their swings have a mechanical look. Those swings are hard work and only for the few who can devote a tremendous amount of time to perfecting them and keeping them together." (Tommy Armour, 1967). Finally, in perhaps the strongest endorsement for rhythm we have read, Eddie Merrins, currently one of golf's preeminent instructors, states, "Learning the right rhythm is vital, because with good rhythm you can get away with a multitude of sins as far as swing mechanics are concerned. If your rhythm is correct, you will make a consistent stroke which means a consistent effect on the ball. But if your rhythm is off, you'll mishit the ball, no matter how sound your fundamentals are" (Eddie Merrins, 1979). Rhythm is of major importance in your swing. Using our system of learning the game, rhythm is easily mastered while your swing is short and manageable. So, pick up your putter and start developing back-and-through rhythm. After a very few swings you should begin to have some sense or "feel" of rhythm in your fingers, hands, and arms as a result of the repeated movements of the weighted putterhead. Are you aware of that feeling yet? If not, don't despair. Later, we will return to rhythm and it's first cousin tempo and give you a number of simple exercises to promote this necessary sensation. For now, let's turn our attention to the crucial business of holding or "gripping" a club correctly.

THUMBS DOWN TO A GOOD GRIP

Of all the parts of your body involved in making a golf swing, only your hands are in actual contact with the golf club. That's pretty obvious. What you may not be aware of is that to a large degree hand position on a golf club controls the direction of the shot you are putting or hitting. If your grip is such that you usually leave the clubface pointing to the right of target at impact, you can assure yourself of being miserable on a golf course. Legendary players such as Ben Hogan, Tony Lema, and Arnold Palmer have found that minor changes in their grip have meant the difference between success and defeat. Yet not one in six amateur golfers holds a club in a way that makes it easier to hit a golf ball. And that's foolish and unnecessary! Your grip is something you can get right before you even start swinging. It takes no more time to put your hands on a club correctly than it does to put them on it incorrectly. So why are there so many poor grips out there? As nearly as we can determine, it's because of ignorance, carelessness, or bad habits. Don't unnecessarily handicap yourself! For those of you who already play, a grip position change will be temporarily uncomfortable. Your hands are going to feel as if they've never touched a golf club before. Relax, it's normal to feel this. In a very short time as you work backward from the hole, your grip will begin to feel "right" again with a minimum of bad shots in the process.

Although there are a number of useful basic grips and numerous variations on these, for the time being we prefer that you hold your putter in the manner we describe below. Many pros such as Nancy Lopez, Bob Rosburg, and Bobby Locke, recommend one grip for all shots. Some professionals, though, prefer to change to a reverse overlapping grip when putting. They believe that this gives the player greater control over the right hand. However, it is just as easy to pull a putt to the left with a reverse overlapping grip as with a standard overlapping grip. Further, as Toski (1978) indicates, you give up some control with the left hand when you use the reverse style.

Plates 1–4 on the next two pages depict the steps involved in making a proper grip. Take a moment and look at these pictures. In Plate 1 you will notice that the golfer's left thumb is placed straight down the center of the shaft. With the thumb in this position the back of your left hand is forced to face the hole or target directly. This is the left-hand grip that many great players and teachers such as Tommy Bolt (Bolt and Mann, 1971) and Arnold Palmer (1963) recommend. When you place your thumb on the club, set it down its natural length along the center of the shaft. Don't stretch it out as far as you can. This promotes floppy wrist action during your swing. After you've set your thumb in the correct position, check to see if the back of your hand faces directly to your left. If it doesn't, shift your hand so that it does. One other thing: hold the club so that the butt of your hand is about one-half inch down from the top of the shaft. This will enable you to have more control over the clubhead while maintaining the club's natural balance.

Now for your right hand. Once again look at the pictures on the following pages. You'll notice in Plate 2 that the golfer's right palm is brought up to the club so that it directly faces his left palm. The palms are, in effect, parallel to each other. This is what you'll be striving for. In Plate 3 as the right hand is closed around the grip of the club, the meaty portion of that hand (the portion just below the thumb) fits directly over the knuckle of the left thumb. Thus the right thumb points not quite straight down but angled slightly toward your left toe. Try this now; it's not nearly as complicated as it sounds. While making your grip, keep your hands close together so that your right pinky is nestled up against your left hand.

Now check the fourth picture in the series. Here you can see that the golfer's right pinky has been curled around the knuckle of the left forefinger. The reason this is done is that in a golf swing your two hands must work together as a single

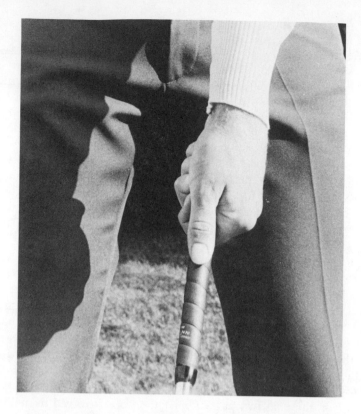

Plate 1

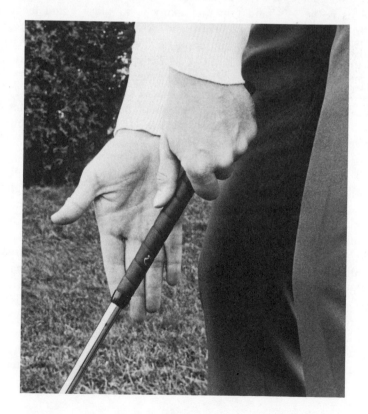

Plate 2

Plate 3

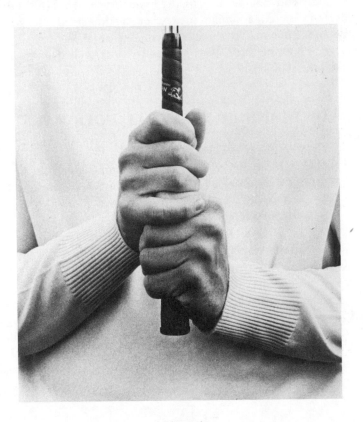

Plate 4

unit. Connecting your hands in this fashion greatly contributes to that desired sense of unity. So with your hands on the club as in Plate 3, lift your right pinky, slide your hands snugly together, and curl your pinky around that knuckle. And that's it! This grip, known as the Vardon or overlapping grip, will take a little getting used to. However, learning the correct way to hold a club will save you years of agony in the form of missed putts, errant irons, and sliced tee-shots.

In addition to correct hand position, proper grip pressure is also an essential ingredient for effective putting and shotmaking. What you will be striving for is a firm but light pressure. We have found that most people, when learning a new skill, tend to hold on very tightly to anything within their grasp. Remember when you first learned to drive a car? That steering wheel was clenched awfully tight. It's the same in golf. Most new, and many veteran golfers hold their club as though someone were trying to steal it from them. A too tight grip will result in a loss of accuracy or distance, or both. In putting, where distance is not a factor, a tight grip will result in a loss of "feel" or "touch." Those of you who play pool or billiards know only too well what happens when you clutch the cue stick tightly. It's the same with putting. You must hold the club with just enough pressure to keep it from slipping in your hands while you swing but not with so much pressure that your knuckles turn white. Somewhere in between these extremes at the proverbial "happy medium" is right. Sam Snead, in his book *The Education of a Golfer* (1962), suggests that you imagine the club's grip or handle to be a bird. If you hold this imaginary bird too loosely, it will fly away. If, on the other hand, you hold it too tightly, you crush the bird. Former PGA champion Dave Marr used a similar idea when he imagined the grip end of a golf club to be an icicle so as to obtain the same sense of firm but *light* grip that Snead urged. Since both of these ideas appear to work well, go with the one you find most appealing.

THE WAY YOU STAND UP TO A BALL DOES MAKE A DIFFERENCE

On any given Saturday morning, on any practice putting green in the world, one can usually find a large number of weekend golfers hunched over a ball in a wild assortment of contorted stances and postures. Heads are tilted cockeyed, shoulders are turned askew, and elbows are akimbo, all in the name of putting. While we are certainly in favor of freedom of expression, the stance and posture we recommend as the one most likely to promote accurate putting is the one known as the "all-square stance." As you can see in the accompanying illustration, imaginary lines drawn across the golfer's toes, through his hips, and through his shoulders are parallel to one another. They are also parallel to the intended line for the roll of the ball. These imaginary lines form a "right" or ninety-degree angle with the face of the putter, which looks down that intended line. This is what's meant by all-square. This square position makes it considerably easier to swing your arms in the pendulum motion necessary to build a consistently repeat-

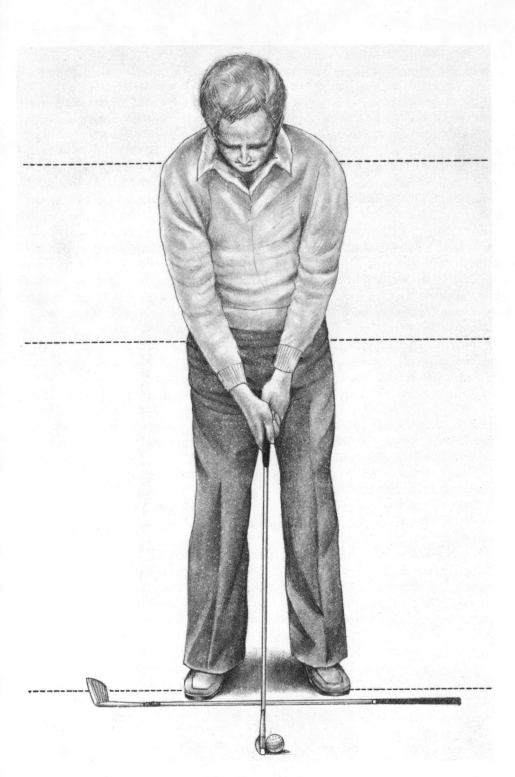

The all-square stance.

able, consistently accurate putting stroke. If you stand up to a ball straight or square, you are most apt to putt straight or square. If you stand up to a ball crookedly, the odds are you will putt crookedly or at least inconsistently. Besides, a square stance means you can make a pendulum stroke with the fewest adjustments needed to compensate for faulty alignment. Aiming in one direction but swinging in another is asking for trouble. There are two good ways to check whether or not you are setting up all-square to the ball. The first way is to practice setting up (taking your stance) in front of a full-length mirror of the kind found in most homes and apartments these days. The information or "feedback" you get from the mirror is cheaper, more immediate and just as valid as having someone take a picture of you with a camera or a video tape machine. While facing it, set up in front of the mirror checking to see if your right and left shoulders are an equal distance from the glass. If they are, you are setting up square; if they aren't you're not. Now do the same with your feet and hips. Several years ago one of the authors of this book (Simek) was playing in a tournament that just happened to have highlights televised on a local station. Although he was close to the lead after the first round, his putting had been terrible. While watching the newscast that evening, he was able to watch himself putting on the sixteenth hole. As the camera was looking directly down the line of the putt, catching him in profile, he could see clearly that his shoulders were misaligned, that is, rather than pointing parallel to the target, they were left of parallel or "open." Grabbing a putter and dashing to the nearest full-length mirror confirmed this observation. A few minutes of practice in front of that mirror was all it took to surmount the problem. The next day his putting was much improved as a result (and he went on to win the tourney in a sudden-death playoff, sinking a fourteen-foot putt on the second extra hole).

Another way to check your set-up is simply to recruit a friend or spouse as a coach and have him stand so that he can look down the intended putting line to the hole. At every major golf tournament in the world, you can observe the pros doing this for one another. It's a big help that can save unnecessary hours of hair pulling and teeth gnashing.

Here are a few more notes about setting up to the ball correctly. A major scientific research team in England (Cochran and Stobbs, 1968) determined that most professional golfers, when taking their putting stance, "had the ball placed (about) opposite their left toe, and their eyes almost directly above the ball" (see illustration). These are features heartily endorsed by Tommy Armour through his informal experimentation with putting styles (Armour, 1967). Having your eyes directly above the ball enables you easily to look down the intended line of roll. This is important as it will help you more readily square the putterface to the target you desire. With regard to your feet, they should be separated enough to encourage a secure but comfortable balance. Most professional golfers achieve this by standing a little knock-kneed with their feet from ten to twelve inches apart.

Our last observation about the putting stance concerns your arms, wrists, and the shaft of the putter. Take a look at the drawing on page 22. This golfer is demonstrating a perfect address position. As you can see, his arms are hanging naturally with his elbows close to his hips. His wrists are arched slightly upward in

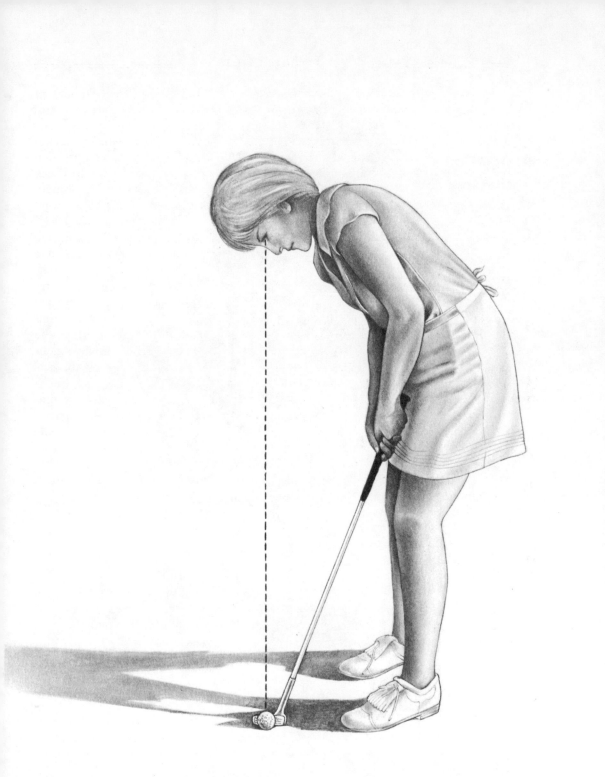

Having your eyes directly above the ball enables you easily to look down the intended line of roll.

A perfect address position.

what the pros call a "high" position. Finally, the clubshaft is tilted about two degrees toward the hole with the putterhead soled flatly on the ground. That is, neither the toe nor the heel of the putter is up in the air.

It is important that the student golfer now take some time to learn the correct stance until it feels natural. This may not appeal to your sense of excitement but it is necessary in order to save strokes on the golf course. Remember, all shots count the same one stroke. This includes the booming two-hundred-fifty-yard drive as well as the six-foot putt, missed because of a faulty set-up. Practice frequently until you can automatically assume the proper stance. Get your stance all-square. Play the ball opposite your left toe. Hold your eyes directly above the ball and place your hands in the proper location with respect to your body and the ball. Take five minutes a day for a week seeking to make your grip and stance second nature. It will pay off for you in the long run.

THE BASIC SWING . . . THE PUTTING STROKE

As you read through the rest of the first half of this book, you will be asked to follow some procedures we have developed based on the work of the noted behavioral psychologists B. F. Skinner and Fred Keller. As we previously stated, these men formulated highly effective methods for shaping and learning various skills. Following these procedures will require some physical practice on your part. However, because success is programmed in from the beginning, this practice is not of the humiliating or painful variety you may have experienced in the past when you began to learn other skills. The practice we propose is absolutely necessary for the simple reason that a golf swing is not an intellectual exercise. We cannot emphasize enough that it is your muscles, not your mind, that must learn the correct action. Jack Nicklaus is on record as saying that he has played in Pro-Am events where some of his amateur playing partners were more familiar with the intricacies of the golf swing than he was. Clearly, if knowledge alone were sufficient for playing par golf, these amateurs he speaks of would be cleaning up on the tour. Of course they are not. If after trying the simple but rewarding practice we recommend, you are unable to spend time on the practice putting green or tee, we direct you to Chapter 13, in which we present various motivational devices and programs to help you establish and maintain a practice regimen.

The easiest way to develop a sound, repeatable putting stroke is to practice swinging between two clubshafts placed on the floor or putting green as in the picture on the next page. When you place the clubs on the ground, set them so that you leave a half-inch leeway on either side of the putterhead. With the clubs on the ground, assume the proper stance that you have now mastered. Once you have set up correctly, gently push the putterhead back a few inches between the clubshaft guides with your left hand and arm acting as a single unit. Now *pull* the putter forward with this single unit. The stroke we are teaching is the touring pro putting stroke which uses no wristiness. Flippy-wristed putting strokes are discouraged because they make it difficult to maintain consistency. Practice the pro stroke a few times. While keeping the putterhead low to the

Plate 5

ground, are you able to make this swing without touching either of the clubshafts? Take it slowly at first. "Easy does it" are the watchwords here. Gradually increase the speed and length of your stroke until it is ten or twelve inches long on the backswing and maybe fifteen to eighteen inches long on the through swing. How many times out of ten can you make this stroke without hitting the club guides?

After you are twice able to make ten in a row, start to concentrate on making that stroke in time with the back and through rhythm you practiced earlier. Remember, push the club back on "back," say "and" just before the putterhead changes directions, and then "through" as you pull the club forward with your left hand. After just a few minutes of practice, you should be able to make a back-and-through stroke nearly every time without touching the guides.

For those of you having difficulty, we have found that the trouble is almost always the result of a faulty set-up. Thus, we recommend practicing against a wall as in the illustration on the following page. As you can see, the putterhead is about one-half inch from the wall while your head is resting lightly against it. This puts your eyes directly over the ball and enables you to see if your shoulders are parallel to the wall. Practice your stroke between the wall and a club guide for two minutes or until you are able to make a short smooth stroke with the proper rhythm. While you are practicing in this manner you will probably notice how easy it is to keep your head steady throughout your stroke. This is very important and will be the last fundamental we discuss before sending you out to stroke some putts. Every great golf champion urges both the beginning and the experienced golfer to keep his head steady while putting. According to Arnold Palmer, this is one of the cardinal rules of golf. Jack Nicklaus tells how his instructor, Jack Grout, would grab a handful of his hair while practicing. If Nicklaus moved his head even a little during his putting stroke or full swing, he would know it immediately in a most painful way. Today Nicklaus has one of the "quietest" heads in the game. From putting to driving, his head moves hardly at all. Despite the seeming simplicity of holding one's head steady, many players report difficulty in identifying if and when they are moving their heads. Fortunately, behavioral psychology has uncovered methods for dealing with this problem.

In our research (Simek and O'Brien, 1978) and that of others, (Ammons, 1956), it has been demonstrated that feedback is important in mastering complex athletic movements. Further, this research suggests that feedback or knowledge of results is most effective if delivered immediately. To that end we snapped a loud clicker, a children's thirty-nine-cent toy, each time the player moved his head. The clicker provided immediate feedback for head movement. In some cases, the head movement, immediately followed by the "snap" of the clicker, occurred early enough to abort the shot. For the most part, however, the clicker served to alert the golfer that he was lifting his head to follow the roll of the ball. The results of this training showed how effective immediate feedback could be. Golfers using this strategy increased headsteadiness and significantly improved their putting. Try it and see how it works for you.

Practicing against a wall.

On the facing page is a listing of ever-lengthening putts, next to which is a column entitled Mastery Criterion. Briefly, Mastery Criterion tells you the degree of accomplishment you need at one step before moving on to the next. It is in this fashion that your golf swing will be shaped and your muscle movements trained to become automatic. Our system of mastery-based instruction maximizes success, minimizes failure, and provides continuous feedback as to how you are progressing. For example, in step three the mastery criterion calls for four consecutive putts to be holed at a distance of two feet. Thus, if you are able to make four in a row at this distance, then you should be able to progress with confidence to the next step in the chain. If you are unable to satisfy this requirement, further practice of the basic behaviors called for at this stage is necessary. Hence, we will ask you to exhibit mastery of such behaviors as headsteadiness and left-hand action through the ball in addition to making a number of putts at various distances.

TABLE 2

Putting Chain and Mastery Criterion.

Step	Shot	Mastery Criterion
1	10-inch putt (between clubs optional)	4 putts consecutively holed
2	16-inch putt (between clubs optional)	4 putts consecutively holed
3	2-foot putt clubs removed	4 putts consecutively holed
4	3-foot putt	4 putts consecutively holed
5	4-foot putt some break	2 holed, 2 out of 4 within 6 inches
6	6-foot putt	4 consecutively within 6 inches
7	10-foot putt	4 consecutively within 12 inches
8	15-foot putt	4 consecutively within 15 inches
9	20-foot putt	4 consecutively within 18 inches
10	30-foot putt	4 consecutively within 24 inches

ON THE PRACTICE GREEN

At this time we would like you to move to the practice putting green and begin working with a real golf ball. (Author's note: If going to the golf course is inconvenient or impossible, we suggest you set up a practice putting cup on a smooth carpet in your home. This apparatus may be purchased commercially at your local sporting goods store, or better yet, with a little ingenuity and some spare materials lying around the house, you may construct or improvise something that will serve as a four-and-one-quarter-inch-diameter hole).

When you get to the practice green, find a hole where the surrounding ground is level, that is, where there is no steep slope or slant to the green. We would like you to start first with short, straight putts. Later we will tell you the ins and outs of what are known as "breaking" putts. For now, drop a couple of balls close to the hole, maybe ten or twelve inches away, and practice stroking them into the cup. You will find that with a putt this short your backswing need not be very long at all. (Bear with us, you experienced golfers.) After a few putts you should be able to get a sense of how hard you need to hit the ball—it doesn't take much. When you feel ready, place four balls ten inches from the hole and sink each one. When you are able to drop four in a row (it's not too tough at this range) move back six inches and practice until you can sink four in a row here, too. It is important that you use the stroke you have been working on so far. "Slopping" it in the hole breeds bad habits that will require extra effort to

27

overcome later. Set up in the manner outlined above and stroke through the ball with the back of your left hand pulling toward the hole. With these short putts you may either practice putting between club guides or merely pretend they are there. After you have successfully dropped four in a row at sixteen inches, move back to two feet and proceed as before. The fundamentals of the stroke remain the same at this distance as they are for putts of any distance. However, the length of the backswing increases as you move farther from the hole. Continue using the same smooth rhythm as you have all along.

DO I NEED TO FOLLOW EVERY STEP?

You might be wondering whether you could skip some of the steps in the chain in favor of completing the program sooner. In our experience this would be a mistake. On occasion, we have allowed a student golfer to pass on to a more advanced level without demonstrating mastery at the previous level. As with social promotions in our public schools, this procedure has proved to be ill-advised. Almost always unwarranted promotions of our research subjects led to swing difficulties further on in the chain. As might be guessed, the best remedy was to return to the original point of difficulty and continue practicing until full mastery of that step was attained. Subjects were then carried through an abbreviated program back to where the problem had become evident. MASTERY IS CRITICALLY IMPORTANT. Skipping steps in this program leads to gaps in the muscle memory of your swing in exactly the same way skipping some of the fundamentals of algebra leads to trouble in working more sophisticated mathematical equations. Skipping steps ends up taking more time rather than less.

ON READING GREENS

As you progress from two-foot putts to three-footers, you begin to contend with breaking putts. For the beginners reading this, breaking putts are those putts that, because of the slope of the land and/or the grain of the green, curve to the right or left despite being struck with a good square stroke. In order to make a breaking putt, you must learn to "read" greens correctly. This will enable you to adjust your aim to compensate for the slope or grain. In other words, you will want to continue making the same square stroke you make on straight putts, only now you will aim to the right or left of the hole as need be and let the slope and the grain of the green pull the ball into the hole. Experience and practice, also known as trial and error, are the best teachers in this area. However, we will make suggestions from time to time throughout the putting chain that will help you plan ahead.

First, on short putts of two feet or less, don't bother to play for break at all. Merely line up your putt to the center of the hole and stroke the ball firmly there. In ninety-nine out of a hundred cases there just isn't enough room on a two-foot putt for the ball to curve if you putt with authority. As you move out to three-footers, though, many times you will need to aim to the right or left of center to some degree. If, when you look at a three-foot or longer putt, you can't readily determine which way the ball will break, here's what to do. Look first at the cup and see if one side is lower than the rest. You can do this by checking to see if there is a thinner layer of earth between the metal liner and the surface of the green on any one side. The thinner side is the side the ball will break toward. Accordingly, you must aim for the other side in order to compensate.

Gary Player (1962) looks in the hole when making decisions on break. If he cannot determine by the relative thickness of the earth layer which side of the hole is lowest, Player then looks to see whether one side is the worse for wear. If there is a worn side, this is apt to be the low one because most putts curve off and strike the low side as they reach the hole. In our experience this insight has provided valuable strategy when all else has failed to furnish the line.

Another tip that we have long used, and which was recently recommended by Johnny Miller (Miller and Shankland, 1974), is to imagine you are pouring a pail of water on top of the green near your ball and the hole. Then you must picture in your mind which way the water will run. The way the water runs is the way your putt will break. Go back to the practice green and try these methods. Play scientist a little; make your best judgment, put a good stroke on the ball, see what happens, and then try it again. Later on, as you become more proficient, we will return to green reading with additional information.

Returning to the mastery chart, you are now at step four—the critically important three-foot putts. Becoming proficient at putts of this length will save you strokes for the rest of your golfing life. On long putts you will be able to relax a little because you know that if you can roll the ball to within a three-foot radius of the hole, you will never three-putt. We will expand on this strategy later in the putting sequence.

Take some time now and practice these putts. First, achieve mastery by sinking four consecutive putts from a single location. Then sink four more consecutive putts, but this time from four different locations. As in the picture on page 30, place a ball at the north, west, south, and east sides three feet from the hole. Use the green-reading skills you have acquired and practice until you can sink four in a row. This is the very best training we know for gaining the experience you need to manage breaking putts and is also the putting practice method used by Walter Travis, possibly the greatest putter of all time (Armour, 1952). Travis wasn't able to hit a golf ball very far off the tee. But, despite this lack of power he won many golf tournaments with his uncanny ability on the green.

One of the most common errors student golfers make at this stage is lifting or turning their heads to watch the roll of the ball. Remember that headsteadiness is a virtue when putting. Take your aim to account for the break, look at the back of the ball, and make your best stroke with your head absolutely steady. Listen with your ears to hear the sound of the ball dropping in the hole rather than looking up with your eyes. This is what is known as the "ear stroke." If you're having trouble making an "ear stroke," go back to the section in this chapter on immediate feedback to improve putting.

With four-foot putts and longer, you will be working under new mastery criteria. Instead of having to hole every putt, you now will be considered to have met the criterion if a designated number of putts end up within a specified dis-

Plate 6

tance from the hole. We have modified the criterion because even the best putters among the professionals are unable to drop them all from beyond three feet. Research has shown that the pros miss one in eight from four feet (Cochran and Stobbs, 1968). So a more useful determinant of mastery is the number of consecutive putts one is able to get within a certain distance of the hole. Of course, it is terrific if you are able to drop a few of these putts. For now, though, simply practice to meet the mastery criterion at each step.

SIMPLIFYING MEASUREMENTS

Instead of measuring every putt you stroke to see if you have achieved mastery, a tedious endeavor to be sure, here is what we suggest for speeding up the process. Using a tape measure, mark off the target area around the hole (on four- and six-footers it's six inches). Place a marker slightly to the right or left of the four main points of the compass so you don't interfere with the progress of a ball about to drop in the hole. This way you will be able to see at a glance whether or not you've succeeded in rolling the balls to within the specified range.

In order to attain mastery at four feet you must drop at least two of four consecutive putts and keep the other two within six inches of the cup. Then before you move on to six-footers, practice breaking putts at this distance. Move around the "horn" using the same criterion, putt one from the north side, the next to the west, and so on. After you have accomplished this, give yourself a hearty pat on the back and then move on to six-foot putts. Again, your stroke is slightly longer. On flat putts of four to ten feet your backswing should be approximately an inch long per foot of putt. Thus, on a six-foot putt your backswing will be about six inches long. The mastery criterion at this step is rolling four consecutive putts within six inches of the hole. This should be followed by the routine we have described for mastering break.

MORE ON READING GREENS

Earlier we wrote of something called the grain of the green. Quite simply, the grain or nap of the green is the direction in which the blades of grass grow. If the grain is predominantly in one direction, like the slope of the green, it can seriously affect the roll of your putt. If you have ever watched a golf tournament, you probably witnessed the pros scrutinize the putting green as if they were detectives searching for clues. Generally, what they are doing is looking for the grain of the green.

There are two popular methods for determining the grain of the green: the easy and reliable, and the easy but unreliable. The easy and reliable method again involves looking at the cup. On three sides of the hole the blades of grass will look sharply crew cut. On the fourth side, though, the edges will appear less distinct, more ruffled and bent over. Once again, in ninety-nine cases out of a hundred, the grain will be growing toward the side that is ruffled. Adjust your aim and force accordingly. For example, if you have a sidehill putt sloping left to right and the grain flows in the same direction, play the ball a couple more inches to the left than you ordinarily would if there was no grain at all. In addition, if you are putting with the grain, stroke the ball a little easier as there is less resistance. Conversely, if you are putting against the grain, stroke a little more firmly, since there's more resistance.

The second technique for determining the grain of the green is known as the shine formula. This is a more common procedure than the first way we submitted, but not as dependable. With this system you must look for light and dark zones in the green. It works like this: when you are standing by your ball and the grass between your ball and the hole looks dull or flat in color, the grain is against you. Grain that looks bright and shiny is leaning away from you and toward the hole. Although much additional information could be written about grain, it is doubtful whether further details would help your putting at this stage of the game. The most important fact about grain is that it has its greatest effect when the ball slows down as it nears the hole. For this reason we promote the cup method for determining grain direction because this is where all the action is.

About the time you begin working on ten-foot putts, your putting stroke should be approximately ten to twelve inches on the backswing. The putterhead ought still to be moving straight back and straight through as it did when you practiced between guides. Once again the mastery criterion target area widens a little, and it shouldn't take you too long to become proficient at this distance.

By now the basic movements of your putting stroke are getting pretty well grooved. After you have attained mastery at ten feet, including the breaking putt routine, we would like you to try the following feedback aids in order to fine-tune your stroke.

THREE SIMPLE FEEDBACK AIDS

Those of you who have played a while know what driving range balls look like. A driving range ball has a red or black stripe around it's equator (see Plate 7). We would like you to obtain a couple of new ones for this particular exercise. They may be purchased for a nominal amount at either a sporting goods store or perhaps your local driving range. Take your newly acquired range balls to a very flat area about ten feet from the hole on the practice green (a spot that's straight uphill with no break right or left would be ideal). Once again recruit a friend to observe, place the range ball in such a way that the stripe points directly down the intended line to the hole. Now put your best stroke on the ball, keeping your head steady, while your friend watches the roll of the ball. If you've put a square stroke on the ball, the stripe will revolve with very little wobble and will point pretty much at the hole when it stops. Stroke a half-dozen additional putts and see what your friend's evaluation is. If the stripe wobbles a lot or if you are finishing consistently to the right or left of the hole, you need to practice stroking between club guides again in addition to practicing the following exercise.

Drop a book (this one will do) on the floor or putting green. Now take the

Plate 7

correct stance so that your putterface is about six inches away and perfectly square to the back binding of the book (see diagram). This time without a ball, make your best stroke. If on your follow-through the putterface finishes perfectly flush to the bookbinding, you are making a perfect stroke. Congratulations! On the other hand, if the toe of the putter strikes the binding first, you are leaving the clubface open, pointing to the right at impact, and this is not good. Practice this very important drill for two minutes or until you are able to follow through with the putterface flush every time. If you are having difficulty achieving this, a thorough review of the preceding parts of this chapter is necessary.

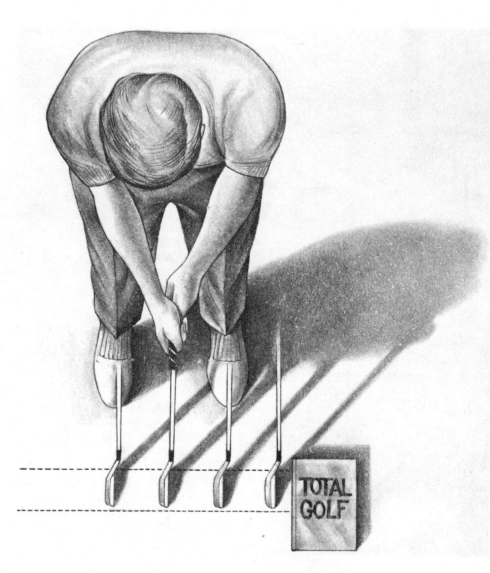

If on your follow-through the putterface finishes perfectly flush to the bookbinding, you are making a perfect stroke.

The final exercise we would like you to try involves striking the ball on the sweetspot of the putter. In the first chapter we told you that Jack Nicklaus concentrates on "contacting the ball with the solidest part of the putter, the sweetspot." The drill we will describe momentarily will help you groove this action. First, however, you need to know how to locate the sweetspot on the clubface. Although club manufacturers often put a mark where they think the sweetspot is, our experience suggests they are not particularly exacting in doing this. A reliable way to find the sweetspot is to hold your putter loosely in front of you at the base of the grip as in the illustration on the next page. Now, with your left forefinger, strike the putterface in various locations. You'll notice that if you bounce your fingertip off the toe or heel of the putter, it twists quite a bit. The sweetspot is the place where the putter twists not at all, but rather bounces straight back. Once you've found this place, mark where it is on the top of the putter with an indelible ink pen.

Now for the sweetspot drill. Rub some colored chalk or pool-cue chalk on one half of a golf ball. When you make your putting stroke, the chalked ball will leave a powdery impression on the putterface. You will be able to see clearly how close you are to contacting the ball on the sweetspot. On the practice green, stroke some ten-foot putts. If the powder mark is off-target, practice until you are consistently able to meet the ball on the sweetspot. To accomplish this task you will probably need to begin practicing very short putts and gradually increase the length of the putt and your stroke.

Upon mastering the drills at a distance of ten feet, move back to fifteen feet and resume the putting sequence. Here your swing changes a little as it becomes longer and the putterhead begins to move a little inside the intended line at the end of your backstroke. This occurs naturally as a result of your physical makeup. Forcing the club to continue straight back on a swing of this length inspires a number of unnecessary complications that are difficult to groove. After pushing the putterhead straight back approximately twelve inches, let it curve naturally toward you five degrees. Some people report having difficulty doing this. They have so well grooved the straight back, straight through stroke that they find it awkward now to let the club come inside. If this is happening to you, we suggest the following remedy. Cut a piece of string twenty-four inches long. Tape this string on the floor so that the first twenty inches are in a straight line. For the last four inches, tape the string so that it curves in five degrees toward you. Place the sweetspot of your putter above the string and stand so that your feet are parallel to the straight section. Your right foot should be opposite the point where the string begins to curve. Now practice your putting stroke, making the putterhead follow the path of the string. You will need to do this for at least two minutes before it begins to feel natural.

The mastery criterion target area changes for fifteen-foot putts to fifteen inches. Mark off this target area and practice until you are able to roll four consecutive putts within it. Then master breaking putts at this distance, using the formula we have previously related.

How to locate the sweetspot.

PLUMB BOBBING AND SPOT PUTTING

The plumb-bob technique for determining break has recently become extremely popular. Although you see numerous variations on this procedure, there is only one correct method. In order to use this technique you must first determine which is your dominant eye. An easy way of making this determination is, first, to hold out an arm at full length. Next, keeping both eyes open, sight a distant stationary object over your outstretched thumb. Now close one of your eyes. If the object remains centered over your thumb, the eye that is open is your dominant eye. But if the object appears to move, your closed eye is the one that is dominant. Once you have determined your dominant eye, you are ready to proceed.

Now, standing three to five feet behind your ball, simply stretch out your arm at eye level while lightly holding the putter between your thumb and forefinger. Using your dominant eye (this means closing the other one), move the putter so that the top of the grip end is in a straight line with the ball and the hole. Next, look up the shaft in the direction of the hole, making certain your head is *not* cocked to the right or left. You will see one of three things. The first possibility is that both the ball and the hole are partially blocked out by the putter shaft. If this is the case, you have an approximately straight putt. The second possibility is that the hole appears to be some distance to the right of the shaft. If so, your putt will break to the right approximately this same distance. In other words, putt along the line of the shaft. The final possibility, of course, is that the hole looks as if it is some distance to the left of the shaft. In this instance your putt will break to the left approximately the same distance. Here again, putt along the line of the shaft. In each of the three cases we said the putt will break *approximately* the same amount you see using the plumb-bob method because there is still the grain to contend with, so be advised. This method takes some practice getting used to. However, once you've acquired the skill, it's an invaluable asset. Such stellar performers as Nancy Lopez and Al Geiberger, who once fired a round of 59 in a tour event, plumb bob nearly every putt and would be lost on the green without this technique.

SPOT PUTTING

For those of you who bowl, spot putting is very similar to spot bowling. Instead of aiming at a target that is a long way off, you aim for an intermediate target which is much closer but still on the path to the final target. For example, say you have a fifteen-foot putt that you have determined will break eight inches to the right. It can be very difficult to aim accurately at a small target this far away. So rather than make guesswork of aiming, align the putterface to a spot on the green three to five feet in front of the ball. This spot (a blade of grass perhaps) should be along the intended line your putt will travel. Now set your feet parallel to an imaginary line running through the ball and the spot on the green. All you need do at this point is stroke along that imaginary line and listen for the putt dropping in the hole. A legal aid for stroking along the intended line of the putt may be found on the ball itself. Each ball has three markings on it. Two of the markings are close together. They are the name and number of the ball. The third marking is located along the equator of the ball as the colored stripe is on a range ball (Plate 8). Because this marking forms a straight line, you may use it to help you on the green. Just as you placed the stripe of the range ball directly down the line to the hole, you may set an ordinary ball so that its marking points directly at the hole for straight putts, or at the spot on the green if you are using the spot-putting method. Now, merely stroke along this visual marker and, once again, listen for the ball to drop.

After you have mastered fifteen-foot putts, your putting stroke has become very nearly second nature. Moving on to twenty-foot putts will serve to stamp in the correct muscle memory. The mastery criterion here is to roll four consecutive putts within eighteen inches of the hole. Before proceeding to thirty-foot putts, also practice until you are able to achieve this level of skill at each of the four main points of the compass. Those of you having trouble with determining break are urged to review the sections in this chapter on reading greens. If you are having trouble gauging distance, we suggest you practice at intervals of one-foot increments out from fifteen feet. In other words, obtain mastery at the six-teen-, seventeen-, eighteen-, and nineteen-foot levels, if need be, before trying again at twenty feet.

"But," you may well be thinking, "what do you do when you're out on the course and cannot stroke half a dozen putts until you get the right distance?" As you continue practicing and gaining experience, you will find it easier and easier to stroke long putts with the proper force. Until you gain that experience, though, here is what to do. Before you go out on the course, stroke half-a-dozen long ones on the practice green. This should give you at least a mini refresher course on judging force. The reason we say hit only a half-dozen long putts is that we would rather you spend whatever time you have before a round practicing the

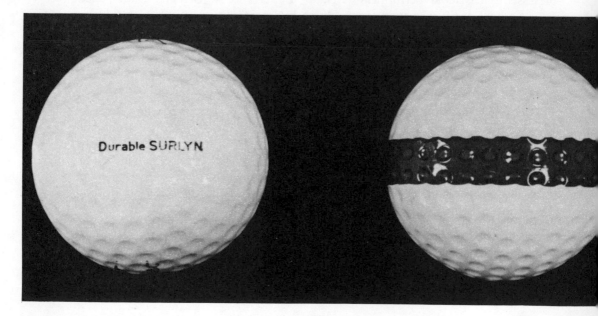

Plate 8

more critical short putts of two to six feet. Practicing these short ones is more re-warding and will provide your muscles with an equal opportunity to remember the correct movements and rhythm. The method we use for gauging the long ones when out on the course is to pretend we are rolling a ball underhand to the hole. We actually go through the movements involved and then visualize the imaginary ball rolling to the hole. The force we would use in rolling the ball underhand is the same force we use in the actual stroke. This method has worked very well in pressurized situations over the years and we enthusiastically recommend it.

Another technique we employ is one we referred to earlier. Using our imagi-nation, we again picture the hole in the center of a three-foot circle. By enlarg-ing the target area to more realistic proportions, we are able to gauge the force necessary to get the ball there more readily. Remember, too, that you have three feet past the hole as well as three feet short or to the right or left of the hole.

The last step of the putting sequence is attaining proficiency on thirty-foot putts. All that you have previously mastered comes into play at this time. The mastery criterion here is stroking four successive putts within thirty inches of the hole. We have found that people who have difficulty here are doing something rather interesting. Although they generally take great pains to line up and aim their putts, they do not stroke along this intended line. Instead they stroke at the hole. Aiming in one direction but stroking in another is deadly to accurate putt-ing. Guard against doing this. After you have achieved mastery from one loca-tion at thirty feet, practice the now familiar breaking putt routine and achieve mastery at this, too.

CONGRATULATIONS!

Through diligent practice you have earned your "black belt" in putting. The skills you have acquired in learning the proper putting stroke will be built upon in the following chapters, but you are well on the way to developing a solid and efficient golf game. The final suggestion we want to make in this chapter is to es-tablish a set routine to be performed on every putt. All of the finest putters in the game have their own particular preshot ritual. Indeed, athletes in many sports develop preshot routines. Basketball players perform the seemingly obligatory three bounces of the ball before tossing the free throw (Nideffer, 1976). Pitchers often tug at the bill of their caps prior to delivering the pitch. A common routine in putting runs something like this: as you walk up to the green look over the general landscape of the putting surface; when on the green look at the final two feet before the hole, decide on the line, take two practice strokes, step up to the ball, put the putterhead behind the correctly aimed ball, look once at the hole, look back to the ball, and stroke. The specifics involved don't particularly matter. Entrepreneur Mark McCormick (1968), possibly sportdom's most influential figure, relates the story of a young pro playing the Far East Tour who included introducing the ball to the hole in his preshot rit-ual. What is important is that the whole operation be done as a single block. This prevents the backswing from being the initial move, thus reducing jerkiness in your takeaway from the ball. In addition, a standard routine provides a framework for dealing with each putt without allowing you to become anxious or lose concentration.

The methods and techniques we have just described are important. However, the mere reading of this chapter will not magically improve your game. Do not lose sight of the fact that *the key to grooving your swing is to zealously adhere to mastering each step of the putting chain.*

3

Chipping
and Pitching

*"Every great player has been able to
consistently get the ball up and down in
two from off the green."*

TOM WATSON

The next link in the chain progression to the full swing is the chip shot. As in
every step of the mastery chain, this step is a simple extension of the swing you
have already learned. Small, easy-to-manage increments will be added as we
move you off the putting green. Although chipping skill mastered in the fashion
we will describe shortly is not difficult, it is an exceedingly important continuation of your swing. The chip shot and its big brother, the pitch shot, are two of
your best stroke savers on the course. Lee Trevino demonstrated this to perfection in the 1972 British Open when he holed out twice from just off the green to
edge out runner-up Jack Nicklaus by a single shot. Several years ago in a match
between former Masters champion Doug Ford and Gary Player, Ford missed
five of the first six greens with his approach shot. Meanwhile, Player missed only
one of the first six greens. The score after six holes? Ford even par, Player one
over par. In every tournament, even the best touring pros miss a few greens per
round. Yet they manage to play in par figures or better. The most striking example of their short-shot prowess occurred when Gay Brewer won the 1967
Masters. Analyzing his victory, Brewer stated, "I won because on the last day I
chipped and one-putted ten times during my 67—and won by one shot." Brewer
hit less than nine greens in regulation figures that day but shot a five under par

41

67. Compare this to the average golfer who usually hits less than nine greens in regulation per round but scores 15 to 20 over par. Clearly Tom Watson's words that preface this chapter are worth heeding.

THE CONE OF CONTENTION AND A HOMEWORK ASSIGNMENT

Tony Lema, former British Open champion, called the area within seventy-five yards of the hole the "Cone of Contention" (Lema and Harvey, 1966). He is exactly right. This is the scoring area and every shot here is important. We could cite additional historical instances of hot or cold chipping and pitching, but there is a better way to bring the impact of the short game close to home. During your next eighteen holes set aside a separate column on your scorecard for the short game shots (putting, chipping, pitching, and sand shots), and record every stroke you make in the scoring area. We bet you will be surprised by the percentage of your total shots taken there. Despite the fact that *most golfers take sixty to seventy-five percent of their shots within seventy-five yards of the hole,* very few bother to practice the skills necessary to manage this aspect of the game. Often golfers we are working with tell us that they don't practice their short game because it is "okay." Their contention is rarely borne out when we ask for a demonstration. However, even if your chipping is adequate, it is important that you continue with the mastery chain. The reason for this is that the chip and pitch shot swings are intermediate steps on the way to the full swing.

Occasionally we hear the following as an explanation for not practicing and mastering these shots: "It's all a matter of feel or touch, isn't it? Either you've got it or you don't." Yes, feel and touch do enter into the short game, but as Toski (1971) indicates, feel is not innate. You will never get the "right" feel until you practice the correct behaviors and fundamentals. Short game skill does not come by wishing for it. The experts' ability around the green is not something they were born with or magically acquired. *They learned how and so can you.* The legendary stars such as Byron Nelson, Ben Hogan, and Sam Snead acquired their proficiency when they were caddies. While waiting for bags to tote, they constantly competed in short game matches in the caddy yard. It was this regular practice that earned them their skill.

Actually, there is no valid reason why you can't be as skilled as the pros around the green. You don't need prodigious strength to negotiate the shorties. Nor do you need lightning quickness. You do need to master some simple basic movements. At our course, Williamsport Country Club, two of the lowest handicap golfers are sixty-year-old gentlemen by the names of Fran Wylie and Henry Parsons. Some of the younger members can outdrive these men by eighty yards off the tee. Yet Wylie and Parsons more than equalize tremendous driving length with their deadly accuracy around the green. In our opinion the major reason people don't spend time practicing the short game is that it doesn't seem as glamorous as slugging a drive. We would like to see a National Short Game Contest to coincide with the National Long Drive Contest. Maybe then chipping and pitching would receive their due.

In this chapter we will describe what you must do to master this aspect of the game. Once again it is very important to attain proficiency at each step. Already you have begun to master the necessary ingredients to accomplish this goal. Back-and-through rhythm continues to be important, so does headsteadiness. Most of all it is critical that you stroke through the ball with the back of your left hand leading the way just as it does when you are putting. The reasons you must lead with your left are twofold. First, the back of the left hand acts as a guide for your swing. Second, the left hand leading helps ensure that you strike first the ball and then the turf. Here is what two professionals have to say on this matter.

Tony Lema states, "For accuracy, we always remember to keep the back of the left hand squarely facing the hole, and the swing is 'square back, and square through.'" Jack Grout, Nicklaus' lifelong golf instructor, echoes that sentiment:

Make sure your left hand leads, not follows, your clubhead through impact, to help assure that the club moves downward, not upward to the ball (Grout and Aultman, 1975).

Clearly, this is a continuation of what you were working on when putting. Indeed, this back of left-hand action leading through the ball is a motion you will incorporate into every swing you make. Pitch shots require it, iron shots require it, and drives require it. It is important that your muscle memory be grooved on these shots.

The mastery chain that you will use to establish muscle memory of the swing at this stage is presented in the following table.

TABLE 3

Step	Shot	Mastery Criterion
11	35-foot chip from 5 feet off green using 7-iron	4 out of 6 within 6 feet
12	35-foot chip from 15 feet off green using wedge	4 out of 6 within 6 feet
13	65-foot chip from 5 feet off green using 5-iron	4 out of 6 within 6 feet
14	25-yard pitch	4 out of 6 within 10 feet
15	35-yard pitch	4 out of 6 within 15 feet
16	50-yard pitch	4 out of 6 within 15 feet
17	75-yard pitch	4 out of 6 within 30 feet

Pull a seven-iron from your bag and practice this left-hand action without a ball for a moment. You will need to make some minor, though important, changes in your stance for two reasons. First, you will note that when you sole both your seven-iron and your putter next to each other, the putter shaft stands more upright than the seven-iron (see Plate 9). Second, the seven-iron is longer than your putter. For these reasons you must assume an open stance in order to more easily swing straight back and straight through. As in the accompanying photograph an open stance is made by withdrawing the left foot an inch or two from the square position. This will keep the left side of your body from interfering with your follow-through. In addition, your toes should be turned out a little as this will improve your balance when you swing. A second look at the picture will show you that the ball is played opposite the midpoint of your stance. This will further ensure that you strike the ball first instead of the ground. For that same reason you must also shift seventy percent of your weight to your left foot and push your hands slightly ahead of the ball at address.

Try this new stance on for size. It's something you will use a lot in your golfing life so take some time to get it right. Choke down on the grip so that your right hand is almost down to the metal shaft. This will give you greater control. Use the grip that you have previously mastered.

Without a ball, practice executing a back-and-through putting stroke using your seven-iron and this open stance. As a result of keeping your weight on your left foot throughout your swing, the clubhead should brush the grass at the lowest part of your stroke. For the time being keep your left wrist straight just as you do when putting.

At this stage we would like you to get out some golf balls and stroke ten to fifteen shots without regard for where the ball goes. Stand about five feet off the practice green and use the stroke you have been working on to bump the ball over the edge of the green. *Don't attempt to lift the ball into the air by scooping at it or flipping your wrists!* Loft was built into the club itself by the manufacturer. Let it do its job. Merely push the club back with your left hand and arm, then pull it through.

An exercise we recommend for "scoopers and flippers" is to practice chipping out of a sand trap or on the beach. If you strike the ball clearly, you will hear a solid click. If you don't strike the ball first by leading with the back of your left hand, the sand will muffle the shot and the ball will barely move. Golfers we have worked with have found this drill particularly effective. One caution, though: this is just an exercise to increase left-hand control. Do not attempt chipping out of a sand trap when you are playing a round of golf. It is far too risky and there are better methods that we will introduce later.

After you have practiced these basic prerequisites, it is time to return to the mastery chain. Find a place on a flat section of green where there is thirty feet of putting surface between the hole and the edge of the green. Drop some golf balls five feet off the green, and with your seven-iron attempt to chip six shots within six feet of the hole; when four of the six shots come this close, you will have achieved proficiency. Use some tees pushed lightly into the green to delineate the mastery target. Remember, you have six feet of room past the hole as well as six feet short of the hole to chip within. Many people are able to achieve this

Plate 9

level of skill by the second or third trial. But if you require more trials than this, don't despair. Briefly review the correct stance and work on the left hand and arm action through the ball while holding your head steady.

FINE TUNING YOUR SKILL

Once you find it easy to roll four out of six shots within six feet of the hole consistently, you might want to see if you are able to increase your skill. Try reducing the target area to a four-foot circle around the hole and use the same criterion of four out of six chips within it.

After you are proficient at this step in the sequence, move on to the next. This time we would like you to move to a place where you are fifteen feet from the edge of the green but a total of thirty-five feet from the hole. Were you to use a seven-iron from this location, the ball would roll far beyond the hole after it hit the green. So instead of a seven-iron, use a nine-iron or a wedge. The additional loft on the nine-iron or wedge will prevent the ball from rolling too much. Use the same stance and swing as before. Make sure the ball carries to the green and then rolls to the hole. Landing in the fringe of the green isn't always safe as it often cuts too much speed off the forward roll or kicks the ball at an odd angle. Practice at this stage until you are able to roll four out of six shots within six feet of the cup. Once you are able to do this you may again wish to fine-tune your skill by reducing the target area to four feet.

By this time you might have guessed that we advocate chipping with a different club to fit each situation. Although some teachers recommend using a single favorite club for all chips, we find this foolhardy. Just as no one treatment is correct for every malady, neither is any one club suitable for every shot around the green. We promote using the club with just enough loft to carry the ball onto the green and let it run like a putt the rest of the way to the hole. Most of the best players and instructors such as Judy Rankin, Tommy Armour, and Billy Casper recommend this method.

It will take some practice and experience, though, to learn which club is best suited for each occasion. However, by paying attention to the results of each chip you encounter when on the course, you will eventually have little difficulty making the proper club selection. As a guide until you gain further experience, we have included the following diagram to assist you in making the proper club selection.

As you can see the wedge is the preferred club only when you have very little green to work with or you need loft to toss the ball over an elevated obstacle. When you have plenty of green to work with, a more straight-faced club is best suited for the job. Rarely is it necessary, however, to drop below a five-iron. The four-, three-, and two-irons are just too long-shafted with too little loft to control easily around the green.

Selecting the proper club.

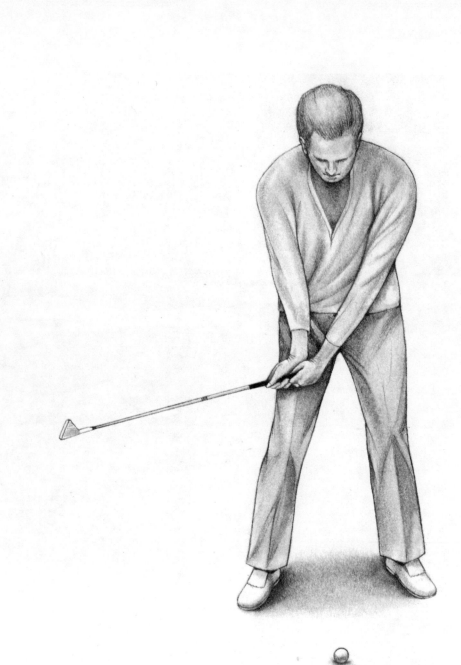

Wrist action.

A NEW WRINKLE

The next step in the sequence involves using a straight-faced club like the five-iron. From a location ten feet off the green, chip to a target sixty-five feet away. Some people report difficulty striking a ball this distance while using a straight-wristed putting stroke. As you move farther from the hole, wrist action becomes necessary in order to increase clubhead speed. It is time to add this component to your swing. The wrist action we refer to is simply a slight hinging motion as demonstrated in the illustration on the facing page. The swing remains basically the same. Your wrists barely break in response to the weighted clubhead and the longer swing of your arms. You must still control the club with your left hand, and you must still strike the ball before brushing the turf. Anyone having difficulty achieving this is urged to undertake the sand-beach chipping exercise we related earlier. Work at keeping your weight on your left foot throughout your swing. Again, this will promote the descending clubhead movement Jack Grout exhorts. Avoid flippiness! Mastery at this step in the chain calls for four out of six chips to stop within six feet of the hole. Attaining this ability level will require some practice, but it will be time well spent.

If you haven't already noticed, you will quickly find that chips break just as putts do. You must play for the break when chipping or face unnecessarily long putts after well struck shots. We instruct our student golfers to "spot" chip as they spot putt. The intermediate target you aim for when chipping must, of course, be larger than the blade of grass you sight when putting. In general we ask our golfers to visualize a half-way target the size of an opened magazine to run the ball over. This image appears to work well, but use your own imagination to develop other possibilities if our suggestion doesn't work for you. The slight hinging of the wrists you master here will also serve you well when you have a tight lie on any chip. When the ball is down in the deep grass that frequently borders a green, you must strike the ball with a more pronounced descending blow. It is important that you put as much clubface on the ball as possible in this situation. A straight-wristed swing simply will not work when the grass is tall, because too much of it gets between the ball and the clubface. It will be worth your while to practice a few chips out of the "deep and wiry," as Bing Crosby used to call it, in order to have some idea of how the ball will react when you are confronted with this condition on the course.

YOUR SWING THUS FAR . . . THE QUARTER SWING

By the end of the chipping sequence, you will have mastered the quarter swing (Plate 10). In the quarter swing your hands are carried to a point just past your right leg on the backswing. Because the follow-through is almost a mirror image of the backswing, your hands swing through the ball to a point just beyond your left leg. This is the impact zone of your full swing, and you must be striking the ball squarely on the sweetspot at this juncture.

Plate 10

PITCH SHOTS

Once you have satisfied the mastery criterion we have presented for chipping, you will want to extend your swing to the pitch shot. The main objective of the pitch shot is to loft the ball high over intervening obstacles such as sand traps and land delicately near the pin without much roll. In order to achieve this, you must swing your left arm straight back as before, but allow your wrists to cock more fully. When your hands reach the half-swing position of belt high, the clubshaft should be pointing nearly straight up to the heavens. This wrist-cocking occurs only at the base of your left thumb as depicted in the illustration on the following page. Do not permit your wrist to cup, collapse, or curl under. These wrist positions twist the clubface out of square alignment and necessitate undue manipulation to correct.

THE QUARTER-TURN DRILL

The quarter-turn drill is designed to provide you with immediate feedback on whether or not you are swinging correctly at this phase. Our golfers have found it to be very helpful, so we pass the exercise on to you.

1. Take the correct address position and imagine you are standing at the center of a huge clock with your body directly facing twelve o'clock.

2. Swing your hands back to the rib-high position.

3. While holding the club exactly where it finishes, shift your body and both feet ninety degrees, a quarter-turn to your right, without moving your hands. Your body should now face directly at the three of the imaginary clock.

4. Now drop your hands, arms, and club straight down so that the clubhead again rests on the ground.

5. You should be perfectly set up to hit a shot in this new direction.

If you find the clubhead twisted to the right or left, you must practice this exercise until you can make the quarter-turn drill four consecutive times and return the clubface to the exact position you originally started from.

The stance for pitch shots is basically the same open alignment as for chipping, though your heels may be separated an inch or two more. While the ball remains opposite the midpoint of your stance, your weight is no longer settled on your left side. Instead, your weight should definitely be centered between the insteps of both feet. If you do this without locking your legs, both knees naturally slide toward each other slightly. When taking your grip you should place your left hand about half an inch below the top of the club. No longer choke down on the shaft. Gripping higher on the club will cause you to stand "taller" and less crouched to the ball and that's just right. When you make the pitch shot swing, allow your knees and body to react to the swinging motion of your arms and hands. While your head remains still your left knee slides toward your right knee about an inch during the backswing. Try this now and see if it isn't so.

51

Pitch shot.

Simply set up with your weight on your insteps and let your arms pull your left knee toward your right knee. If this isn't occurring, you are locking your legs and hips. Stop for a moment and shake them loose. Then try it again. Don't overdo it now. Forcing this action often leads to excessive head movement. Perform the quarter-turn drill again and check whether your left knee is reacting naturally.

DOWN AND THROUGH

As a result of the slight coiling of your body on the backswing followed by the downward/forward motion of your arms on the return or downswing, both your left and right knees will shuttle slightly toward the target as you swing through the ball. Let them. All the movement of your knees we have just described occurs normally as the result of setting up properly and swinging your left hand and arm. You need not worry about what to do with them because they will move by themselves unless you freeze your lower body.

Take five minutes now and make twenty to thirty practice swings to accustom yourself to the swinging motion of your left arm. Casually, observe your knee action and convince yourself that they naturally perform as we report. The rhythm of the swing is still back and through. If you haven't yet grooved this aspect of your game, you should return to the previous steps in the mastery chain and ingrain it there. Do not neglect this feature of your swing.

Find a location twenty-five yards from the hole (or a makeshift target on the practice range) and hit ten to fifteen shots without regard for mastery. After you have struck these practice shots, it is time to return to the mastery chain. First, practice until you are able to pitch four out of six balls within a twenty-foot diameter surrounding the hole. Once you can accomplish this regularly, reduce the target area to a ten-foot bullseye, and practice until you are able to land four out of six shots within this zone.

At this stage you are making approximately a half-swing (Plate 11). Your hands reach about hip high on both the back- and downswings. What is called for now is practice at increasing distances from the hole. This practice will accomplish three important things. First, it will stamp in the fundamental movements. Second, it will help you become accomplished at judging distance and the force necessary to hit the ball to the hole. Third, as you move farther from the hole you will naturally increase the length of your swing. The thirty-five-yard shot calls for a swing that is only slightly longer than that required by the twenty-five-yard shot. Here your hands are carried back to approximately rib high. The mastery requisite at this stage is pitching four out of six shots within a fifteen-foot diameter of the hole.

If you encounter difficulty achieving mastery on the fifty-yard shot, there are several interventions you should attempt. First, simply drop back to forty yards away and gradually increase the length of the shot by five-yard increments until you are able to achieve pitching four out of six shots within fifteen feet of the hole. This strategy worked well for our students and it may for you as well. While working at the easier, shorter distances, review, one at a time, the basic stance and swing fundamentals. Make certain you are aimed correctly. Head-

Plate 11

Plate 12

steadiness is critical. Your left hand and arm need to be in control of the swing while your right hand goes along for the ride. Rhythm remains back and through. Before you proceed to seventy-five-yard pitches, attain mastery at fifty yards.

THE THREE-QUARTER OR SHOULDER TO SHOULDER SWING

The swing for the seventy-five-yard shot requires that your hands swing to about shoulder height on your backswing and follow-through (Plate 12). Some golfers, though able to make a swing of this length, simply cannot hit the ball seventy-five yards. There is nothing wrong or bad about this. Physical limitations are valid considerations. If you find yourself in this situation, you must simply accept your limitation, and determine the maximum length you are able to hit the ball with a three-quarter swing. Don't attempt to hit the ball farther by swinging faster or harder. Jan Stephenson, *Golf Magazine*'s All-American wedge player for 1979, states, "Never hit a full shot with a wedge because accuracy, not distance, is important" (Stephenson, 1979). We concur wholeheartedly. The mastery criterion for a seventy-five-yard pitch shot (or whatever your maximum distance may be), is hitting four out of six balls within thirty feet of the pin. Again, if you are having difficulty succeeding at this level of proficiency, simply drop back to a distance midway between this step and the previous one.

THE PITCH AND RUN SHOT

There are many variations on the basic pitch shot that prove extremely valuable on the golf course. One such variation is the pitch and run shot. This shot is preferred when you need to knock your ball over an expanse of fairway but there remains plenty of "green" room to work with. Also, this shot is especially effective on windy days. Although there are any number of tricky ways to transact a pitch and run shot, all you really need do is switch from a wedge to a less lofted club such as a six-, seven-, or eight-iron. Choke down on the grip a couple of inches and make the same swing you have been perfecting. No other modifications are necessary. This shot will fly slightly lower and run a long way, so remember to plan your strategy accordingly. After you have attained mastery at each distance with your basic pitch shot swing, go back and practice the pitch and run using the same mastery criterion as before. Other finesse strokes from around the green, such as the cut-lob shot, will be discussed in later chapters as these variations call for changes in your swing not applicable to the mastery chain.

If you follow the program we have outlined in this chapter, your short-game arsenal will be formidable indeed. There is no valid excuse for not mastering the skills we have presented. Each step builds on the one immediately preceding it. Nothing we ask you to try is beyond the ability of the average player. If you want to improve your game and swing, you must attain competency at each of these steps.

4

Irons
and Fairway Woods

"Irons are the offensive shots of golf."
BEN HOGAN

"The same fundamentally sound swing that produces good shots with the other clubs likewise produces good long iron shots."
MASON RUDOLPH

Although first-rate putting, chipping, and pitching represent the major portion of a golfer's game, it is precision shotmaking with the iron clubs that often distinguishes the advanced player from the less skilled. The immortal Ben Hogan (1948) writes that, "Good golfers attack a golf course . . . (while) a faulty iron player must immediately go on the defensive, avoid as many errors as he can and rely on his short game for any help at all in cutting down his score." Adding further weight to Hogan's statement, the golf research team of Cochran and Stobbs (1968) statistically determined that iron approach shots are indeed where most professional golf tournaments are won. The necessity for solid iron play should be readily apparent to anyone playing the game. A simple look at the scorecard of any regulation sized golf course will tell you that fourteen or more holes per round require iron shots of some description. How well you negotiate these shots can have a significant impact on the score you mark down for each hole.

If you have followed the program we have described thus far you are ready to progress to this next link in the golf chain. Mastering iron shots, and later fairway woods, will require two additions to your current golfing skills. First, a modified address position is necessary to accommodate the longer swing. The new address position will enable you to maintain balance and facilitate a fuller body turn. Second, more effective legwork is needed to extend the three-quarter swing to the full swing that will propel the ball longer distances. Before these changes are attempted, however, it is critical that you master the fundamental body and arm movements necessary for putting, chipping, and pitching. This will groove your arm swing up through the three-quarter swing position enabling you to now concentrate on making a more complete turn.

ADDRESS POSTURE AND BALL POSITION

It is almost impossible to hit a decent iron shot if you crouch over the ball as if you were robbing a safe. It is equally hard to hit it well if you are standing up stiff and straight. Unfortunately, these descriptions are a reasonable facsimile of the contortions some golfers naively adopt as address posture. The many instructional pieces that state that you must stand up to the ball comfortably and naturally are correct. But what does that actually mean? In point of fact, there are aspects of posture that you should not adopt even if they feel natural. As with other learned behaviors the correct address posture will come to feel comfortable and natural with practice. The following exercise will put you into the best posture to swing a golf club effectively.

1. Grip the intended club in the correct fashion (See Chapter 2).

2. Stand straight with your feet together and . . .

3. . . . let your upper arms rest lightly on your chest.

4. Bend from your waist until the clubhead is soled flat on the ground.

5. Separate your heels approximately eight inches for the nine-iron (more for the longer clubs).

6. Bend your knees in about three inches.

And there you have it, the perfect comfortable and natural stance. Oh, you say you don't have it yet? Well there is only one way for you to get it and that is to practice. For many people it comes quickly but others will have to spend five minutes a day rehearsing this posture at home so that it can occur spontaneously out on the course.

While we are working on the address you will also have to adjust the position of the ball as well as the center of your weight. Because you'll want to use a descending blow with your irons and fairway woods, the best placement for the ball is just before the lowest point of the arc of your swing. That low point for most people is approximately two inches inside their left heel. Use this ball posi-

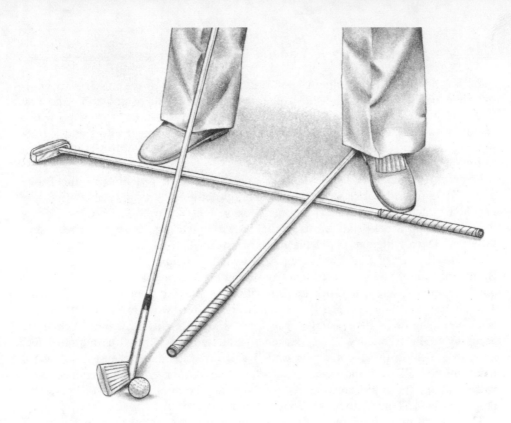

Ball position for normal shots with irons and fairway woods.

tion for all normal shots with your irons and fairway woods. Some golfers push the ball back to the midpoint between their heels. This placement encourages a chopping motion in their swings that is most undesirable. When on the practice tee we urge you to cross some clubs on the ground as in the accompanying illustration to guide this ball position.

As in chipping and pitching, the location of your weight at address greatly contributes to your performance of the full swing. Since you will want to shift it there during your backswing anyway, the place to put sixty percent of your weight is on the instep of your right foot. You will not hit the ball "fat" with the bulk of your weight on the right instep if you follow the swing skills we present in the remainder of this chapter.

Much has been written over the years on the topic of making the perfect back-swing turn. Often, golf students are urged to make a full turn with their shoulders, while restricting the movements of their hips. We find this suggestion to be perhaps the worst bit of advice ever pushed on unsuspecting golfers. No other golf tip that comes to mind has promoted such flat-footed swinging—not to mention acute lower back pain. Supposedly, by restricting the hip turn, tension is "coiled up" for quick release on the downswing, resulting in extra distance. Un-doubtedly, tension is stockpiled on the backswing using this method. Unfortu-nately, the release of this coiled-up tension is not going to increase distance. That's right, uncoiled tension will not increase distance. Rather, it is the shifting of weight from the right foot to the left foot while swinging your hands in smooth synchrony that results in good distance. You can prove this fact to yourself right now by walking outside and throwing a baseball or football. The first time throw the ball with only your hand, arm, and shoulder (in other words stand flat-footed) and chuck it as far as you can. On your next effort add leg action by taking a step when you throw. We bet your second throw goes much faster and farther than your first.

Legwork is crucial for success in every ball sport. Can you imagine Jim Bibby of the 1979 World Series Champion Pittsburgh Pirates hurling a ninety-five-mile per hour pitch without that awesome kick/weight shift he has? Could Terry Bradshaw whip a pass sixty yards in the air without using his legs? Do you suppose that Dave Kingman could blast the home-run ball as he does without stepping into the pitch when he swings? How many tennis championships would Bjorn Borg win if you prevented him from using his legs on his serve?

In a similar fashion, legwork is also critical in making a powerful golf swing. The phenomenal Sam Snead (1979) states that golfers who do not use their legs when swinging are, "two pistons away from still more distance and much more accuracy." The legendary Walter Hagen was quoted as saying, "the minute I feel my legs stiffening up, I don't turn well. I can just look out because I know I'll have the ball all over the place" (Snead, 1968). Other great golfers who have written about the importance of legwork include Tommy Armour (1952), Ben Hogan (1948), Tom Watson (1975), and many more.

There is no mysterious secret to using your legs correctly when swinging a golf club. If you watch any of the consistent tournament champions on the pro tour you will notice that their left knee kicks in toward the right on the backswing. After that it slides back to the left on the downswing. This leg action first shifts their weight emphatically to the right where it is then powerfully pulled to the left. The reason it is important to initiate the downswing with the left knee is that this action has the effect of pulling your left arm and hand down at the proper angle of attack.

Golfers who "hit from the top" by starting the downswing with their hands and shoulders throw the clubhead out of the true path and dissipate a great deal of power in the process. You can avoid coming over the top of the ball by using your legs properly. To make this movement, simply push your left knee in behind the ball on the backswing (see Plate 13 for full swing knee action). Then slide your knee in the direction of the target while holding your head steady. Head swaying results in swing-arc changes that are next to impossible to coordinate. Many golfers, young and old alike, find it necessary to raise their left heel slightly off the ground on the backswing—even on short iron shots. This is something we can recommend if you are having difficulty making the proper turn. Moreover, this move has the advantage of preventing the classic golf-swing error, the reverse pivot. In the reverse pivot the golfer's weight remains stuck on the left side throughout the backswing, then falls back on the right foot during the downswing. This is exactly the opposite of effective leg action and generally results in topped, pulled, or sliced shots.

Plate 13

UP AND AT'EM!

It's time to get up and start practicing again. So, stand up and without using a club begin grooving the muscle memory of the correct leg action. As you swing your hands away from the address position kick your left knee in so that it points inches behind the ball, then as your hands pause briefly at the top of your backswing, slide your left knee toward the target. Perform this action a dozen times while concentrating solely on the motion of your left knee. You will find it easier to maintain your balance when you add leg action to your swing if you will widen your stance slightly. Separate your feet a couple of inches wider than you would for a pitch shot. Since we teach the square stance for all normal full shots, square up your stance, too. Remember, your shoulders and hips need to be parallel to the target just as your feet are.

Once the leg movement begins to feel natural make ten more practice swings pairing the correct leg action with the back-and-through rhythm you have previously mastered. In a short while the new motion will begin to feel comfortable and well timed, usually with a minute or two of practice. Next, pick up a nine-iron and make fifteen to twenty swings without hitting any golf balls. If you are experiencing difficulty in making a turn, allow your left heel to rise slightly (no more than an inch). Check to see if your weight shifts more readily. To initiate the downswing merely replant your left heel firmly on the ground. Upon doing this your left knee will automatically slide toward the target as it should. The only caveat about raising the left heel is that it must return to the exact place from which it left. This is not difficult to achieve but is critical to perform. Failure to do so will result in errant shotmaking.

For those golfers who are able to make the correct pivot while keeping their left heel on the ground throughout the swing, you have a choice between two ways of beginning your downswing. You may either slide your knee toward the target as we have previously mentioned, or you may start down by rolling your weight to the outside of your left foot. The resultant body action is the same with each technique but many of our student golfers report greater success using the latter method. A little experimentation will tell you which way works best for you.

THE MASTERY CHAIN FOR IRON SHOTS

As we have stated before, simply reading the instructions we present throughout this book is not enough to ensure competence in any given facet of your golf game. A demonstration of mastery is the only way to ensure that your muscles have learned the correct responses. Failure to attain mastery at a particular step suggests that you had best spend additional time practicing.

TABLE 4

Mastery Criterion for Irons and Woods.

Step	Shot	Mastery Criterion
20	100-yard shot	4 of 6 within 40 feet
21	125-yard shot	4 of 6 within 45 feet
22	150-yard shot	4 of 6 within 54 feet
23	175-yard shot	4 of 6 within 66 feet
24	200-yard shot	4 of 6 within 90 feet

Table 4 is that portion of the chain that pertains to iron-length shots. As always, the mastery criterion for passing to the next level accompanies each step. You will notice that the distances at which to achieve mastery extends from one hundred to two hundred yards. Many golfers, however, simply do not have the physical ability to strike their irons (or even a wood) one hundred seventy-five to two hundred yards. Other golfers, though, will be capable of rifling a long iron two hundred ten yards on the fly. Thus, it is important that each golfer find his optimal length for each club in his bag. Trial and error is the only method you have available for making this discrimination. As a guide, though, we suggest that if you have to jump all over the ball in order to hit a nine-iron one hundred twenty yards it is likely that it is not the correct club for you at that distance. Some readers will need a five-iron or more to accurately reach one hundred twenty yards. Use whatever club it takes to cover the distance. For those of you who already play, because you once hit a seven-iron one hundred sixty yards does not mean you are capable of consistently hitting a seven-iron that distance.

For the shorter hitter the mastery criteria listed in Table 4 are too difficult. In the past we have allowed these golfers to pass this step by landing only half of their shots within the target area. The reason that we have been so generous is that for many golfers these distances are at the outermost fringe of their range. Many of their shots will be on target but fail to meet criterion only because they fall short. If you have no difficulty reaching these distances you should use a stricter mastery criterion such as four out of six shots within the designated area, rather than the three of six suggested for the shorter players. The method that we have taught you for the longer shots follows directly from the skills you have mastered going through the chain.

Often we are asked if the same backswing/takeaway used for pitch shots should be used for longer shots. Generally, the golfer who asks this question has some experience with the game and somewhere along the line has been told that you must make a "one-piece" takeaway, that is, a backswing where the wrists are prevented from cocking before the hands reach hip height. The one-piece takeaway was espoused by such great stars as Byron Nelson (1966) and Gene Littler (Littler and Collett, 1962) and the vogue for it lasted many years. More recently, however, such stars as Johnny Miller (Miller and Shankland, 1976), Tom Watson (1975), Ben Crenshaw, and *Golf Digest* Master Instructors, Bob Toski and Jim Flick (Dennis, 1974a) have been advocating an early set of the wrists during the takeaway for a number of very valid reasons. First, by setting the angle of your left wrist early you promote additional left-side control of the golf club. Also, you are more able to place your left wrist in the proper square top backswing position while your swing is slow and easy to manage. This square alignment of your wrist and forearm is achieved when you set your wrists so that wrinkles form beneath the vee between your thumb and index finger as in the accompanying illustration. In addition Dennis (1974a) states that it is possible to gain more distance as well as more accuracy with this type of takeaway because there is less of the "rebound" of the club shaft and wrists at the top of the backswing that frequently occurs when you delay the wrist set.

If, however, you set the angle with your right hand in control rather than your left, the early set will cause you trouble. This is the reason we have stressed left-hand control so strongly in this book. Without the left hand, arm, and side guiding the club, your right hand and shoulder will overpower your swing at almost any point resulting in a botched shot. Obviously, this is all reversed if you are a lefthanded golfer.

Early in his golfing life the first author (Mr. Simek), like many others, was a devotee of the "one-piece swing." In working with golf professional Joe Lewis he found that this forcing of the one-piece action was very unnatural and resulted in streaks of erratic play. Mr. Lewis, one of the finest golf instructors we have ever worked with, cultivated and shaped an early set of the left wrist, greatly improving the consistency of play. For these reasons we submit that the early set of the left wrist is a plausible alternative to the one-piece swing. Moreover, our research has demonstrated the efficacy of this approach.

A NOTE ON THE ADVANTAGES OF THE FIVE- SIX-SEVEN-WOODS

Because the five-six-seven-woods have more loft than the long irons we heartily recommend them to the twice-a-week golfer. Getting the ball airborne is much easier with these woods, which are also excellent for use from the rough. Unfortunately, these clubs have the unmerited stigma of being "old men's clubs" and that is why they are scorned by the average golfer. Recently, the first author, who is twenty-seven years old, purchased a six-wood that he consistently employs with great success (to the dismay of his opponents). Try one of these clubs, it is apt to become your favorite weapon.

At this point you should be in control of the game from the green through the fairway and it is now a relatively simple task to extend your swing to the tee.

Square alignment of the wrist and forearm.

5

Driving, or What to Do With the Fourteen Least Important Shots in a Round

"I'm going to swing the driver so easy that the ball is never going to stop rolling."

A longhitter
quoted by
TOMMY ARMOUR

By following our program up through the irons and fairway woods your basic full swing has become ingrained. There are still a few minor changes to make in addressing the ball plus a honing into the "square slot" at the top of your backswing but these are details. The swing you use for the long irons and fairway woods is virtually identical to the one you will want to use with a driver. The only difference being that for irons you use a steeper, more descending swing to get the ball airborne, while with the driver, the ball is perched on a tee just waiting to be swept into the air.

The best way to ensure a sweeping type motion is to set a little more weight on your right side at address and to lower your right shoulder a little so that your left shoulder stands taller than your right. Take your driver and practice this adjustment to your stance in front of a full-length mirror for a minute. Don't exaggerate this position too much. Just relax your right shoulder and arm.

67

Plate 14

Let your right elbow bend slightly and rest close to your right side. Our students report that this stance makes them feel as though they are ready to spring at the ball from below. See if you don't have a similar feeling. Because the ball is on a tee and you want to make a sweeping motion you will need to advance the ball slightly so that it is in a line directly opposite the inside of your left heel (Plate 14).

Many people are careless about this placement and it usually proves costly. If you address the ball somewhere in a line off your left toe, you may lunge at the ball, resulting in a skied drive and a white ball mark on the top of your driver. If this happens check your address position.

Further stance alterations include: separating your feet to approximately the width of your shoulders, and positioning your left arm so that it appears as though the back of your left wrist is about in a straight line with the ball. At this point, the heel of that palm should be only one hand's width from your left leg. Special care should be taken so that you don't open your shoulders when you make these adjustments. A good way to learn to attend to the proper variables when addressing the ball is to set twelve to fifteen balls in a row about two feet apart. Then address each ball correctly while a friend gives you feedback as to how you're doing. Proceed from one ball to the next without hitting any shots. This drill is simply to get you to pay attention to how you are setting up to the ball. These minor adjustments in address will allow you to apply your well-groomed fairway swing to the task of achieving long, *accurate* drives with the ball teed up.

The driver is the most difficult club to manage because of its small amount of loft. Loft produces backspin which partially inhibits sidespin from carrying the ball off line. A club like a nine-iron has so much loft that it masks sidespin almost completely. With the driver, on the other hand, any variation of the clubface off square alignment at impact will send the ball careening into the deep rough or trees. Therefore, it becomes very important that swing fundamentals be performed precisely.

Square impact is exceedingly hard to achieve when the club is jerked back and down in an overzealous effort to rip the ball a long way. An incident in a factory that we recently observed illustrates this kind of over-effort particularly well. In this factory the second shift would come in and set the machines to run at a nice, steady speed. By twelve o'clock when the shift was over, the workers had produced a pretty good output because there were no breakdowns. At eight A.M. the first shift would come in and see what the second shift had accomplished. Feeling that they must do as well or better than the second shift they would crank up the machines. Things ran well briefly, then the timing began to miss. First, the product's quality would start going down. Then something jammed in the machine putting it out of commission for as much as an hour before it could be cleaned and used again.

The golf swing is similar in that if you swing at a smooth, even pace you will get a solid output. However, if you turn up the juice various parts are going to jam. The quality of your shots diminishes until you need major rehabilitation by your local pro to repair the damage. Remember: you can swing no faster than the weakest links in your swing can withstand. In fact, pros such as Tom

69

Weiskopf (1973) and Jack Nicklaus (Nicklaus and Wind, 1969) suggest that you swing at only eighty percent of this amount, holding something in reserve. This keeps all parts of your swing well below the red warning lights that forecast trouble.

How does one discover the best speed or tempo at which to swing? Here are a few clues. Swinging so fast that your body is pulled off-balance is ineffective. Your weight must not be allowed to roll to the outside of your right foot on the backswing. If the hub of your swing is yanked off-center it is only luck that will bring it back. The best method to establish solid balance is through the following legwork exercise. Take your driver and address an imaginary ball on some soft ground. Tamp your heels into the earth about one-half to three-quarters of an inch. Now make fifteen to twenty swings. Your heels should come up and down in the impressions you made. If you are chopping up the footprints you are probably forcing yourself to swing faster than you are able. Slow down.

At the top of your backswing your grip should be as lightly secure as it was when you addressed the ball. Many people clutch the club so hard when they yank it away that their hands tire and separate at the top of the backswing. You can learn if you are doing this by placing a penny between the heel of your palm and the grip. If when you swing the penny drops out you are losing control of the club.

Lighten up your grip and make a smoother swing so that the penny stays where you put it. You should be able to swing ten straight times without losing the penny.

SHAPING YOUR SWING AT THE TOP

There are three critical junctures in your full swing. The last of these, impact with the ball, is basically a product of the first two. The first juncture is the address position. If you set up to the ball poised and square you make your golf life immeasurably easier. We have discussed the importance of stance and posture more than once in these pages. If you take care to address the ball like a golfer rather than a hockey player, you have received our message.

The second critical juncture in your swing occurs at the top of your backswing. Ben Hogan (1948) and Tommy Armour (1952) are just two of the hundreds of professional golfers who have expressed concern about that segment of the golf swing. More recently a book by Dick Aultman (1970) and the Editor of *Golf Digest* helped make countless golfers aware of the importance of the proper top of backswing alignment. For many years our teaching professional Joe Lewis and his father Bud Lewis of Manufacturer's Country Club (Philadelphia, Pa.) have espoused similar top of backswing geometry, though using different methods to achieve it. Quite simply the desired position at the top is a clubshaft pointing directly at the desired target with the clubface at a forty-five-degree angle to the ground (Plate 15). With the club in this position at the top you are all set to pull the trigger and swing through the ball. No further club manipulations are necessary. Once you are in the "top slot" simply kick off your downswing as you learned in Chapter 4 and let 'er rip!

Plate 15

Unfortunately, few average golfers swing the club into the "top slot." Generally, their club finds its way to either the laid-off position or the crossed and blocked position. In Plate 16 our model is demonstrating the laid-off position. As you can see, the clubshaft is pointing wildly to the left of the target. With the club over there all the golfer can do is cut across the ball in an outside-to-inside motion causing a pull or a slice. Many golfers swing to this position and suffer from banana ballitis. Occasionally, slicing stems from picking the clubhead up and outside the correct takeaway path. If you have mastered the basic swing through the chain back from the green, this should not be a problem for you. If it is, you should return to an abbreviated mastery chain beginning on the green but emphasizing (that is practicing past criteria) those areas where you feel that you lose control of the swing.

Though at first trying to stay in the slot will feel as if you were swinging the club abruptly inside, you are not actually doing so. The feeling will pass within an hour of practice.

Some golfers start out correctly but lay the club off as they progress through their backswing. Joe Lewis has developed the following novel strategy to combat this problem. Imagine that you are standing at home plate of a baseball diamond with second base and straight-away center field being your target. If at the top of your swing your club is not pointing precisely at second base but instead is pointing at shortstop or third base, on your next swing try to place the clubshaft down the first-base line. It will feel awkward briefly, but your shots will soon straighten out and your swing will feel less cumbersome. Recruit a friend or fellow practicer to give you feedback on how you are doing. Have him stand ten to twelve feet behind you looking at the target you've selected. Immediately after each swing have him call out how many inches to the left you were that time. No comment is necessary beyond the location of the clubshaft at the top of the backswing.

In Plate 17 our model is demonstrating the crossed and blocked position. Here the clubshaft points severely to the right of the target while the clubface points at the sky. Tournament caliber golfers are continually having someone check to see if they are in the slot or have crossed the line. They do this because the crossed and blocked swing leads invariably to hooking, pushing, and other nightmarish (to the touring pro) trouble. Just as with the laid-off position, a golfer can cross the line by swinging the club too quickly inside on the backswing. The remedy here is also to return to the short shots and regroove your backswing.

Again, though, many golfers are able to take the club away properly but somehow cross the line further on in their backswings. For golfers who aim at second base but have grooved their swing toward first base, attempting to lay the club down the third-base line works wonders. Ask a friend to help out again and soon you'll be on the proper track. Your mastery assignment at this stage is to make ten practice swings in a row, hitting the proper top of backswing slot each time. Don't cheat. Start over after each off-line swing.

Plate 16

Plate 17

Having completed this feedback homework on the backswing slot you are ready to attempt mastery of the driver. Because we don't all hit the driver exactly the same distance the mastery criterion will vary for each person. This is fair because being three degrees off line at one hundred yards will land the ball only five yards off course while the same error at two hundred yards will send the ball ten yards off course (Cochran and Stobbs, 1968). On the next page is a diagram that shows how the target area increases as the length of the drive increases.

If you are consistently able to drive the ball two hundred yards, look across the chart at the two-hundred-yard increment. You will find that you are allotted a target zone of thirty yards. Set up markers delineating this space on the practice area. To achieve competency with the driver you must land seven out of ten shots within this range. The concern here is not how far you can hit the drive but hitting accurately at your natural distance.

ON TEEING THE BALL

Once you have achieved the muscle memory of good driving, there are some tactical advantages from the tee that you should be familiar with. The seemingly simple act of teeing the ball correctly could reduce the average golfers' eighteen-hole score by two shots per round. There are three prime considerations to take into account when teeing off. First, how high should the ball be teed up? Bernie Krick, head pro at Williamsport (Pa.) Country Club states that, "there is no one perfect height for all golfers. This is because different drivers have clubfaces of varying depth. A golfer using a shallow-faced driver should naturally tee the ball lower than a player using a standard or deep-faced model. The basic guideline, however, is to tee the ball so that approximately half of it shows above the top of the driver when the driver is soled behind the ball."

The second tip is derived from the USGA's rules of golf. While every golfer knows that he must tee his ball between the tee markers, many golfers are unaware that you are allowed a space of two club lengths deep behind the markers as well. With this in mind you might think that the serious golfer would locate a smooth, level lie from which to tee his ball. Remarkably, he rarely does so. More often he is preoccupied with standing as close to the markers as humanly possible to avoid adding more distance to the hole. Rather than sacrificing a yard or two to drive from a good, level lie, he throws caution (and balance) to the wind. Little does he realize that the yard he thinks he has gained will actually cost him ten to thirty yards in distance. He also has increased the probability of an off-line drive caused by missing the driver's sweetspot.

And finally, the most important factor in setting up for the drive concerns which side of the teeing area one should swing from. Many amateur golfers give no thought at all to this crucial decision. They simply plunk the ball down in the center of the teeing area between the markers and think they are doing the smart thing. Alas, they are not. Each hole on a golf course has its own ideal place from which to take a second shot. Whether you face a reachable fairway

Table 5
Mastery Criteria For Drives

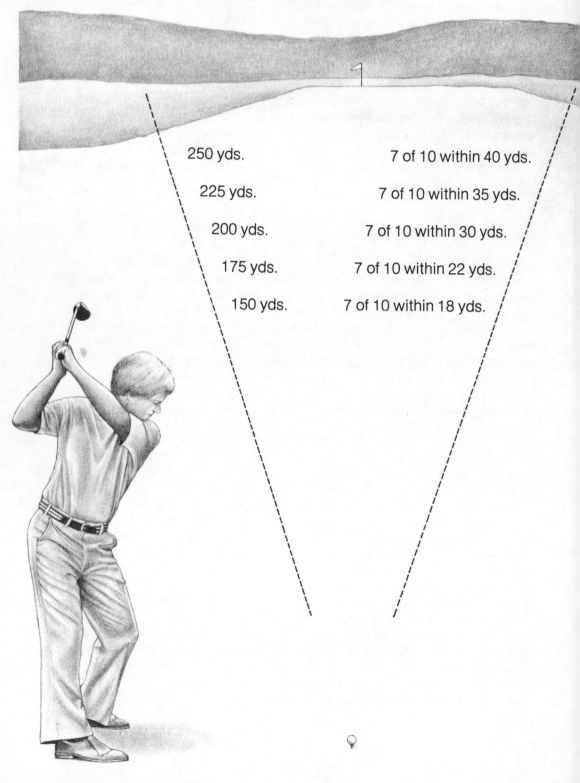

250 yds.	7 of 10 within 40 yds.
225 yds.	7 of 10 within 35 yds.
200 yds.	7 of 10 within 30 yds.
175 yds.	7 of 10 within 22 yds.
150 yds.	7 of 10 within 18 yds.

bunker, trees that block off free access to the green, out-of-bounds, a creek or stream, or whatever, there is usually something out there to be avoided. You should identify where you want the ball to go rather than where you don't want it to go. Then correctly teeing your ball can help you put it there. The smart way to begin each hole is to tee the ball on the side of the driving area closest to trouble, and aim away. For example, if there is a bunker you can reach on the left side of the fairway, you should tee the ball on the left and aim out toward the right. Doing this gives you the widest possible landing area away from the hazard. By aiming out to the right, even if you hook the ball you'd have to hook it very badly to run it all the way across the fairway and into the bunker. If you hit a straight drive you'll be on the right side of the fairway in perfect shape. And, though you'll end up in the right rough if you slice the tee shot, that's not so serious a problem as landing in the sand. If you use your head and eyes when you tee the ball, you will save a lot of strokes in the long run.

DEVELOPING A ROUTINE

In Chapter 2 we pointed out the importance of following a set routine on every putt. That advice applies equally well to every shot from the putt to the drive. As before, this preshot routine provides a framework from which to deal with the forthcoming shot. It also helps alleviate tension, and it forces the golfer to focus on the situation at hand. Your preshot drive ritual should include:

1. Aiming for the spot where you want to hit your second shot.

2. Teeing the ball up correctly.

3. A light practice swing to remind your muscles that they are on call.

4. A waggle or forward press and a deep breath to reduce any tension.

You may add a step or two to this ritual if you like but keep it as similar to your preparation for other shots as you can. Once it is established follow it on every drive without exception.

A FINAL WORD ABOUT DRIVING

When average golfers talk about driving ability their overriding concern is usually power. You will hear them mention with awe the long ball hitters of the game. "How do they do it, and more importantly, how could I do it?" they wonder. The eighty to one hundred shooter will buy all the gimmicks advertised in the back of golf magazines to increase his length off the tee. Included among these aids are: steel inserts, special clubhead weighting, "kick-step" shafts, acrodynamic clubheads, graphite shafts, English-size golf balls that have no distance restriction, specially designed exerciser clubs, and even custom tees that are constructed to minimize clubhead speed loss at impact. Although the average golfer does indeed have an obsession about driving power, statistical studies show time and again it is driving accuracy not driving power that is most important to good golf. (Brown, 1969, Cochran and Stobbs, 1968, *Golf Digest*, 1968). Interviews and questionnaires filled out by pros invariably list precision driving before they list belting the long ball (Nieporte and Sauers, 1968). The fact of the matter is that long hitting just isn't very important to winning golf. The legendary power boys off the tee, such as Jim Dent and George Bayer, actually have decidedly undistinguished records of victories on the tour. The truth is that if you are playing hole number one, it is better to be two hundred yards down the first fairway than three hundred yards down the tenth.

It has been our experience that you had better look out when you hand a driver to a 90 shooter. Usually you can see the misguided soul grit his teeth, tighten his grip, and tense his entire body for the impending blow. The swing he then makes can only be described as rigid, ungainly, mechanical, and full of sound and fury signifying rough. Rarely does such an effort lead to a booming drive. More often the result is a feeble "banana ball slice." But because the golfer's body feels tight and powerful such behavior persists. Not one golf book, instructional article, or club pro we have encountered has once mentioned any beneficial effects from tensing the body. Instead, almost every one has stated, in one form or another, that to hit a long drive you must stand relaxed and make a fluid, rhythmical swing. Although that seems somehow paradoxical, physiological studies have proven that a relaxed muscle will react far more quickly than a stiff, rigid one. Furthermore, studies have demonstrated that striking the ball on the sweetspot will result in longer, straighter drives. Our research has shown that golfers who learn the swing through a chaining mastery-based system are more likely to strike the ball closer to the sweetspot and consequently hit the ball farther and straighter, with the emphasis on the latter quality. Accuracy is the key to winning golf, and focusing your attention on additional power is a sucker bet. There are a number of swing adjustments, the "late hit" for example, which are recommended to increase power off the tee. Unless you are aiming for the PGA Championship we suggest you avoid monkeying around with your basic swing. These adjustments are more likely to increase your score than your distance.

Several chapters in the second half of this book will deal specifically with ridding your swing and game of the tension that is robbing you of more effective and enjoyable play. For now, however, you will best serve yourself by working on the final shaping of your swing. Take some time and practice the lessons detailed in these pages. The mastery program will guide your efforts toward a precise and powerful swing.

6

Trouble Shots and Finesse: A Mastery Approach

"Three of those and one of them make four!" (A description of Walter Hagen's ability to recover to a par.)

ARTHUR CROOME

Mastery of the fundamental swing from putting through driving is the key to competent golf. If you have zealously followed our program, muscle memory for all of golf's basic shots will be at your beck and call. In a just world, that would be enough to guarantee success in any match you play. Unfortunately, life, especially on a golf course, is not fair. It is ladened with obstacles, sand traps, and unlevel lies that require adjustments to your basic swing. Since you can't adjust something that you have never learned, we have not introduced these problems until you had the basic swing down pat.

In our previous research we have not included training for finesse and recovery shots because they represent a variation of no small magnitude on the fundamental swing. Our goal was to establish muscle memory for the basic swing. We did not want our students digging in the sand until that basic goal had been established. But, as golfers say, "Out on the course, the ball is not always sitting up fat and sassy, begging to be hit." During a round, you will have to play your approach shots as they lie. Occasionally, this means that the ball will be above your feet, below your feet, or even higher than one foot but lower than the other. If the slope of the ground is severe you will need to make adjustments in your stance and swing to accommodate the unlevel lie.

79

Difficulties with the lie of the ball are not limited to hills. Finding your ball buried up to the number in sand, is not an uncommon occurrence. Since there is no way to avoid an occasional pilgrimage into the pits, a golfer must be prepared to deal with sand traps and other obstacles which golf course architects seem to love. The golfer, therefore, must be taught sand play even though this skill represents a hitch in our backward-mastery chain.

In the first two studies we conducted, we took the coward's way out by not teaching sand play at all, and it cost us. One of our subjects shot an 87 while taking six shots to get out of one trap. Needless to say he was a little disconsolate after such a harrowing experience. He had simply never been taught how to handle this situation nor had he experienced any actual practice in sand. Although the average golfer may have experienced some instruction in sand play somewhere down the line, he, too, is handicapped by a lack of practice in escaping traps.

Lack of familiarity with shots that frequently occur is a serious shortcoming in any golfer. In addition to recovery shots there is effective finesse play around the green that the sophisticated golfer should master to complete his education. We have developed a minimastery program to teach the swing variations required for finesse and recovery shots. Our experiments with this program are, as yet, incomplete but the principles are theoretically sound. As always we will begin with the easiest finesse/recovery shot and progress to the more complex as each small, manageable step is mastered.

THE TEXAS WEDGE

Your putter isn't limited to use solely on the green. Under certain conditions this is the best club for a short roll over the fairway and onto the putting surface. This is not, however, the best shot every time you miss the green with your approach shot. Only if the grass is cut relatively short and is growing toward the green should you attempt the so-called Texas Wedge. Links lore has it that in Texas, when the wind blows so hard that a sand storm can take the paint finish right off your car, diehard golfers have found that the most effective shot is to roll the ball on the ground and to keep it out of the wind. Hence the name for the putter, the Texas Wedge.

There is nothing tricky about using the putter from off the green. The stance and stroke remain the same but now you must strike the ball with slightly more force as the longer grass of the fairway will slow the ball down more quickly. Before attempting this shot under actual playing conditions it is wise to get some experience with it in practice. The mastery chain for cultivating this useful skill is presented in Table 6.

TABLE 6

The Texas Wedge Mastery Chain.

Step	Shot	Mastery Criterion
1	1 foot off edge of green, hole 15 feet away	3 out of 4 within 3 feet of the hole
2	3 feet off edge of green, hole 15 feet away	3 out of 4 within 4 feet of the hole
3	5 feet off green, hole 25 feet away	3 out of 5 within 5 feet
4	10 feet off green, hole 40 feet away	3 out of 5 within 5 feet

Everything you have learned about putting applies to stroking the Texas Wedge shot. Headsteadiness, rhythm, left-hand control, address position, and so on are still important and not to be slighted. However, these are skills that you have already mastered so you are free to concentrate on the force of the shot. Before you attempt to meet mastery on each of the four shots listed here, stroke a couple of balls and see what happens. If you are overshooting the hole you will need to lighten up a little and vice versa, of course, if you are leaving the shot short. Allow your muscle memory of the putting stroke to work for you. Simply adjust the force of your swing.

SAND PLAY

Many greens are surrounded these days by sand traps. Learning to deal competently with these hazards will reduce the anxiety you might feel when you try to shoot over or out of them. If you are just learning the game you might not be aware that the rules of golf do not allow you to sole your club in a hazard. Touching the sand at address or on your backswing will cost you one penalty stroke. This can be avoided by simply holding your club slightly above the surface of the sand as you address the ball.

The easiest shot from the sand is, once again, the putt. Here too, it is appropriate to attempt this escape route only if the sand is smoothly packed, and there is no lip to the trap. All you need do is roll the ball through the trap, up to the hole. Joe Lewis is so good at this shot that he sometimes has his caddy tend the pin for him. He holes this exaggerated putt so often that he is sometimes accused of aiming for certain unlipped traps just so he can show off to the incredulous dismay of his opponents.

For the time being, however, our goal is simply to escape the trap and roll the ball to within fifteen feet of the hole. Further practice on your own will enable you to reduce that large bullseye to a smaller, more precise target. The stroke for making this shot is identical to your putting stroke, with even greater emphasis on headsteadiness. Any head swaying at all will almost certainly cause you to hit the sand behind the ball resulting in a second chance to try this shot and another stroke on your scorecard.

Before using a putter from the sand trap, make sure the following prerequisites are met:

1. The ball must be lying clean.

2. The sand between your ball and the edge of the trap must be packed and smooth.

3. There should be no lip to speak of on the trap.

Take some time one evening, when your activities won't bother anyone, to master this technique. Locate a trap where the above conditions may be found. Practice until you are able to roll five out of six shots within fifteen feet of the hole. When you finish please remember to rake the trap so that those playing the next day will find the course in the same playable condition as you did.

Your introduction to sand shots has been made particularly easy by starting out with the putt from the trap. Many times, however, you won't be able to use this shot because the lip of the trap is too steep. Therefore, it is necessary for you to learn the simple variations on your pitch shot swing that will enable you to negotiate sand.

Before you run over to your club's practice sand trap you ought to obtain the golf tool best suited for this shot. The sand wedge has been specially designed with a large flange (see illustration) to more easily extricate a golf ball from sand traps. This is why many pros including Tommy Armour have called the sand shot the only shot in golf that you can buy. Avoid unnecessarily handicapping yourself by rationalizing frugality. The sand wedge will pay for itself many times in your golfing lifetime.

Once you have obtained the appropriate instrument for sand play you are ready to learn the next skill. The basic sand shot with the ball lying fairly clean is much akin to the pitch shot swing you have already mastered. The major difference is that with the sand shot you do not hit the ball. Instead you aim between two and four inches behind the ball and slice both sand and ball onto the green. As in the illustration on page 84, your stance and clubface should be open slightly. You need to dig your feet into the sand in order to supply a secure foundation from which to swing. Pay particular attention to how heavy or how tightly packed the sand is when your spikes dig in. This will give you some information on how far you need to take the club back.

As always headsteadiness is a must. So, too, is an unhurried swing. Joe Lewis instructs his students to change the rhythm line from "back and through" to "soft and through." Superhuman strength is not necessary in playing this shot. You must merely dislodge a shallow handful of sand. The phrase "soft and through" seems to convey just the right idea of the force required. It is impor-

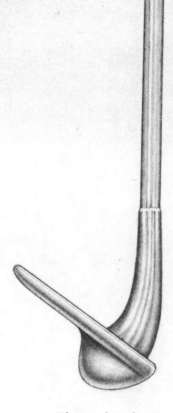

The sand wedge.

tant to be aware that the second part of that phrase is just as important as the first. You must swing through the sand and ball and finish with your hands about shoulder high as you do in your three-quarter swing. Every club pro or magazine golf writer that we have encountered stresses this point. Quitting on the swing will leave the ball in the trap. It is essential that you follow through.

Place a few balls in the trap and with the sole purpose of getting the ball out try a dozen trap shots. Aim at a spot two or more inches behind the ball and use a soft and through three quarter-swing. Some golfers do better if they imagine that the ball is lying on the center of a dollar bill and then try to splash the whole bill out of the trap. If this image works for you, use it. Your mastery goal for this shot is simply to get the ball out of the trap and onto the green nine times out of ten. Continued practice of this shot will enable you to hone that mastery target area down to the size of a child's wading pool. At first, though, take some pressure off yourself by aiming for a large target and working on your swing.

Many golf courses and country clubs are currently using power rakes to smooth out their sand traps. This lessens the chance that your ball will lie clean in the trap. More likely it will plug or be buried so that a different strategy is

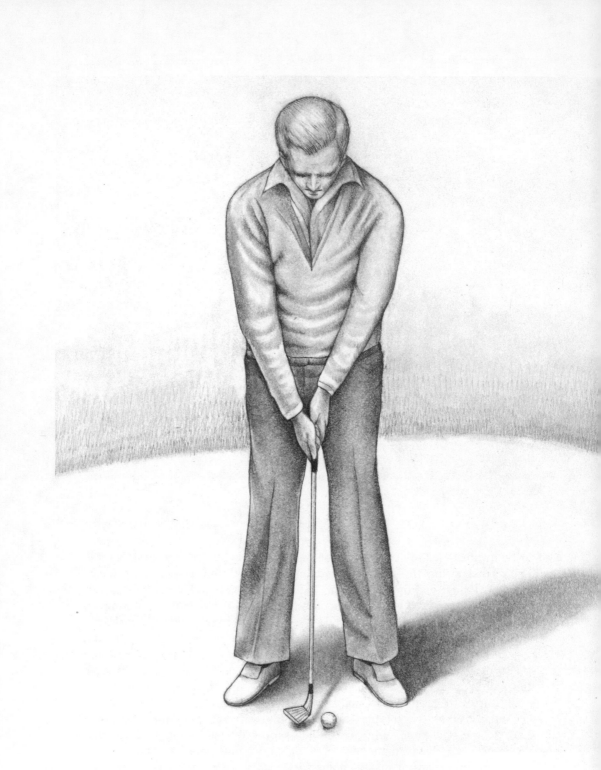

Your stance and clubface should be slightly open for a sand shot.

required to get it out. For the plugged or buried ball a more pronounced descending blow is necessary. This descending blow is made by abruptly cocking your wrists on the backswing followed by punching the ball on the downswing. Many pros call this the V-swing (see page 86) because that shape accurately describes the path the clubhead must make for a buried sand shot (Mills, 1973; Stacy, 1979). The best way to learn this V-shaped swing is to stand in the trap in such a manner that you will hit the bank on the backswing if you don't abruptly set your wrists. Practice this swing without a ball for two to three minutes until it begins to feel comfortable.

Another adjustment you need to make on this shot is to close up the clubface at address. Turn the clubface a few degrees toward your body. If you leave the clubface open as for an unburied ball you won't be able to cut deeply enough into the sand. By closing or hooding the clubface you can prevent this from happening. In addition to shutting the clubface you now must move your aim up toward the top quarter of the ball rather than two to four inches behind the ball. This, too, will help explode the ball out of the tight lie and onto the green. However, as you will soon find out, hooding the clubface and playing the top quarter of the ball will increase the amount of roll the ball will take.

Occasionally, you will face a shot where the ball is buried in a greenside trap but the hole is only a short way onto the green. In this situation there isn't much chance you will knock the ball close to the pin even if you play the shot perfectly. Under such conditions it is wise to relinquish any hope for a miracle and simply get the ball somewhere on the green. Although you are apt to bogey the hole you need to remember that a bogey is much better than the double bogey (or worse) that you might make if you tried to play the shot too cute and left the ball in the trap. Discretion really is the better part of valor in this instance.

One final comment before you begin to practice buried sand shots. You must aim a few feet to the right of the pin in order to compensate for the closed clubface which will send the ball to the left. Continue to use an open stance but pretend the hole is a few feet to the right of where it actually is. Practice will tell you exactly how much.

As you begin to practice buried lies, start with balls that are only one-quarter buried. Don't make learning this new skill unnecessarily difficult by squashing the ball so deeply into the sand that you need a shovel to get it out. Gradually work up to that level of difficulty. After you have punched four out of five one-quarter buried shots onto the practice green, try some shots where the ball is buried halfway. Only when you are consistently able to blast four out of five of these shots onto the green should you attempt shots where the ball is more deeply plugged.

There are many other variations on these two basic sand shots and you will encounter them all once you are playing regularly. What to do about these numerous variations, however, is beyond the scope of this book. In order to attain some degree of mastery over them you must experiment, practice, and even take a lesson or two from a qualified pro. He is best suited to helping you learn all the variations on a theme a golfer can experience in greenside sand traps. Follow his technical advice and then construct your own personal mastery-based program to increase your skill.

The V-shaped swing.

FAIRWAY BUNKERS

Around the green is not the only place you can find yourself in sand. Fairway bunkers are strategically placed throughout good courses to catch errant golf shots. Here again, your first line of attack is to get out. If the bunker has a fairly steep front bank it may be all you can do to smack the ball with a pitching wedge hoping to get fifty yards farther down the fairway. It's a rare bunker where the golfer is able to employ the shallow-faced long irons with any chance of success. Once in a while the safest and smartest shot is to chip the ball out sideways onto the fairway. Although this "lateral move" is a galling thing to have to do, it is a much better tactic than battering the ball into the bank of the trap a half-dozen times. Use your head before you use your body. If you are a four-iron distance from the green but the height of the bunker will allow you no more than an eight-iron, do the smart thing, play the percentages and use the club that has enough loft to clear the bank. A good pitch shot will put you back in the ballgame.

Obviously, the most important aspect of this long shot from the fairway bunker is to make solid, clean contact with the ball. If even the smallest amount of sand comes between the clubface and the ball, the shot will be muffled. Head-steadiness, of course, will be a big aid toward making crisp contact. There are adjustments one can make to increase the probability of striking the ball solidly. First, address the ball midway between your feet. From this position it is easier to strike the ball before hitting the sand. Next, reduce your swing to a crisp three-quarter action. This will be less difficult to perform in the sand than the full swing.

The best way to learn how to deal with this type of shot is to begin by tapping some chips out of the trap. Building on this miniature swing in small increments will allow you to experience successes while you become accustomed to swinging through the sand. Make sure that when you start practicing this shot you keep your weight on your left side. This will aid you in making a sharp descending blow. Sitting back on your hind foot while scooping at the ball is not an effective method of escaping the trap and will tend to increase the likelihood of flaws creeping into your normal swing.

Follow a reduced version of the basic chain after you are able to tap four of five chip shots out of the bunker.

As you can see in Table 7, the mastery criterion target area has been widened by twenty-five percent over the same distanced shots from off the fairway. Because of the added variable, sand, this is a more reasonable target to shoot for.

TABLE 7

Shot	Mastery Criterion
50-yard pitch shot	4 of 5 within 20 feet
100-yard shot	4 of 5 within 50 feet
125-yard shot	4 of 5 within 55 feet
150-yard shot	4 of 5 within 60 feet
175-yard shot (optional for those physically able)	4 of 5 within 75 feet

DOWNHILL LIES AND OTHER RUBS OF THE GREEN

Were golf played solely on smooth, level lies, as on the driving range, the game would be much easier, and far less interesting. Uphill, downhill, and sidehill lies are there to be dealt with even on the ostensibly flat courses of the Midwest. There these unlevel lies occur in the form of gullies, banks, dips, run-off ravines and so on. To negotiate these obstacles, you must make some changes in your basic stance and swing. As with other variations on the basic swing, lack of practice will add many unnecessary strokes to your score.

Not all unlevel lies are fearsome though. In fact one such lie is welcomed by many golfers. This lie, of course, is the uphill lie. Here the slope of the land encourages the 80- through 90-shooter to make a better backswing turn because most of his weight is automatically set on his right foot. Also, the uphill shot is much easier to get airborne, thus overcoming the fear of dibbing a shot along the ground. Despite the built-in advantages of an uphill lie, there are a few dangers that call for attention. First, there is the tendency to hit a hook or pull hook from this position because the ground rises in front of the ball making it difficult to drive the clubhead straight through to the target. Next, the extra height one gains from an uphill lie cuts down on distance, in effect turning a six-iron into a seven-iron. And finally, there is the sensation on the downswing of being unable to shift one's weight back to the left side and this generally results in an awkward lunge at the ball.

The experienced golfer develops muscle memory for this swing with uneven footing through practice. He then naturally counteracts the inherent imbalance of his swing. In order to master the necessary skills you should begin as usual, with the shorter irons, and progress back to the fairway woods. Find a gently inclined slope from which to start. Later on you can play mountain goat and try severely inclined ski-type slopes if you so desire. A few practice swings without a ball will tell you that a chopping motion is good for moving large chunks of earth but little else. A sweeping motion is much more effective. One thing you can do at address to promote a sweeping motion is move the ball slightly more toward the target than it is in its standard placement (about in a line with your left heel is perfect).

Were you to hit a few shots with a nine-iron at your normal target you would find that they fall short and to the left of the pin. Your first strategy to correct for this change in trajectory is to use a longer club. In addition, you must learn to ignore the target and aim for an imaginary flag a few yards to the right. Be sure that you set up absolutely square to this new target. Many golfers think that they are all-square when in fact they have assumed a closed stance. This closed stance exacerbates the possibility of a nasty hook rather than allowing a soft draw to result. So be doubly careful that you are aiming and swinging for the imaginary target zone. When attempting to attain mastery use the enlarged mastery criterion you worked with on fairway bunker shots.

SIDEHILL LIES

Bypassing downhill lies temporarily, the next common situation you will face on a course is the lie in which the ball is either higher or lower than both your feet. Sidehill lies present a new problem to the serious golfer chiefly because his natural swing plane will be modified in accordance with the terrain. Thus, on shots where the ball is above your feet your swing flattens out and becomes more like the one you use to hit a baseball. Conversely, when the ball is below your feet your swing becomes more upright, like that of a ferriswheel, for example. Shots from these angled lies will behave irregularly, too. The general rule is that the shot will curve in the direction that the slope faces. This means a shot with the ball above your feet will hook to the left while a shot with the ball below your feet will slice to the right.

As before, you need to adjust your aim accordingly. The most important thing you must do at this time is to maintain your balance. Falling into or away from the ball will have unfortunate results. Good legwork and a steady head are worth their weight in strokes. Find a spot on the driving range where you can practice shallow sidehill lies using short irons. After you have attained a modicum of success there you may progress to more angular sidehill lies and longer clubs.

Some final advice for these shots. Choke down on the grip of the club for sidehill lies where the ball is above your feet. Use one club more than you think you need for shots where the ball is below your feet. Mastery for sidehill lies should be established using the same criterion as on shots from the fairway bunker.

For shots from downhill lies begin by adopting a closed stance in which your right foot is pulled back an inch or two from the square position.

DOWNHILL LIES

These lies were reserved for last because they are less easy to handle than the other shots from unlevel terrain. The main difficulty here comes from the fact that the downward slope of the fairway makes it harder to get the ball into the air. In effect the downhill slope reduces the loft of whatever club you are using, i.e., a six-iron becomes a five-iron. Besides the lower, bulletlike flight pattern, the second problem inherent in shots from downhill lies is that standing with your right foot above your left largely obstructs making any backswing turn at all with your body. A slashing arm swing is what golf instructors generally witness. Although the natural tendency for this shot is for the ball to fade or slice to the right, a novel approach will reduce the amount of slice and increase both the amount of backswing you are able to make and the length of the shot itself. Begin by adopting a closed stance in which your right foot is pulled back an inch or two from the square position (see illustration). In this way you set your body free to make a fuller turn. While a closed stance usually results in a hook, in this instance the hook counterbalances the normal tendency for this shot to slice. Such touring pros as Billy Casper (1966) use this method and report great success with it. Begin practicing downhill lies on gently sloping fairways using a short iron. Take it easy for a while. Rhythm, tempo, and headsteadiness are as important as ever. Play the ball back in your stance, toward the higher foot. Slightly behind the center of your stance is a good starting point. Use the mastery criterion established previously in Table 7 and gradually refine your skill.

THE LOFTED PITCH SHOT

(Beginners, attempt this shot at your own risk.) The final shot in our mastery-based system of instruction is the cut lob or lofted pitch shot. The lofted pitch shot is a very handy manipulation that could save you many strokes around the green. We did not discuss this shot earlier in our chipping and pitching chapter because the particular hand action required in this shot would have interfered with the learning of the basic swing. Moreover, this is a very risky shot. You should not gamble with it unless you have taken the time to master it. If you haven't mastered this shot, try a regular wedge for the fat part of the green.

The lofted pitch is the preferred shot when you need to pop the ball over a sand trap but have an extremely small portion of green to work with. The lofted pitch will fly high and land most tenderly without much roll. To execute this shot use the most lofted club in your bag (a sand wedge is ideal). Next, open up both your stance and the clubface. This will force you to pick the club up just barely outside the intended line of flight. Doing so will put extra side and backspin on the shot that will help stop the ball quickly. Ball placement at address should be opposite your left heel so as to increase the height of the shot. Stand up now and swing at an imaginary ball. Make the backswing you have long since mastered, but on the downswing do not permit your right hand to cross over your left as it ordinarily would. Instead, as you swing through the ball keep the back of your left hand pointing toward the sky. Many touring pros

The lofted pitch shot.

state that a good method for achieving this is to imagine there is a glass of water positioned on the clubface as you swing through. Try to swing so that the glass can ride on the clubface and not tip over. The reason for not allowing the hands and clubface to turn over is that when they do little backspin is imparted to the ball. With no backspin the ball will run over the green and into trouble.

The hand action of the cut lob is very unnatural and will take many hours of practice to master. At first you may dribble many of your attempts along the ground but don't give up. Practice the move in slow motion ten to twenty times before increasing the pace in small increments. When you begin to hit real balls be less concerned with where the ball goes than with how you finish the swing. You should be striving for a short follow-through with your head held behind the spot where the ball was addressed. Your hands should stop no higher than waist high when they swing through. As you increase the number of times these things occur on each swing you will begin to notice the ball drawing to a stop more quickly. To achieve mastery on this shot you will need to find a spot on the practice green where the pin is located closely behind a sand trap. When you are able to stop the ball within twelve feet of the hole on four out of six attempts you will have attained competency on perhaps the touchiest shot in golf. Good going!

SOME FINAL WORDS ON THE PHYSICAL SIDE OF THE GAME

The program we have presented to you in this half of *Total Golf* has been designed to give you the fundamental skills you will need in order to play your best game. You are unlikely to acquire these skills if a *cursory* reading of this book is the extent of your "practice." For the beginners in the audience, six weeks of diligently practicing this system will put you on the level of play most golfers attain only after years at the game, if then. For the veteran players, six weeks of scrupulous practice at the beginning of the season will enable you to pick the pockets of all those golfing buddies whose green's fees or club membership you've financed over the years. Isn't that a pretty thought?

7

Baserating for Golfers

"Every golfer is capable of improving his game if he will keep the necessary records which can be evaluated and analyzed."

M. S. KELLIHER

A young man walked into our office one day looking very dejected. He was a student in Mr. Simek's Introduction to Psychology class and had learned of our research on improving performance in various sports. The lad had hoped to make the varsity golf team but failed to by a couple of shots in the qualifying rounds. Let's tune into the conversation that ensued that day.

"Mr. Simek, I love to play golf and really want to improve my game. I want to become a good golfer but right now my game stinks," he began.

"What is it about your game that smells so bad?" I asked.

"Well, I'm just hitting the ball terribly, and I was wondering if that behavioral psychology you talked about in class could help my game."

"Possibly," I replied. "What are your shots doing that you don't like?"

"I don't know; I guess I'm just not striking the ball well."

"What are your shots doing that you don't like?"

"Ah, I don't feel like I'm swinging the club as I visualize."

Once again I asked, "What are your shots doing that you don't like?"

"Well, I think I don't quite have the proper feel for a good swing."

The client was responding in vague generalities that didn't answer the question I put to him. He expected that in some miraculous manner I would divine what he meant by "not striking the ball well" or "not feeling like I'm swinging the club as I visualize." I had no way of knowing from what he said whether he

95

was slicing his tee shots, pulling his iron approach shots, three-putting on the greens, or all of these and more. After explaining to the young man that I couldn't effect a change on something that wasn't described accurately, we continued the interview.

"What shot are you having difficulty with?"

"Okay, I'm hitting the ball just miserably off the tee, kind of slashing my iron shots, and making a . . ."

"Whoa, whoa," I said. "Apparently you're having difficulty with a number of different aspects of your game. We are going to have to get a specific picture of each problem. However, no professional athlete attempts to correct every aspect of his total performance all at once, nor should you. It's an impossible task. It's much better to concentrate on only one problem rather than a large number of difficulties. This way we can build a solid program in that one area and have a better chance of modifying a particular target behavior." These are basic concepts of behavior modification (Malott, *et al.,* 1971). By systematically eliminating trouble areas and increasing the desired behaviors of the player's game, one at a time, his score will improve steadily.

"All right now," I said, "which shot is causing you the most grief?"

"Yeah, it makes sense to work on one thing at a time," he said. "Well, I suppose it's my tee shot that's the worst problem right now."

"Okay, your tee shot isn't up to par. Tell me what the flight pattern looks like." Learning that the tee shot was the major problem was a good start. Now I wanted to obtain a more precise description of the problem. Imprecision is the bête noir of behavioral psychology. You simply cannot modify behavior that you are unable to describe accurately.

"The flight pattern of my drives? Ah, well, I slice the ball off the tee. The shot moves from left to right in the air and most often winds up deep in the right rough." Once we were able to pinpoint the problem precisely, the next step was to determine the frequency with which this pinpointed or target behavior occurred in his normal game. Gaining an exact count is critical for two reasons. First, we need to know exactly where the person is starting from. Second, after we have acquired the starting level, known as the baseline or baserate, we will be able to see conclusively whether or not his game is improving. That is, whether or not the intervention chosen to combat his targeted problem has been effective. Consequently, my next question to the young golfer referred to this issue.

"How many times during your last round did you slice your tee shot?" Not surprisingly, he couldn't supply an accurate count.

"About six or maybe up to ten of my drives were sliced, I guess," he answered. Approximation and guessing are normal not only for golfers with flaws in their game but also for many clients coming to psychological clinics with problems in living. No matter what reaction needs to be altered, accurate measurements are essential for producing changes. There is a semi-famous story told in psychology classes about Ogden Lindsley, the pioneering Kansas behaviorist. As the story goes, Lindsley was attempting to reduce the bedwetting of a small child. When he based his treatment of rewarding the child on whether or not he had remained dry all night, no progress was forthcoming. However, when

Lindsley measured the amount of wetness and rewarded the child for wetting less and less over a series of nights, the child quickly learned to control his bladder. Wet or dry was simply too general a measurement to pick up the child's subtle improvement. Similarly in golf you must specify the current behavior and the desired change.

The interview with my student golfer ended as follows:

"Six or ten isn't quite as exact as we need. So if you want to work on this with me, here's what I propose. Before we do anything else I would like you to keep track of every sliced drive you hit in your next five rounds. Take another scorecard along and label the first column 'slices.' Mark down each slice you hit off the tee. If you have other problems, keep track of those as well in order to see which behavior is likely to yield the most improvement in your game. Bring the cards with you when you come back to see me. We'll decide what to do next at that time. Agreed?"

"Agreed. See you in a few days."

During the following two months we met once a week at the local driving range. Every session began with a review of the latest information he had gathered on various aspects of his golf game. In addition to slicing tee shots, he was frequently short of the green with his approaches, and often left his first putt below the hole. Let's look at the data he gathered and the improvements he made. In the five baseline rounds he sliced an average of eleven tee shots per eighteen holes while recording scores of 83, 80, 81, 84, 82. His putts finished below the hole from seven to thirteen times per round, and he was short with his approach shots almost half the time, averaging eight and one-half short approaches each round.

His slices off the tee might have been the result of several different swing problems. Accepting his description of the problem, we trained his daily playing partner to record the flaws that were most likely to be causing his slice: overly quick rhythm, head movement, and a laid-off position at the top of the backswing. We would not recommend that you take on this much bookkeeping yourself, but since an observer working under our supervision was available, it was possible to speed up the process. Baseline for the five rounds mentioned earlier showed that all of these problems occurred frequently in his play.

Over a period of six weeks he was able to correct each of these problems and demonstrate that a new skill had been learned. His last five rounds were 73, 72, 77, 70, and 70. Short approach shots had decreased to two per round. He was now leaving only three putts below the hole each round and slicing only one drive for each nine holes played. I observed an eighty-three percent decrease in the number of times he was off the square position at the top of his backswing. There was an eighty percent decrease in both the number of shots where his head moved forward inappropriately and in the number of hurried full swings.

All of this was accomplished because I could identify the problem from his records and discover the effects of our interventions. This would not have been possible if he had not continued to record the outcome of each shot. The record-keeping of proper swing fundamentals helped to identify particular swing errors and beneficial changes in mechanics.

The method of data collection we employed in this example is based on standard applied behavior analysis precepts originally developed by Ogden Lindsley and later modified specifically for golf by William P. Brittain and Lawrence F. Hurr (1974). This is the only recording system that we have seen that provides enough information to help you improve your day-to-day play. At this point we will present a description of how you may utilize this method to improve your own game.

THE BASERATE GOLF DATA COLLECTION SYSTEM

Behavior change is impossible unless you pinpoint the behaviors that need to be increased or decreased in frequency. Examples of specific, concrete behaviors include: the failure to push your left knee down and in behind the ball on your backswing, slicing your drives, pulling your short irons, or moving your head toward the target on the downswing. Do *not* attempt to quantify vague generalities such as: not "feeling right" when you swing, or hitting "bad" medium-length shots. Such descriptions are impossible to quantify precisely because they have no definite meaning.

Although you will be concentrating on one and only one behavior at a time, you may choose up to four behaviors to record. The best choices for improving your game are the behaviors that are causing you the most difficulty. Ed Feeney whose behavior change program saved Emery Air Freight two million dollars, indicates that in industry you concentrate your recording and feedback on those behaviors that most clearly affect the profit/loss ratio. Similarly, in golf you focus on those aspects of the game that are costing you the most strokes. If missing putts of ten feet and under is setting you back twelve shots per round, it is foolhardy to start recording your distance off the tee.

As noted in the preceding example, the first step in correcting the problems in your game is to identify them. No intervention can be successful until you have targeted the behavior that needs to be changed. This can only be accomplished by keeping shot-by-shot records of your play. To collect this information on your game, take an extra scorecard with you when you play. Label a separate column on the card for each specific, concrete problem you are experiencing. These are the target behaviors and effects that you will be recording during that particular round of golf. The label for each column should clearly refer to the target behavior. According to Brittain and Hurr (1974), abbreviations or anagrams make satisfactory labels.

Before attempting any interventions, you should record each error that you want to decrease or the desired behavior you would like to realize; do this for three to five rounds. This will furnish you with a reliable baseline of the pinpointed trouble. For example, if one of your targeted problems is sliced tee shots and you slice your drive on the second hole, place a mark under the appropriate column in the box on the card opposite hole two. *Record every sliced drive you hit no matter how slight.* This is critically important as you will never resolve a problem if you refuse to report it when it occurs. This is similar to the necessity of accurately recording what you eat when you are trying to lose weight. The excess calories will wind up on your hips whether you record them or not, so if you consumed them, be honest about it. You must know how many slices you are really hitting, so record every incidence of this target behavior when it occurs.

At the nineteenth hole of each round, simply total the number of marks in each column. Place that number in the box the scorecard provides for eighteen-hole scores. You will use that tally when you graph your daily progress.

If there is one portion of this system that is integral in demonstrating how your game is shaping up, it is graphing the frequency of your target behaviors. The graph presented for this purpose was developed by Brittain and Hurr and is reprinted below. For the interested reader, these graphs and specially designed target behavior recording forms may be obtained from Dr. William P. Brittain, Department of Psychology, Montclair State University, Montclair, New Jersey.

Using this graph is very simple. For those of you who become nervous at the mere sight of a graph or chart, fear not. We will review the graph step by step so that you will have no difficulty employing it. First, look at the right-hand side of the page on which the graph appears. You will notice the headings "Behavior," "Name," and "Course" each followed by a blank line. On the line labeled "Behavior" indicate the specific nature of the problem you wish to tabulate. This means you will need a separate graph for each target behavior. For the "Name" blank fill in your name. On the line labeled "Course" write in the name of the golf course you will play when gathering this data.

Below the graph is a series of rectangular boxes preceded by the title "Date." Here you simply place the date of each round you play. Above the date of the round is the graph where you will plot two things. The first step is to graph the frequency of target behaviors you have faithfully recorded on the spare score-

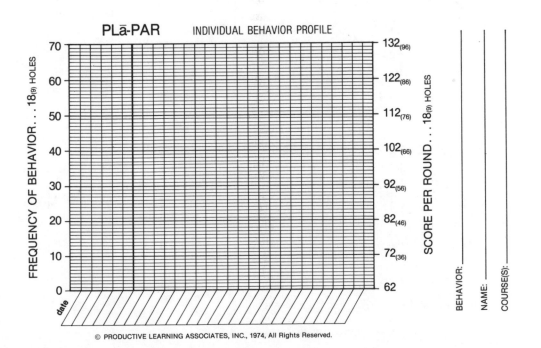

card. To do this simply count the correct number of horizontal lines and place a dot on the one that corresponds with target behavior total. The numbers along the left-hand side of the graph labeled "Frequency of Behavior" will help you locate the correct line. For example, if you struck sixteen sliced tee shots on April 8, plot that number on the graph above April 8.

The second thing you must plot above each date is your total score for that round. The numbers along the right-hand side of the graph labeled "Score Per Round" will help you find the line that corresponds to your eighteen-hole score. *Record the date of the round, the frequency of target behavior, and your eighteen-hole score the same day you play.* Use different colored ink to plot frequency and eighteen-hole score.

Once you know what is happening to your shots, you must then experiment with possible alterations in your play to increase the frequency of good results. Draw a vertical line down the graph at the date you initiate a new treatment. Label that line to indicate the nature of the change as in the example below.

Return to the chapter that pertains to the troubled area of your game. When you identify the appropriate approach to changing your game, give yourself several rounds to see if it is producing any effects. After you begin practicing and playing with new swing strategy keep recording the target behavior and your eighteen-hole score. It is impossible to know if your swing modifications have been effective unless you continue shot-by-shot recording. For instance, suppose you hit twelve sliced tee shots and had an 86 on July 7th. Three rounds later on July 15th you fire a 79 while slicing only four tee shots. It would appear the intervention you have initiated is working, as both the frequency of the target behavior and your eighteen-hole score have improved. Often a particular tactic will take more than one round to assimilate before your shots and scores show any improvement. Remember, you are trying to learn a new skill that will eventually

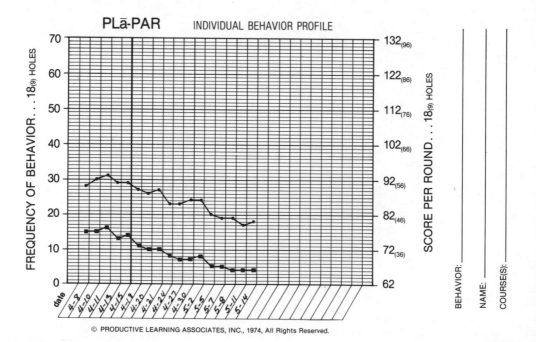

improve your score. At this point learning the skill is more important than your total per round. A similar situation occurs in behavior modification for weight loss (Craighead, O'Brien, and Stunkard, 1978). It is more important to learn new eating behaviors than it is to lose weight immediately. In the long run learning these new behaviors will improve your score just as learning new eating behaviors helps people eventually maintain weight loss.

Occasionally, certain behaviors may be controlled solely by keeping a record of them. We found this to be the case in our research when we instructed a student golfer to keep a count of the number of times he left his approach shot short of the green. Because we suspected that the golfer's mere recording of the problem would decrease the incidence of this behavior, we had a playing partner keep an accurate tally of the times he was short of the green with his approach shot. Once we had a baseline we then allowed the golfer himself to keep track of this aspect of his play. The data showed that recording alone could result in an increase in the number of times he reached the green on his approach.

From time to time you will be able to increase or decrease your target behavior, but see no effect on your total score. This sometimes happens because other parts of your game camouflage improvements in your swing. This is the reason recording only your eighteen-hole score does not provide you with enough information to evaluate specific improvements. In our original research on mastery-based golf instruction, we wanted to control for this variable when we collected our data. Thus, we took measurements at many different distances to ascertain the players' skill with each club. In one phase we even placed stickers across the clubface to see if our golfers were hitting the ball on the sweetspot.

LOGS AND DIARIES

This is not the first golf book to acknowledge the value of record-keeping. Gary Player (1962) emphasized keeping a record of your play and more recently Frank Chinnock (1976) has recommended shot-by-shot recording. Unfortunately, other golf writers have failed to distinguish between keeping accurate records and writing postmortem diaries of the round. To have your record-keeping help you, you must avoid vague musing about your game. Logs and diaries that are filled out at the nineteenth hole or at night before bed will give you information laced with inaccuracies. Further, if you spend your time in a literary description of the tree you were behind or the frustration you felt, you are missing the point. An accurate count of the number of times you hooked the ball is an absolute necessity if you are to improve, but writing a short story about your sports self-concept is not a productive way to better your game. If you are interested in writing about the traumas of golf most certainly jot down your thoughts and feelings about the game. However, if you wish to improve your golf scientifically keep a count of your specific swing behavior and outcomes.

It is not that we are against casual clubhouse reverie. Certainly, going over one's round is a lovely way to spend an evening. The problem is that it is simply not possible for most people to recall exactly what happened on each shot, let alone what they were thinking about before, during, and after the shot. Even if this were possible, it seldom happens because it isn't very rewarding to remember what really happened rather than what you wanted to happen. Fritz Perls (1969), the charismatic Gestalt psychologist, relates a short parable that clearly elucidates this point:

> Memory and Pride were fighting. Memory said, "It was like that," and Pride said: "It couldn't have been!" And Memory gave in.

Shot-by-shot recording as you play the round is the only way to accurately discover the state of your game. Similarly, charting those records over a series of rounds is the best way to make use of this information. Keeping a diary or log of ill-defined generalities may be fun but you'll never change your golf behavior if you remain at that level of description.

RECORDING THOUGHTS

Not all thoughts are necessarily uncountable or vague. There is no reason to avoid recording thoughts if you specify them clearly and simply record whether or not they occurred, leaving out all the window dressing and self-dramatics.

A thought is a behavior. It can also stimulate other acts which may affect your play. It is possible to record thoughts just as you record actions, but you must treat the thoughts as reactions only you can observe and count. Then, just as you would for any other behavior, you can keep track of the number of times you felt anxious, the number of times you dumped on yourself, or the number of rage reactions you experienced in a round. List them on a spare scorecard and plot them just as you would any other behavior. Then evaluate your attempts to control these reactions by looking at the graph. Be certain to indicate on the graph when you begin any new treatment. Throughout the second half of this book, we will present a number of highly effective strategies for dealing with these mental and emotional states as well as for improving your concentration. These tactics include relaxation training, thought stoppage, hypnosis, and Rational-Emotive Therapy for golfers.

GOLFER, KNOW THY GAME

The great majority of golfers, amateurs as well as professionals, do not precisely know which part of their game is costing them the most strokes. To prove our point, an enlightening example of meaningful record-keeping was IBM's coverage of the 1967 and 1968 Men's Professional Golf Tour. Their purpose was to determine the shot-making abilities of various touring pros (*Golf Digest,* 1968 and Brown, 1969). IBM kept track of such aspects of each player's game as: score per round, percentage of greens hit in regulation figures, percentage of drives in the fairway, length of drive, number of putts per round, number of greens negotiated in less than two putts, number of greens three or more putted, skill with the irons, stroke-saving ability, and overall shotmaking ability. This type of data accurately delineates the strengths and weaknesses of each golfer's play. Thus, a pro looking at the printout of his game for 1967 would know specifically which part of his total golf required practice in order to improve his chances for the following year.

Golf is clearly a sport where what you don't know will indeed hurt you in the long run. The system we have presented here is designed to be tailored to your game as it actually is. It will spotlight those flaws in your play that need remediation while highlighting improvement in your golf that may otherwise be camouflaged when only eighteen-hole scores are recorded. A golfer we once worked with told us, "You know, I never really knew my golf game before. I thought it was my driving that was adding the most shots to my score but this recording system showed me I was hitting eighty percent of the fairways off the tee. Instead, it was my pulled approaches and sloppy chipping and pitching that was hurting me the most. Now I know which part of my game to work on."

Ogden Lindsley writes that "The hardest thing (about this system) is to get people to do it, not to get it to work." Clinical psychologists all over the world have found that keeping accurate records has been demonstrably effective in helping their clients make behavior changes. You may not need the service of a psychologist to help you cope with problems in everyday living, but you do need shot-by-shot record-keeping if you are serious about improving your golf game.

In addition to using the graph as an indicator of improvement, a review of the scorecard you use for baseline recording will often shed light on your play. For example, if most of your recorded errors occur during the first few holes of each round, perhaps you aren't warming up properly. And maybe you find that you consistently make a particular error on certain specific holes. If that's the case, a closer scrutiny of what is actually happening on those holes is in order. Brittain and Hurr (1974) tell us that often golfers begin their round well but finish poorly. They suggest the answer to this problem lies in one of two directions. Possibly they are tiring by the late holes; perhaps they are not as physically fit or as young as they thought. The second direction concerns slipping concentration. In the case of the out-of-shape golfer, a *light* exercise program would be beneficial to both his golf and his physical well-being. For the golfer whose concentration is not what it could be, a number of suggestions to improve this aspect of his game will be presented in forthcoming chapters. And all golfers, regardless of their problems, will stand to benefit from the shot-by-shot record-keeping we suggest. You will find that your game may improve simply as a result of having a specific goal in mind before each shot (Kelliher, 1970).

II

The Psychological Side of Golf

8

The Mental Game or How to Break Par Without Breaking Your Nerves or Your Clubs

"Golf is very much like a love affair: if you don't take it seriously it's no fun; if you do, it breaks your heart."

LOUISE SUGGS

The psychological problems that impair the performance of golfers are more abundant than the water hazards at a Florida course. Although each golfer has his own unique style of golf neurosis, the problems usually reflect either anxiety about his ability to make a given shot or temper tantrums that leave him so enraged that the club becomes a murderous weapon rather than the fine tool it must be to achieve a good score. These problems are not independent but often go hand in hand. However, for the purpose of clarity we will begin by discussing how to dispel the gremlins that produce golf's fears and later in the chapter analyze the game's rage-provoking frustrations.

Nerves, anxiety, choking, or a lack of confidence are all names for the agonizing fear that can grip a golfer as he approaches an important shot. This anxiety is most well known for the infamous effect it has had on touring professionals but it most certainly can be found out on the course with the weekend golfer as well. Although Tommy Armour (1967) christened golf anxiety with the painfully descriptive name of "yips," these feelings have been familiar to golfers for as long as the game has been played. It is hard to name a legendary player whose competitive career was not shortened by the yips. Of the early players one can add Harry Vardon, Bobby Jones, and Craig Wood to the aforementioned Tommy Armour as victims of terminal golf anxiety. More recently, anyone who followed golf through the sixties still winces at the image of Ben Hogan playing perfect golf from tee to green but freezing on every short putt. The story of Sam Snead is similar but somewhat less pathetic because of Snead's ingenious and fairly successful use of a modified croquet style of putting. In the current decade rumors have it that Arnold Palmer and Billy Casper have met the yips and been conquered.

Anxiety can strike any golfer in any situation. It is not limited to the old or the professional nor is it limited to the putt. One can clutch on the drive off the first tee, at the water-hole, or on the chip that could enable one to break 90 for the first time. The fact that golf anxiety seems to increase as you get older probably reflects the old army philosophy that eighteen-year-olds make better soldiers because they are not smart enough to realize that they could be killed. Similarly, the young golfer may not be realistic enough to seriously entertain the thought that he could miss the shot and blow the round, lose the money, ruin his reputation, or endure any of a thousand other misfortunes to which we attach such great importance.

The golf literature contains descriptions of anxiety that are as good or better than any psychologist has ever written. It is hard to pick up a copy of *Golf Magazine* or *Golf Digest* without finding some reference to fear on the links under such titles as confidence, concentration, self-control, or tension reduction. While Armour's writing is perhaps the most descriptive, Julius Boros, Sam Snead, Al Geiberger, Carol Mann, Jane Blalock, Dave Stockton, and many others have been effective in recording the anxiety that comes hand in hand with an important golf shot.

The problem of golf anxiety has been clearly identified but what does one do about it? Like the patient who wants to find out how to get rid of what he's got, not what it is called, the anxious golfer may be disappointed with these descriptions. When it comes to getting rid of the yips the golf literature offers little help. The most frequent suggestions are to relax and become more confident. Obviously, if the golfer could relax he would not be anxious nor would he be looking for help with his nerves. The fact that he cannot relax is the problem. Telling him to relax without telling him how offers no solution. As Alex Morrison observed some three decades ago, "It is only at the nineteenth hole that the average golfer enjoys any relaxation" (Morrison, 1946).

One might make the argument that the key to becoming relaxed is to become confident. While it is true that the confident golfer is not likely to be anxious at the same time, the suggestion that one should become more self-confident is only helpful if it is accompanied by some directions on how to achieve this blissful state. Many golf authorities have suggested that confidence can be built through practice. They are partially right in that increased practice will give you more confidence in your physical skills. Former PGA Champion Chick Harbert (1978) suggests that if you become nervous facing three-foot putts you should practice them until you make ninety-nine out of a hundred. That seems like a good suggestion but practice will not cure the yips. In reality, practicing on the putting green or going through a bucket of balls with your five-iron bears little resemblance to trying to sink a crucial putt or hit the last green in a close match on the course. Ben Hogan was known to enjoy practice more than he enjoyed playing yet anxiety destroyed Hogan's game. It doesn't seem likely that more practice would have given him the confidence to make the putts that he so often yipped. With perhaps the best golfing skills yet seen and a practice schedule that was merciless, Hogan had more right to feel confident than anyone. Yet, no one who saw the Open in 1959 or the Masters in 1966 will ever forget his anxiety. As has been observed by many including Bobby Jones, those who suffer worst from the yips on the course are able to make all of those shots in practice. Unfortunately, the only way that one can really build confidence is by making those shots in a round where they mean something and if they mean something the anxiety is likely to prevent you from making them. One cannot become more confident until one begins to make the shots and one cannot begin to make the shots until one has become less anxious or more confident. This represents an inescapable dilemma, a golfer's Catch-22.

Chick Harbert's emphasis on practice is correct to the extent that mastering the mental side of golf is totally irrelevant unless you have learned the necessary physical skills. It is literally impossible to play a psychologically confident game of golf without having command of the basic shots. Unfortunately, having the prerequisite physical skills is not sufficient to avoid the mental anguish to which golfers so often fall prey.

From a psychological standpoint the important thing to recognize about the yips is that it is one example of a more general phenomenon called performance anxiety. It is characterized by nervousness or fear of what will result from one's actions. Golf anxiety is no different from any other anxiety about how well you will perform. If the boss is looking over your shoulder evaluating you for a promotion you are likely to botch something that you have done correctly a hundred times before because of your anxiety. If you are in the middle of a passionate scene with the lover of your dreams you may just experience enough anxiety so that nothing happens. These situations are exactly the same as trying to sink a two-foot putt in the club championship. Anxiety is not specific! It is the same reaction whether it occurs to a pianist in front of an audience or to a middle-handicap player on a hole where he has a stroke coming.

One of the authors (Dr. O'Brien) once had a student who complained that she became so anxious when taking tests that she had to grip the pencil very hard or else it would fly out of her hand. She went on to say that she would find her hand twitching so badly that she would try to write her answers quickly between twitches. Compare her description to that of the great British Champion Harry Vardon:

> I have never felt nervous when taking part in a golf tournament; this lack of confidence which overtook me when I was playing a short putt was something altogether worse than nervousness. As I stood addressing the ball, I would watch for my right hand to jump. At the end of about two seconds I would not be looking at the ball at all. My gaze would have become riveted

on my right hand. I simply could not resist the desire to discover what it was going to do. Directly I felt that it was about to jump I would snatch at the ball in a desperate effort to play the shot before the involuntary movement could take effect. Up would go my head and body with a start and off would go the ball—anywhere but on a proper line . . . (Vardon, 1912)

Isn't it obvious that the student and the golf master are talking about the same devil. Anxiety is anxiety but it is a devil that can be beaten. There are sound psychological techniques of demonstrated efficacy to increase relaxation, reduce anxiety, and even to prevent it from occurring without resorting to dangerous tranquilizers or other drugs. These techniques have made impotent males potent and text-anxious collegians "A" students. There is no reason that they cannot be just as effective for the golfer. Unfortunately, these techniques are rarely among a person's first reaction to feelings of anxiety. They require training and effort, but, on the other hand, easier, off-the-top-of-the-head solutions to anxiety are seldom effective. Thus, mastering these techniques is worthwhile. The yips can be conquered but only through conscientious effort in a psychologically sound program.

If you are feeling anxious or nervous about something including a golf shot there are really only a few things that you can do about it. First, you can try to feel less anxious or try to relax. Once your anxiety has gotten to the point where it is noticeable this technique almost never works. The more you strive to become less nervous, the more nervous you become. Try to remember the last time that you had lunch with an important client and noticed that your hand was a bit shaky as you sipped your soup. If you focused your attention on that hand to make it stop shaking you probably wore some of that soup home. The more you tried to shop shaking the more tremulous you became. Similarly, the first date you had with that special girl or guy may have been the impetus for a little extra perspiration. The act of trying to control or hide the sweat will simply make you so anxious that you could drown.

When you begin to get anxious standing over a putt, your first response is likely to be an attempt to "get hold of yourself" or bring your nerves under control. When a golfer tries to control his body his muscles become tense, not relaxed, and his anxiety will increase rather than abate. Listen to Tommy Armour's description of how his anxiety proceeded through his muscles in steps of increasing tension and see if it doesn't sound painfully familiar:

First under tension, the grip tightens, then the forearms, the shoulders, the body and legs stiffen in a chain reaction, then finally the brain tightens and you are hopeless. Sheer luck and animal instinct gets you hitting the ball in a wild way. (Armour, 1967)

Armour's description shows that the yips are more than just the anxiety. It also includes the player's self-defeating response to that anxiety. The more the golfer tries to inhibit the anxiety, the more tense and anxious he becomes. In fact it is exactly the golfer who prides himself on his self-control who will have the most enduring problem with the yips. The self-made golfer who has always relied on his command of his body is the golfer who is most likely to believe that he can conquer anxiety through the sheer weight of his will just as he has mastered the other aspects of his game. A list of those "Name" golfers who have been most devastated by the yips, e.g., Jones, Armour, Hogan, Wood, Palmer, and Snead, is also a pretty fair list of the grittiest players ever to pick up a club. Psychologically, their response of attacking their anxiety is likely to have magnified it to the point where tournament golf became a nightmare.

It is not possible to will yourself into feeling calm. If something is making you nervous no amount of telling yourself to stop being nervous is going to be helpful. What is worse, the realization that you cannot control the nervousness, leads to even more anxiety. It is not surprising that Hogan, Jones, and Armour should have been so badly victimized by the yips, nor is it difficult to guess which of the current glamour professionals are likely to be yipped off the tour. To conquer anxiety you must recognize that the problem cannot be overcome simply by practice and determination. If it were not for the self-fulfilling nature of this problem, we would present a list of likely candidates for the coming years but the authors do not wish to start anyone going in that direction. You can be sure that as scientists we have such a list in order to check our predictions in the future.

You may now be willing to accept the notion that if you try to control the anxiety by trying to force yourself to become less anxious you will simply get yippier; but you may wonder why it isn't possible to put the anxiety out of your mind. That is the possible reaction that is second in popularity. It has one advantage over simply trying to force yourself to become more relaxed. It is not as likely to lead to an increase in tension but neither will it do anything to reduce it. The reason it does not work can be most easily shown by a small example. Try to forget that there are 103 tournament-class golf clubs in the state of Florida. Just put the number 103 out of your mind! Do not think about it! You will have the same amount of success trying not to think of that number as the anxious golfer has in trying not to think of the water hazard, his hook, or the possibility of missing the easy putt for a birdie.

If you read what golf authorities write about anxiety you will find that the writers fall into two broad camps depending on whether or not they have ever experienced a nasty yipping streak. Those like Tommy Armour who had a full dose of the yips are likely to believe them to be incurable. Not surprisingly, Armour offers little in the way of effective treatment for the problem. Others like Sam Snead offer mechanical variations in an attempt to forestall anxiety. Tony Jacklin once observed that an unorthodox grip gives you something to concentrate on so that you spend less time worrying about the shot. Generally, however, the experienced yipper fails to be helpful to others because he has yet to find a solution for himself.

The younger golfer may have difficulty understanding what all the fuss is about. Since he has felt some anxiety in his tournament play but no real self-doubt, he cannot truly grasp the problem of the anxious golfer. In fact, if he does become nervous he is often surprised at the occurrence. When David Graham choked on the seventy-second hole of the 1979 PGA Championship at Oakland Hills he described the situation of sudden anxiety perfectly: "It didn't hit me until I got to the 18th tee. Just as I started my backswing I kind of woke-up to what was going on and I hit a dreadful tee shot." After two chips from the rough, Graham was four feet from the pin but he missed the putt. "I felt very confident," he continued, "but I hit it twelve inches by. I said to myself, My God! What's going on here." (Associated Press, August 6, 1979) Graham had now experienced real anxiety.

Compare Graham's description to Dave Stockton's memory of his thoughts as he set up for the fifteen-foot putt that was to win the 1976 PGA. "I really wasn't nervous preparing to make that putt in the PGA at Congressional. Putting is my forte, and I was really enjoying myself . . . But I don't try to put those thoughts (anxiety) out of my mind, really. That's the fun of the game. That's what we're there for" (Stockton, 1977). For Stockton the more that was riding on the shot the more of an enjoyable challenge it became. Since the young golfer has not re-ally felt the full force of anxiety, his suggestions of how to deal with it are usually limited to a slightly different waggle or more practice. They are not likely to have much impact on a solidly formed anxiety response. Remember, trying to put the anxiety out of your mind does not work. How many tourna-ment courses are there in Florida?

The golf writers are correct in diagnosing the problem. The golfer must be-come more relaxed and more confident. He must also learn not to think about his fears. What the anxious golfer quests for and usually does not find is a method for doing what the professionals suggest. In the next four chapters you will be taught ways to achieve these goals.

For the golfer whose problem is uncontrollable rage rather than anxiety, the information in these chapters can be just as useful. If you are known for the hel-icopters that you make when you fling your putter through the air or for the nicks in your clubs from chopping down trees, you know the frustrations that can enflame a golfer's temperament. It would not serve our purpose to recount the fiendish depths to which course architects seem to go to provoke the emotional golfer; it is only important that you recognize the fact that it is not the course, the missed putt, or the sliced drive that ruins the temperamental player's game. It is his emotional reaction to those events that does him in.

Unfortunately a trip through golf literature in search of ways to control your temper is likely to be disappointing. Each book contains the same descrip-tions of Lefty Stackhouse punching a tree to punish his right hand and Ky Laffoon dragging his clubs behind his car. Those articles that go into more detail will mention Ivan Ganz hitting himself in the leg or the head while recounting how Tommy Bolt threw his clubs into a lake or had to play the eighteenth with his two-iron because he had broken the rest of his sticks. While these stories are entertaining, they do little to help a golfer get a grip on himself.

Golf temper problems have been viewed as reflecting immaturity, personality arousal differences and, most recently by Wiren, Coop, and Sheehan (1978), too much traffic on the corpus-collosum which connects the two halves of the brain. Yet it is difficult to see how explanations such as these are going to help the golfer who has just played a frustrating shot. Certainly, he cannot stand on the tee waiting to grow up or inject some sort of chemical to quiet his corpus-collosum. What can he do? The most common answer to that question has been well stated by Lanny Wadkins (1973) in his advice to juniors: "(Emotional Control) is something (you) learn the hard way through a few bad experiences." The example usually attached to this advice is Bobby Jones. It is said that Jones gained control of his temper because he found that the consequences of his emotional overreactions were so punishing that he gave up blowing his top. The young golfer is told that he will learn the hard way when his temper has cost him enough strokes. One only has to count the number of quite adult golfers with temper problems to realize that this advice is hardly enough to solve the problem.

The golf world seems at a loss for anything constructive to tell the temperamental golfer. This is most easily seen in a recent *Golf Digest* article by Polly Pendleton Brown (1979) called "How to Keep Your Temper Out on the Course." Although Miss Brown provides some interesting observations on anxiety and concentration, and tells some funny stories of people breaking their clubs, her only real advice for temper control is to relax so that you play better, are less frustrated, and less likely to become emotional. These suggestions are hardly earth-shattering news to the rage-prone golfer.

Like Damn Yankee, uncontrollable rage really is two words. You can learn to control your temper, even to become frustrated without becoming enraged, if you will spend your time changing your self-messages about frustration and learning to establish a stable emotional state before you start.

As Jane Blalock (Blalock and Netland, 1977) among others has indicated, golf is not an emotional game. In boxing or football controlled rage may be an asset. In a game that demands the finesse and fine motor control of golf there is no place for emotions. We strongly disagree with Wiren, Coop, and Sheehan's caution that a golfer can become too unemotional. It may be possible to hurt one's game by becoming unconcerned or unmotivated but that does not mean that one should ever be anything but totally calm out on the course. Some of the greatest champions in the history of golf have been some of the least emotional people while they were playing it. Hagen, Trevino, Hogan, Suggs, and Whitworth were all completely dedicated to golf yet they would leave their emotions at home when it came to playing the course. Anyone familiar with golf lore can also name a dozen players whose emotional involvement kept them from maximizing their talents.

It is difficult to name a golfer who achieved greatness in either amateur or professional golf until he had achieved emotional control. In the case of golfers like Hagen, Trevino, and Jacklin it is clear that they had learned a philosophical approach that allowed them to tolerate the ups and downs of the game long before they swung their first professional club. For others, like Julius Boros, Bobby Jones, and Tom Watson, controlling the emotions was a painful learning experience.

It is not psychologically useful or defensible to attribute this variety of emotional styles to some sort of unspecifiable personality difference. The differences are in the way that people have learned to handle their emotions not in some inborn diversity in how easily their emotions are aroused. The golfer who believes that he is just overly emotional by nature is giving himself an excuse for not learning to control his reactions. Such a belief stands in the way of developing good emotional control. Wiren, Coop, and Sheehan (1978) believe that each golfer has his own level of arousal which is best for him. But, attributing lack of self-control to an individual's natural emotional style, is not helpful in overcoming the problem. There are techniques that will help a golfer to stop overreactions to his bad shots as well as to his good ones. He can be trained to stop his emotional self-stimulation, control his self-accusations, and identify the early stages of his overreactions. These techniques are the psychological interventions which will be most effective in ridding your game of its emotional horrors. Historically, the psychology of golf has been limited to describing the problem. Yet, you do not have to live with anger or anxiety on the golf course. It is possible to modify the occurrence of these emotions just as it is possible to change any other aspect of mental golf.

The importance of the mental side of golf has long been recognized. Initially psychological factors that effected swing mechanics were the focus of attention. Early golf instructors (Dunn, 1922) were quick to perceive the need for fluid motor performance. The paradox that they discovered was that to consciously try to make the correct flowing swing resulted in becoming all thumbs or hopelessly mechanical. As Dunn (1922) put it, "The player's attention must be on what is to be done not how it is to be done. . . . The actions involved in doing the thing are to be correct automatic performance, the result of distinct paths in the nervous system, ploughed out by repeated practice of the right kind."

Almost forty years later Sam Snead (1961) reached a similar but more colorful conclusion about the role of thought in swinging a club. He stated that playing good golf involved three important skills: grip, stance, and swing. Then he said, "Put them together on the practice tee or range. *Memorize* each facet *with your muscles*. Then just *relax* and *swing it*. You don't think about eating. So groove your golf swing and forget it. Why poke yourself in your golfing eye?"

Recently, Wiren, Coop, and Sheehan (1978) have reached the same conclusion as Dunn, Snead and so many others on the limitations of conscious effort in producing a graceful swing. Interestingly, they have interpreted this difficulty in light of the current rebirth of split-brain research. They suggest that the inability to think through a swing reflects the distinction between the left hemisphere or verbal side of the brain, which they call the "Analyzer" and the right or nonverbal side of the brain which they call the "Integrator." The golfer's problems occur when the Analyzer, which should set up the shot, interferes with the Integrator's job of making the shot or vice versa.

These fifty years of observations, from Dunn to Wiren, Coop, and Sheehan, offer an unquestionably valid caution on the role of the brain in swing mechanics. Yet, psychology has come a very long way since 1922. We are past the point where our goal is mere description, and it is difficult to see how these observations can be applied to improving one's game. The problem lies in the fact that being told that you ought to switch on a certain neural pathway or side of the brain when you start your swing leaves you right where you were before because it is impossible for you to directly control brain functions. What you need to know is what behaviors you must engage in to attain the neurological states that these theories describe. How do you actually change your behavior so that you can do what Snead recommends—"Learn it and forget it"—when it comes to taking the shot?

Happily, there are many techniques that will allow you to let your body make the correct response once you have grooved the swing. You can employ behavioral methods of self-control to effectively change your behavior and your reaction to stress by changing the consequences of your actions. You can modify the experiences that you have without trying to change brain function which is inaccessible to you.

In the next five chapters we will present a variety of techniques to help you attain control of the psychological and emotional side of your game. All of these techniques have demonstrated efficacy with a broad range of psychological objectives but as yet, there have been few investigations in sports to confirm the successes observed with other tension problems. In the area of sports psychology, scientifically sound treatment research has been rare so we will begin with the technique that has shown itself to be the most consistently effective in reducing sports tension. Chapter 9 outlines a program of relaxation training to help you remain calm on the course. There is no better technique for coping with stress than learning how to remain relaxed.

Closely akin to relaxation training is hypnosis, the oldest method of producing an unruffled game. In Chapter 10 we present various ways to help your game hypnotically and introduce the most influential and glamorous of the mental techniques; visualization. If you become tense or lose your concentration in your matches, these procedures can be of considerable benefit. The improvements that you can achieve through hypnosis and visualization are the result of normal mind-body interaction. Neither of these techniques is supernatural in any sense. Contrary to popular belief, if you can't play the game, visualizing Jack Nicklaus' form or the perfect flight of the ball isn't going to do a thing for you. Similarly, hypnosis is not a magical panacea for transforming you from Mr. Hacker to Dr. Pro. These techniques can be useful but their limitations must not be lost in a smokescreen of popular magazine fantasy.

In Chapter 11, three brief techniques are introduced to help you rapidly gain control of your game when your emotional state begins to deteriorate in the middle of a round. Negative practice, thought-stoppage, and abbreviated stress inoculation training have received little attention in the sports world, although behavioral psychologists have demonstrated consistent progress with these methods in other areas. This lack of experimental data on sports problems is significant, however. The reader should pay particular attention to evaluating techniques on the basis of the evidence from research rather than simply accepting the endorsements of well-known golfers. We do not mean to suggest that the professional golfer who promotes a given psychological technique is trying to mislead the golfing public. On the contrary, the endorsement is usually quite sincere. The problem lies in the fact that the professional is so skilled at the game that in his hands even a thoroughly worthless procedure may seem beneficial if it coincidentally occurs at the same time as one of his many streaks of superb golf. In order to write a scientifically responsible book we must point out that only relaxation training is supported by a substantial amount of sound scientific evidence. Visualization and hypnosis lack this kind of support but self-reports and case studies suggest that these techniques can help some golfers. Negative practice, thought-stoppage, and stress inoculation represent behavior-change operations that have worked in other areas but as yet have not been established as effective procedures for athletic problems. They are theoretically sound and they may be the most efficient approaches to golf tension because they can improve your emotional control at little cost in terms of time and effort.

Chapter 12 presents a different approach to emotional control. Using Rational Emotive Counseling (Ellis and Harper, 1978) we attempt to teach you a philosophy that prevents overly emotional reactions. This chapter is particularly relevant to temper control problems. If blowing up on the course is your current golf torment, we believe that you should read this chapter next and then return to reading the relaxation, hypnosis, and negative practice material in the usual chapter order. The REC is designed to help you keep your game in perspective. Conscientious application of a rational-emotive approach will enable you to face the game's frustrations with a philosophy that puts you in control of your reactions whether they are rage, fear, depression, or ecstasy. In combination with the other techniques we describe, this philosophy can put the fun back in your game.

In the final chapter of this section, Chapter 13, we teach you systems to improve both your physical and mental practice. This may be the most important chapter of all because it is impossible to master any of the other methods we propose unless you practice. The techniques that we present to groove your swing are based on a program of practice to allow you to master each step in the swing chain. Similarly, there is no way to learn to become relaxed or to change your philosophy without rehearsing new thoughts and different self-messages. Practice can be fun, rewarding, and enjoyable if you know how to program pleasure into your practice routine. We believe that you can learn to do exactly that and practice, painlessly, much more often than you have in the past.

9

Relaxation Training

"Think in such a fashion as to relax yourself!"

SAM SNEAD

There can be little doubt that being relaxed on the golf course is the most important aspect of the mental game. The list of golf professionals and teachers who have singled out tension as the golfer's number one enemy includes almost every famous name in golf. In our view the best evaluation of the importance of being relaxed was made by Julius Boros (1976), when he said, "Excessive tension is the major problem of most middle and high handicap golfers." Anxiety on the course can make your putting unsteady and inaccurate. It can also inhibit your swing to rob you of power. Learning how to relax is the simplest way to bettering your game once you have mastered the physical rudiments of the swing. Relaxation is the key to confidence, tempo, and judgment. As Alex Morrison astutely observed, "If the word 'concentration' had been erased early from the golfer's dictionary and 'relaxation' substituted for it, fewer players would be struggling to break a hundred and club handicaps would be much lower than they are" (Morrison, 1946, p. 6). The techniques described in this chapter are fully capable of putting you in control of your golf anxiety, just as they have succeeded in reducing the fears of others both in and out of athletics. Study them well and get your nerves off the course.

Most golfers experience anxiety as increased muscle tension. They become tight and their swing becomes short, choppy, and hurried. In this chapter we will

117

teach you various methods for inhibiting anxiety through reducing muscle tension. The program we are going to outline is designed to rid you of this problem for as long as you continue to practice the relaxation exercises, but it is not, in itself, a stop-gap measure. For an immediate impact on your game, we have devised a brief, tension-controlling intervention employing the principles of the full relaxation program. If you follow the instructions below you may be able to gain limited control of your anxiety, but you should master the full relaxation program to ensure lasting effects.

The first thing that you must do is identify the situation in which you become anxious. Try to recall the last time you really tightened up on the course. Now, pick up the appropriate club and stand over a ball. Try to recreate that stressful shot. Address the ball, close your eyes, and take yourself back to that putt to halve the hole or the tee looking down on the water hazard. Can you imagine the situation vividly enough that you begin to feel anxious and your muscles start to tighten up? If you can't, you are going to have to wait until your next sojourn around the course to discover what muscle group needs to be unwound, or at least spend some time practicing more vivid imagery of the stressful situation so that you can locate the anxiety. If you are already able to produce those anxious feelings, try to identify the location of the tension in your body. Is it in the grip? What about your neck and shoulders? Maybe your anxiety shows itself in the legs and knees. It may even be in your hips or in your gritted teeth. If you feel as if your whole body tenses up, try to zero in on the area that seems to have become the most rigid and pressurized. Many golfers find that they experience tension in different areas of the body depending on the nature of the shot they have to make. Tension may be greatest in the legs off the tee and in the grip and shoulders on the green. For this reason you should not change the anxiety-inducing image, say from putting to long irons, as you try to locate your constricted muscles.

Once you have identified the muscle group that seems the tightest, we want you to try to increase the tension in those muscles. That's right, *increase* the tension! For example, suppose that your neck and shoulder muscles were the tightest. For five or six seconds try to push your chin into your chest, but do not allow your chin to touch it. At the same time hunch up your shoulders so that you feel stress in your shoulder muscles. This may be accomplished by exaggerating a shrug. If you have any physical problems of the neck and shoulders, do not do this exercise! We want you to feel tension in the muscles, not pain. Discontinue the exercise immediately if it hurts you.

At the end of six seconds let go, all at once! Let the muscles relax. They should feel tingly and heavy, yet rather airy and unencumbered. This feeling should continue to increase for another twenty seconds or more. In that time set up your shot and let 'er go! Don't hurry! You have at least thirty seconds, probably closer to a minute, before you feel your anxiety start to return. That's a lot of time.

If you misalign your shots or haven't grooved your swing, this method will not help you. But if it is only anxiety that is blocking the smooth execution of your shots, the intentional overtightening of your muscles will push the pendulum enough so that it will come back to a point of relaxation. If you allow twenty seconds for the relaxation to build, you will be able to perform the swing calmly. It is a good idea to inhale and hold your breath as you tense the muscles, and exhale when you release the tension. After the tension is released you should be breathing deeply, slowly, and rhythmically through the nose as you approach the shot.

Your shoulders and neck are perhaps the hardest muscle group to tense when you are on the course because of the awkwardness of the resultant stance. Yet, this tensing is not nearly so noticeable as you imagine. In most cases the people that you are playing with are into their next shot rather than watching what you are doing. You can even perform the muscle tension while they are shooting. In any event, few of us are going to look as natty on the course as Jan Stephenson or Gary Player, so why not concentrate on your score rather than your appearance. This technique is intended to help you make a more relaxed golf swing under stressful conditions. For many people it seems to do just that.

We will talk about producing relaxation in the other muscles as we proceed through the full muscle relaxation procedure. Before we leave the stop-gap measures however, we should mention the special aspects of relaxing the legs and the grip.

To relax the legs, you must straighten and lock the knees as you try to push your feet through the ground. It is easy to pull a leg muscle and even easier to produce a charley horse with this exercise. Quickly release the tension if you feel yourself beginning to cramp. The timing is the same as before. Hold the tension for five to six seconds. Make the legs rigid and lock the knees. When the six seconds are up, abruptly release the tension and watch the knees fall back into a relaxed bend. For at least the next thirty seconds your legs should feel a sensation of floating and tingling, but little tension. Again, there is no need to rush your shot. You have plenty of time to line up and execute the shot without hurrying.

In putting, tension is most often felt in the hands. In order to relax your hands you can either try to strangle your putter for six seconds and then allow your hands to relax to a light grip, or you can make a very tight fist for six seconds and feel the tension ooze out of your fingertips when you release the tension. The latter method may be preferable because professional golfers such as Dave Stockton (1977) and Dutch Harrison (Kemp, 1978) have independently reported that suddenly releasing and shaking out the tension from a tightened fist successfully induces relaxation. Either way, when you hold the club for the actual shot, your hands should feel light and loose around it. You will now "feel" the club for the putt you wish to make rather than trying to crush the grip on your putter. Johnny Miller (Miller and Shankland, 1976; Dennis, 1974) has made the point that the light, relaxed grip is also a key to success off the green. In his view the muscles tighten when you grip the club strongly, and those tight muscles react more slowly than long, relaxed muscles. Faster muscle reaction leads to more power, and a light grip is associated with relaxed muscles. When you tense the hand muscles for six seconds and then make your shot, after you

119

have released the tension and allowed the hands to relax, your grip will feel loose. Miller advocates gripping the club as lightly as you can. He reports that all of the long hitters of his acquaintance hold a similar view on the constriction and power loss caused by a tight grip.

The short-cut relaxation that we have just described is the least efficient way to use relaxation training. We present it to you only on the slight chance that you will run into a situation that provokes uncontrollable anxiety before you have mastered the full program of relaxation training which has been so generally successful. However, if your physical skills are sound, this six-second preshot routine could enable you to hit rather than yip many of your stressful shots. The relaxation produced in this way will not impede your judgment or limit your physical performance, but if you can master it in this abbreviated form, it may well significantly relieve your anxiety.

As with any worthwhile skill, learning how to relax takes time and work. If you are playing any kind of competitive golf, be it club, high school, college or professional, you will find that the time it takes to master relaxation is well worth the effort in lowered scores and greater joy derived from the game. Actually you may even find that the time you lose practicing relaxation is more than made up for in the time you no longer spend in abject depression over your game or endless post-mortems over your poor shots.

These skills are particularly valuable to the professional golfer. If you make a living at this difficult game, the stress that you encounter on the golf course is more extreme than that met by even the most ardent amateur. While it is possible for you to attain a state of relaxation by reading the procedures we describe, it would be worth your while to find a competent behavior therapist to help you implement an individualized program of relaxation training. A professional can respond to your personal concerns and difficulties in a way that is impossible through the printed word. Should you decide to take such a step we recommend that you seek out a behaviorally trained psychologist for the agreed upon purpose of learning how to relax. Do not be afraid to check out the psychologist's credentials. You want someone with a behavioral approach who specializes in these techniques. Relaxation can be learned quite nicely without the danger of tranquilizers or other medical interventions. Similarly, there is not likely to be any need for long discussions about how you felt toward your mother when you were three. You should be learning how to relax, naturally, without drugs or the need for long-term therapy. The easiest way to locate a behavioral psychologist is probably to contact the Psychology Department of a university and ask them to recommend one.

THE FULL RELAXATION PROGRAM: RATIONALE

Modern relaxation training, through alternately tensing and relaxing muscle groups, was first introduced by University of Chicago physiologist Edmund Jacobson in the mid-thirties. While there are a number of theoretical explanations for the phenomena that he observed, a serviceable approach is the simple premise that all bodily functions have refractory periods. That is, if you maintain an activity for a period of time and then stop, your body will resist resuming that activity until it has rested. Jacobson (1938) noted that anxiety seemed to be reported when a person experienced tension produced by a shortening of muscle fibers (Bernstein and Borkovec, 1973), just as Tommy Armour (1967) noted that anxiety produced muscle tension and inhibited movement. But Jacobson did not stop at describing this reaction. He suggested that if one wanted to decrease anxiety, it was necessary to decrease muscle tension. This could be done simply through a spring principle that allows muscles to snap back to a relaxed or elongated state after they have been tensed or strongly compressed. Thus, if a muscle was being maintained at a moderately high level of tension and you intentionally increased that tension to a higher level, when you let go of the spring it would snap back to a stretched-out position rather than to the position of moderate tension present before the stress was increased. The muscles would return to a position that was more relaxed than the state they had been in before the tension was increased. Like the male refractory period following sex, the muscle requires a short period of rest before it can tense up again.

If one can relax one muscle group in this way, it might also be possible to continue through the various muscle groups of the body to produce a thoroughly relaxed individual. Jacobson went on to demonstrate that indeed one could induce relaxation by progressively tensing and relaxing various muscle groups. Unfortunately, his procedures were lengthy and cumbersome. Their general application had to await a more practical format. That format was provided by a psychologically sophisticated psychiatrist named Joseph Wolpe.

In the fifties Wolpe (1958) reported a successful muscle tension and relaxation technique that took roughly ten percent of the time of Jacobson's original program. With this new tool, Wolpe initiated a program of research which demonstrated that experiences that would normally produce anxiety would be nullified if the person was relaxed when they were encountered. This finding has much significance for the anxious golfer.

In addition to improving the procedure and investigating its effects, Wolpe went on to apply a relaxation-based treatment to phobias, generalized fears and other anxiety reactions. His methods were remarkably successful with simple fears, and have been extended to the area of sports anxiety. It has been possible to reduce a boxer's anxiety to the point that he won the championship of his division and to decrease the anxiety of a professional golfer who went on to win the U. S. Open. That's right, the U. S. Open!

These early reports have led to further success in reducing sports tension with relaxation training. Dr. Robert Nideffer (1976) has reported positive effects with both golfers and divers. He indicates that similar self-relaxation techniques have been successful in a variety of sports including baseball, skiing, hockey, tennis, and track. He reports a particularly impressive improvement in a college shot putter who broke his own conference record in successive meets after having had little success earlier in the season. Recently, the second author (Dr. O'Brien) had occasion to use progressive relaxation with a professional boxer, resulting in marked improvement.

Some of the most impressive demonstrations of improved athletic performance through relaxation have been reported by Richard Suinn (1972, 1977) in his work with the United States Team in the 1976 Olympiad. Suinn's particular variant of progressive relaxation training, which he calls Anxiety Management Training (Suinn and Richardson, 1971), is the program that is most similar to the self-control procedure that we formulate for you later in this chapter.

These case histories are interesting and suggestive of positive effects to be gained from relaxation training in both amateur and professional sports. However, controlled research is required before any strong conclusions can be drawn. The first author has recently completed a test of the efficiency of relaxation with golf teams from three high schools. The results, which will be reported in more detail when we talk about visualization, demonstrate that relaxation training can produce measurable gains in a golfer's scores over the course of a season (Simek, Miller, and O'Brien, 1980).

The first thing that you must do to use relaxation on the golf course is to be able to distinguish when tension or anxiety is a problem for you. For most golfers this does not present much of a challenge. They are altogether too familiar with their fears on the links and have no need of help in recognizing them. It is possible, though, that you have learned your anxiety so well that you tighten up without even being aware of it. Since these cases are the exception rather than the rule, we will not dwell on them here. If you have difficulty recognizing your anxiety, we would endorse Nideffer's perceptive observation that when you find yourself breaking your normal preshot ritual, the chances are that you're experiencing some interference from stress. If this happens to you often, you are a candidate for relaxation training.

Progressive muscular relaxation has two significant drawbacks as a procedure to reduce anxiety. First, it requires practice. It does not really require much practice, but it does need to be practiced consistently. Second, it often works too well! When these two limitations are combined, they may lead the golfer who quickly overcomes his anxiety through diligent practice to stop practicing relaxation because he no longer has a problem. Naturally, once he stops practicing he loses the ability to relax easily and his anxiety returns. When that happens, he assumes that the relaxation training has failed, and that he therefore must grin and bear a never-ending battle with his nerves. Nothing could be further from the truth. If you can relax your muscles and practice this training, your anxiety will very likely be among the missing when you pull out your clubs.

FULL RELAXATION PROGRAM: METHOD

Enough description, let's get to it! Find yourself a comfortable chair (a recliner is best) and remove your shoes, glasses, or contacts. Loosen any tight-fitting clothing. If you are on a bed, couch, or recliner, lie back and make sure your entire body feels comfortably supported. If you are in an armchair, put your feet flat on the floor and uncross your legs. This procedure takes about twenty to thirty minutes when you are new to it so make sure you have the time to complete the exercise. It is best if the room is relatively dark and quiet, but at least in the beginning leave enough light so that you can read the instructions. If possible, choose a time of day when you will be free of sudden noises and interruptions. One of the authors (Dr. O'Brien) once relaxed a client in his office in a comfortable chair next to his desk. Unfortunately, no one had told his secretary to hold incoming calls. Shortly after completing the relaxation exercise, a loud intercom buzzer went off in the relaxed client's ear resulting in a serious challenge to the state high-jump record. Do not make this mistake! It is difficult to get relaxed again if you have just been scared out of your skin. Just as relaxation inhibits anxiety, established strong anxiety will prevent relaxation.

There are any number of good programs for progressive relaxation. There are also several tapes available to help produce the relaxation response. The best self-relaxation procedure we have seen was written by Spencer Rathus and Jeff Nevid (1977) in their fine book, *BT/Behavior Therapy: Strategies for Solving Problems in Living*. Their systematic procedure for tensing twelve muscle groups is presented below. Take a moment to read through their list.

How to Tense Each Muscle Group

1. Tense the hands and wrists by clenching your hands into tight fists. Try this slowly at first so that you will determine whether your fingernails are too long for the exercise. If they are, trim them or keep them angled away from your palms as you make tight fists. You should feel the tension in your fingers, along the backs of your hands, and, to a lesser degree, on your wrists.

2. Tense your biceps by bending your arms at the elbows. This is usually what children do in response to the adult request to "make a muscle." However, do not also clench your hand into a fist. Focus on the biceps only, keeping the rest of your arm as relaxed as possible.

3. You can see what it feels like to tense your triceps (the backs of your upper arms) and the tops of your forearms by lying on your back on a couch and pressing your hands down flat against the couch. After you have practiced this a couple of times, you will be able to reproduce the tensing sensations in your arms without pressing against an opposing force.

4. Tense your forehead by frowning hard, so that you can place your hand on your forehead and feel wrinkles.

5. Tense the middle of your face by scrunching up your nasal area. Keep your forehead smooth as you do so.

6. Tense your mouth region by pressing your lips together hard. Many practitioners of progressive relaxation instruct their clients to bite their teeth together hard. This can be costly to dental work. Others suggest you press your tongue against the roof of your mouth. We note that this can cause discomfort.

7. The feeling you should experience while tensing your neck is the one you obtain when you press your forehead forward against your hands. If you try this sitting, keep your head vertical and do not bend your back. If you try this while lying on your back, keep the back of your head against a pillow or a mat—do not lift it. After you practice this a couple of times and attend to what the tension in your neck feels like, you will be able to reproduce the sensation without

using your hands. Practice this a couple of times and then take a brief break. You may be tired.

8. In order to experience tension in your shoulders, stand with your back against the wall and press your shoulders back against the wall. Then reproduce the sensation while sitting or lying down, without actually pressing your shoulders against anything, but just, in effect, stretching them back.

9. Tense your abdominal region by "sucking in your stomach" hard.

10. Tense your thigh muscles by lying down on a couch or a bed, straightening out your legs hard, and pushing your legs out from your body. Do not push out your toes or your heels alone. Stretch your legs forward, as if trying to be an inch taller. As you do so, you should be able to feel tightness in the tops of your thighs with your hands. Do not stretch so hard that you develop a muscle spasm or charley horse.

11. Tense your calves by drawing your feet back up toward your face while you are lying on your back or reclining. Again, do not tense so hard that you develop a muscle spasm.

12. Tense your feet by curling your toes, as you had made a fist with your hands. Be careful: Toes are not as flexible as fingers.

Following the Rathus and Nevid program you will be going through each muscle group beginning with the hands. We recommend you use the following seven-step strategy for relaxing each muscle group.

1. Tense the muscle.

2. Feel the tension in the muscle.

3. Hold the tension for five or six seconds.

4. Say the word "relax" to yourself as you release the tension in the muscles all at once.

5. Feel the muscles relax as you let go! Feel them tingle! Feel the sense of heaviness in the muscles at the same time that you experience almost a floating sensation in the muscles. The muscles may feel like they will rise by themselves but at the same time feel difficult to lift.

6. Enjoy the feeling of relaxation for thirty or forty seconds.

7. Repeat steps one through six a second time.

Please take a moment now to go over the order of the muscle groups that you are about to relax. Try the relaxation procedure with your eyes open the first time through so you can read the directions. The next time you sit down to do your relaxation program, close your eyes as you begin the procedure. You will find it's easiest to remember the order of the muscle groups to be relaxed if you break the list into sections that follow a natural sequence, such as:

1. Hands, Biceps, and Triceps

2. Forehead, Nose, and Mouth

3. Neck, Shoulders, and Stomach

4. Thighs, Calves, and Feet.

Ready? Lean back in your chair and relax. Take three deep breaths; inhale and exhale. Try to feel the air going down into your lungs. For some of you smokers or New Yorkers, that much air may come as a shock to your system, but you will start to feel calmer as soon as your breathing becomes deeper and more rhythmic.

We will begin with your hands. Make tight fists! Hold those fists for five or six seconds. Now say the word "relax" and all at once release the tension in your fists by opening your hands. Feel the tension drip from your fingers. Allow your hands and wrists to feel warm and heavy for thirty to forty seconds. Now repeat the procedure. Notice the warmth and tingling as your hands become more and more relaxed. Really feel the relaxation in your hands and wrists over the next forty seconds. Let your hands return to the arms of the chair after the second tensing. As you proceed through the rest of the program try not to engage in much activity with those parts of the body that have already been relaxed. Let your hands rest easily.

At this point your hands should feel very relaxed. Move on now to your biceps and repeat the procedure using the same time limits. Remember to tense each muscle group twice with a thirty- to forty-second break in between each tensing. It is very important that you observe and remember the feelings of relaxation in your muscles. When you move on to a new muscle group, you should allow more than the prescribed forty seconds between tensions of the same muscle group. You may wish to rest for a full minute between groups. After you have finished the second tensing of the biceps and allowed yourself time to enjoy the feeling of relaxation in those muscles, you should proceed to the triceps, following the program described by Rathus and Nevid. Continue through their list all the way to the feet, using our seven-step relaxation procedure outlined earlier.

After the second repetition of the tension-relaxation sequence of your feet, we would like you to add three new steps to the relaxation procedure. First, we want you to relax your eyes. Golfers' eyes are all too often a prime location for interference from anxiety. A darting glance can wreak havoc on setting up and executing a tough putt. Having removed your contact lenses, close your eyes and tightly, but carefully, squint them up. When you first close your eyes, you should see some flashes of light which are followed by a more even darkening of your visual field. Again hold for five seconds and release the tension as you say "relax." It is not necessary to open your eyes. Just let them return to a normally closed position and feel the heaviness in your eyelids. Your eyes should feel very comfortable remaining closed, whereas previously they may have seemed like they wanted to open as you went through the program. As with all other steps, repeat the eye tension a second time thirty to forty seconds later.

125

Now that your eyes are relaxed, the second thing that we want you to add is a total relaxation of all the muscles at the same time. Tense everything at once! Make sure you don't miss the neck, shoulders, and mouth. Hold it for four to five seconds then let go as you say the word "relax." Your body should now feel really heavy. Notice how relaxed you feel. Just wallow in that pleasant sense of fluid, loose musculature.

Your body has become totally relaxed and your thoughts may well have gone in the same direction. In case they have not followed the body's lead, we have one final request to make of you, in order to get rid of your troublesome thoughts as well as relax your body. As you are lying calmly relaxed with your eyes closed, imagine that you are staring down at a light blue golf ball. See the golf ball in front of you! Visualize it! See the dimples and the shine! Now imagine that it is starting to grow. Watch it get bigger and bigger, and as it does it will turn a darker and darker blue. Watch it getting bluer and bluer . . . as it becomes softball size . . . then basketball size . . . then so large that it begins to blot out your whole visual field. All you see now is a dark, deep blue field. That field is going to turn into a deep royal blue, velvet theater curtain. Feel the heaviness of the curtain and the smooth, furry texture of the velvet. Feel it rubbing against your skin! . . . Now feel that curtain coming down over your thoughts . . . wrapping up your mind . . . covering up all of your cares and thoughts so that only the deep blue velvet is left. Feel yourself continue to relax more and more as you lie back enjoying this carefree existence.

It is not necessary for you to memorize this procedure or have someone read it to you, although having it read to you certainly will produce the desired effects. The most sensible way to use this thought relaxation script is to memorize the key points in a few words such as:

1. Blue Golf Ball

2. Larger and Darker

3. Blue Velvet Theater Curtain

4. Blot Out All Thoughts.

If you can remember those four phrases and have read the actual procedure, you should be able to wing it, without reading, and produce the desired effects. You can then use it to talk yourself into a calm state of mind. This procedure allows you to do what Arnold Palmer (1963) recommends, that is, to put aside all your thoughts and concentrate on the ball.

After completing the program, open your eyes. You should feel relaxed but not sleepy, and carefree but not lethargic. It should be around twenty minutes since you began exercising, although by the end of your training you will be able to perform the same functions in five to ten minutes. The key to this intervention as in most other golf skills is practice. To master these techniques you should practice at least once a day and preferably twice. We know that you have a busy schedule, but you will find that one practice session is easily accomplished at night before going to sleep and the other can usually be squeezed in sometime during the day. If you are able to practice twice a day, you should have this down in a maximum of two weeks. The less you practice, the longer it will take you to master relaxation techniques.

It is important that you keep a record of your practice sessions. Start a log to note the date, time, and length of each relaxation session. Then in a final column, rate how relaxed you felt from one (little or no relaxation) to ten (totally relaxed) immediately after the exercise. These ratings will give you valuable information on your progress toward calmer golf.

As you get more and more proficient at relaxation training, you will need to spend less time doing it. You will also discover that you can combine muscle groups so that you can produce the effect in four steps instead of the original twelve. These four steps are:

1. Hands and Arms

2. Head, including Eyes

3. Neck, Shoulders, and Stomach

4. Legs and Feet.

Do not neglect your thoughts of a total-body tension-relaxation as you abbreviate the procedure. Pay particular attention to your breathing as well. Always begin each session by establishing a rhythmic pattern of deep breathing. As a fifth step in the physical relaxation series, you may want to tense your chest muscles by taking a deep breath and holding it for four or five seconds. Then exhale with the word "relax" as you release the tension in your chest. Your breathing will then return to a deep, rhythmic pattern. We are suggesting therefore that in your abbreviated practice you add two more steps:

5. Breathing and Chest Tension

6. Total Body Relaxation.

The above program will produce relaxation for most people. In fact, it is possible that you will fall asleep on occasion during the procedure. That is not a bad sign. How much more relaxed can you get than to nod off? Most people have little difficulty achieving a relaxed state with the abbreviated procedures if they practice even minimally. If you practice very diligently, you may even be able to establish such a strong link between the feelings of relaxed muscles and the word "relax" that merely saying the word will produce those sensations. Imagine how useful such a skill might be when you are staring at an important putt or waiting to tee off in a close match at eighteen. Although our concern is with golf, once you can initiate relaxation in this simple way, you can also reduce tension in the face of stress in business or interpersonal relations.

No matter how well you learn this procedure, you must not forget the need for continued practice. If you do not take yourself through these exercises at least once a week, they will lose their effectiveness for you no matter how well you learned them initially.

The relaxation program that we have just described is the one whose effectiveness has been the most thoroughly substantiated, although there are a number of other relaxation approaches to anxiety. This relaxation technique depends on the fact that tension on the golf course is a learned reaction. Nobody takes up the game feeling up-tight on every shot. You have to learn to be anxious about sand traps, four-footers, and club championships. You learn to be anxious about these situations by repeatedly encountering short putts and negative results over many experiences. This learning is helped along by modeling. Professional golfers, opponents, and partners tell you how anxious they get and demonstrate the anxiety for you. Yet, whatever is learned can be unlearned! The link between a golf shot and anxiety can be broken by preventing the anxiety from occurring. Relaxation stops the anxiety so you can learn to feel relaxed in what had been a stressful situation.

The relaxation procedure described above is intended to enable you to turn on relaxation in any situation. The repeated pairing of the word "relax" and deep breathing with the release of muscle tension will enable you to achieve a relaxed feeling in yourself by simply taking a deep breath and saying "relax." This occurs through the same learning-by-repetition principles that established your anxiety in the first place. For some golfers, however, a briefer, more specific attack on anxiety is all that is necessary. The shorter program described below may well be enough to overcome your general anxiety on the course. We have derived this program from Suinn and Richardson's Anxiety Management Training but tailored it specifically for golfers. We believe it is the most productive and efficient way to use progressive muscle relaxation.

The weakest part of the relaxation exercises that we have just taught you is the technique for relaxing your mind. Many people have difficulty visualizing when requested to, and others find that what may be a relaxing image to us, does nothing for them. Suinn and his colleagues have developed a practical solution to this problem. They have their clients develop an individual relaxation scene that the client identifies as most effective in making him feel calm. This represents a major step forward in the use of relaxation approaches.

ANXIETY MANAGEMENT TRAINING FOR GOLFERS (AMTG)

Week 1

AMTG includes an abbreviated form of progressive relaxation, but, in our view, it improves upon the standard relaxation format by helping the individual to identify those instances that make him anxious as well as by having the individual provide his own imagery to induce relaxation. At this point we would again like you to think about some lie or situation on the course that wrecks your nerves. Try to imagine that you are actually in that situation. Get as much detail as possible. Note the texture and color of the grass, the discoloration of your clubhead, and the color of the tee. See the name and number on the ball. Get into it as much as you can, and as you do, try to identify when you start to feel anxious. What are the first signs from your body that you are getting tense? Is it tightening in the neck? A squint? Dryness in the mouth? A tendency to straighten up as you are over the ball? These are just some of the possibilities. The start of your reaction may be quite unique, and only you can identify it.

Let us give you an example of an anxiety scene so that you will know exactly how to build an image that will make you feel anxious.

Imagine yourself with a four-foot, downhill putt on the seventeenth green. You lie two on this par four but one of your opponents has already sunk his twelve-footer for a birdie and your partner missed his from thirty-five feet. They are one up in the match so if you do not sink this baby it's all over. You look down the line of the putt. It appears that it breaks slightly from left to right. Imagine yourself walking around to address the ball. Feel each step. Hear your spikes on the grass. Feel them dig in. Look down at the ball. Feel your hand around your putter and your arms as they get into address position. See the name on the ball and the color and grain of the grass. Think about how important the shot is. Remember how you blew a three-footer on fifteen to put the team down. Think about how you hooked your drive on sixteen and were out of the hole. This is your chance to redeem yourself and make good! Again, look at the line of the putt. Check it out! Is that break really there? How hard do you dare hit it? Now do your waggle and take the shot.

Did you hole it? More importantly, did you experience anxiety? If this scene works to make you feel anxious, feel free to use it, but it is probably better if you tune in to your personal stressors by writing your own scene on the lines provided below.

_____

_____

_____

_____

Once you have written your scene, sit back, close your eyes, and take yourself through it. On the lines below write your bodily anxiety signals in the order that you noticed them.

1. _____
2. _____
3. _____
4. _____

We now have an idea of what will make you anxious out on the course and of how that anxiety shows itself. We have still one more task to engage your writing skills and imagination. So far we have developed a scene to make you anxious. Now you must create its counterpart, a scene to help you relax. Try to picture a scene in which you feel totally calm. Some examples might be:

1. Lying on the beach on a nice sunny day.

2. Playing a familiar piece of music on an instrument.

3. Watching a ball game in a comfortable chair in front of the TV or listening to your stereo.

4. Taking off in a jet plane or taking a long trip by boat or train.

5. Dancing at your wedding reception.

6. Nursing a baby or holding your child as you rock him or her to sleep.

Try to make the scene as vivid as possible. For "lying at the beach," for example, you might imagine the following:

You are lying on the beach. Feel the hot sun on your arms and legs. Feel the cool ocean breezes. Notice the scratchiness of the blanket underneath your body. Feel the hot grainy sand on your feet and hands. See the blue sky and white puffy clouds. Smell the ocean spray and feel the dampness. Listen to the sound of the surf beating against the shore. Focus on that rhythmic sound of the waves breaking and returning to the sea. Then tune in to your own feelings of relaxation, peace, and serenity. Lie there, soak up the sun, listen to the surf, and relax.

Write in a relaxation scene of your own on the lines below. Feel free to use the one we have described only if it really makes you feel calm and you have experienced relaxation at the beach. Otherwise, use your own scene. A word of caution here: avoid sexually stimulating fantasy. Some of our clients have succeeded in reducing their anxiety in this manner but they report some interference in their play from the sexual arousal. Make it as realistic and striking as you can. Try to write into it bodily sensations as well as the sights, sounds, odors, and tactile sensations associated with the experience. Try to get your skin to feel the hot sun, dampness and/or breeze to make it as vivid as possible.

_____

_____

_____

_____

_____

The next step is to return briefly to the progressive relaxation format that we used earlier. Take yourself through the relaxation procedure as described previously, but conclude the exercise by putting in your own scene. Our eventual aim is to produce the same feelings of relaxation that we obtain from the complete tension-relaxation program by using only a deep breath and a relaxation scene. Begin each exercise session with three deep breaths and conclude with your relaxation scene. You should practice this routine once a day for at least a week. If it is possible for you to get in two practice sessions daily, it would be beneficial, but a minimum of five sessions in seven days is required.

Week 2

Once the progressive muscle relaxation has been learned, the next step is to produce the feelings of relaxation without first tensing the muscles. Begin by taking a breath and slowly exhaling. Again, breathe in and exhale deliberately. Take a third breath and slowly exhale as you think the word "relax." Now go through your body beginning with your hands. Let your mind produce the feelings of relaxation that you previously achieved through tensing and relaxing your muscles. Feel each muscle group become warm, heavy, and relaxed. Take fifteen to twenty minutes to go from your hands to your feet. After you have finished with your lower extremities, take three more deep breaths and initiate your relaxation scene. Use your senses to develop the scene as vividly as you can. Get lost in it! Feel as though you are really there! Notice the surroundings and build them into your fantasy. Let yourself sink into the feeling of a carefree, tensionless existence. Enjoy it for a while, a minute or two, so that you begin to get comfortable being calm.

After you have been fully relaxed for a few minutes, bring your anxiety scene into focus. Think about that four-footer but as soon as you feel any anxiety, bring back the relaxation scene. Mentally, leave the green and return to the beach. At the first sign of any tension, bring yourself back to the rhythmic calm of the surf. Whether you feel any anxiety or not, do not spend more than ten seconds imagining your anxiety scene. Then take some deep breaths, exhale slowly, and visualize your relaxation scene. Hold that scene until you feel completely comfortable. Then, after about a minute, begin the anxiety scene again. Let it go a little longer this time. Spend twenty to thirty seconds imagining yourself getting ready for the shot. Now, take a deep breath and bring the relaxation scene to mind again. Repeat the twenty- to thirty-second anxiety scene three more times, relaxing for a minute between each take.

You may wish to break the process we have just described into two steps. The first week would be spent learning to relax without muscle tensing. Then, in the second week you would practice using the relaxation to reduce the nervousness produced by your anxiety scene. Whether you spend two weeks on this step or use the combined system and do it in one, practice of the nontensing relaxation instruction should be engaged in at least twice a day for fifteen to twenty minutes for a full week. It takes some effort to be able to recapture the feelings of relaxation in your muscles without first tensing them. If you wish to begin using the relaxation scene to defuse your anxiety scene, you should add ten minutes to each of these practice sessions. If you feel that you are not having problems instituting relaxation without tensing, we believe that you should move on to challenging your anxiety scene at this time.

Nideffer (1976) offers an excellent word of caution about your relaxation practice, and we would like to echo and expand on it. This is not something that can be forced. It requires passive concentration rather than active effort. Jack Burke (1966), who in 1956 won both the PGA and the Masters has called this feeling "concentrated relaxation." Try to get lost in your relaxation scene and the warm, heavy feeling of relaxed muscles but don't try to relax. As you repeatedly practice these techniques, you will feel the sense of relaxation come on as if somebody turned off your tension (but you cannot actively try to pull the switch). This is where your records of your practice can be invaluable. Don't become discouraged or quit practicing. Don't rush it or move too quickly from one step to the next. It will come but some people require more practice than others. It can't be forced!

The greatest leap in this procedure is going from tensing muscles to produce relaxation to becoming relaxed without a preliminary muscle tension. Fortunately, this most precarious step is also the least important skill to acquire. It is more convenient and faster to learn to relax without tensing exercises, but all of the results of the other steps can also be accomplished if you continue to use tensing exercises to make your muscles relax. Each practice session will be longer but the relaxing effects should be exactly the same.

The theoretical underpinning of this technique relies on breaking the bond between your anxiety and the situation that makes you anxious. This is achieved by repeatedly experiencing your anxiety scene while the relaxation stops you from being anxious. You are actually rehearsing a calm approach to the anxiety scene. This means that if your anxiety scene does not really make you nervous as demonstrated by tension returning to your muscles, restlessness, more rapid breathing, etc., you have to make that scene more vivid or find a more stressful scene. On the other hand, if you stay anxious when you turn on your relaxation scene, it means that either you haven't practiced your relaxation scene enough and are rushing the process, or you are allowing too much anxiety to build up before the relaxation scene is introduced. If the problem is the former, more practice is called for. The latter problem obviously calls for shorter exposures to the anxiety scene.

The best way to break a learned link between a situation (four-footers) and your reaction to it (anxiety), is to prevent that reaction from occurring while it is being unlearned. If you engage in competitive play as you go through this stage of the procedure, you are threatening your barely learned relaxation responses with a full blast of anxiety. That will undermine your program but not necessarily defeat it. The best way to gain control of your course nerves is to learn to be relaxed over the winter when you do not have to play. If you must continue to play, don't forget that you have been working on becoming relaxed for only three weeks while you have spent years becoming anxious. Practice does make perfect! Your ten-plus years of practice at being nervous have made you awfully good at it. You may find that when you have a touchy lie and anxiety wells up on the course, your attempts to breathe deeply and turn on your relaxa-

132

tion scene have no affect. At that point you have tried to stop a tank with a pistol and gotten rolled over in the process. (You'll have to wait until your pistol eventually grows up into a bazooka but each time it gets smashed by the tank its growth is impeded.) You are not ready yet to try AMTG techniques out on the course. If you proceed too quickly it will interfere with learning the relaxation.

By the end of the second week you should be able to quickly establish relaxation without tensing. Breathing plays an important role during this period. Your slow rhythmic breathing should be well established and begin to make you feel relaxed in and of itself. Many golfers, such as Byron Nelson, Gary Player, and Bobby Nichols, have advocated controlled deep breathing as a method of defusing the tension associated with an important shot (Kemp, 1978). Their experience suggests that this is an important technique to master.

Week 3

During the third week you should begin each practice session by making yourself relaxed using the method that you have found to be most effective. Breathe deeply and allow your muscles to relax. By this time you are probably quite proficient at relaxing. Deep breathing may be all that is necessary for a feeling of relaxation to develop, but do not worry if you continue to require a more extensive program.

After you have achieved a relaxed state, initiate your anxiety scene but let the anxiety build somewhat further than you have before. Then shut the scene off by breathing deeply and returning to your relaxation scene. Your goal for this week's practice session is to be able to take yourself all the way through to the successful conclusion of the shot while retaining the ability to turn off your anxiety at any point by changing your breathing and returning to your relaxation scene.

Practice is crucial at this juncture. Two sessions of forty minutes a day is ideal but you can benefit from as little as half an hour of daily exposure. You should be capable of achieving relaxation in ten minutes, allowing twenty to thirty minutes for repetition of the anxiety-scene/relaxation-scene sequence. Four to six repetitions is ideal. By the end of the week you will be able to stop yourself from feeling anxious at any point in your anxiety scene.

Week 4

Your efforts at becoming relaxed without first tensing your muscles should continue this week. Practice relaxing by deep breathing and passive concentration on the relaxed feelings of your muscles. Direct your practice toward developing feelings of relaxation before you begin your relaxation scene. If you have practiced the program as described over the first three weeks, it is likely that you will feel very calm even before the relaxation scene is begun.

You may find that by the fourth week you are having difficulty becoming anxious during your anxiety scene. This week is a good time to write a second and third tension-producing anxiety scene from your golf experiences. If you have recently faced a situation that produced overwhelming anxiety on the course, use that as the topic for your second anxiety scene. Even if the first anxiety image continues to make you tense, you must develop other scenes so that you can learn to relax in the face of those situations as well as you are learning to control your nerves in the first scene.

There are two important new skills to be mastered this week. They are interrelated, so you must learn one before you try to practice the other. You may recall the comparison that we made earlier between trying to use your amateurish relaxation skills against your professional anxiety, and trying to stop a tank with a pistol. Let us carry that analogy a little bit further. How could you stop a tank with a pistol? There probably isn't any way that would be effective. But suppose that you were face to face with the driver of the tank who told you that he was going to run you down as soon as he could get in and get the tank rolling? Now you can stop the tank simply by using your pistol to keep the driver from getting into it. You can also stop your anxiety before it gets rolling but you have to learn the early warning signals.

How does your tension begin? Look back at the list that you made earlier. What is the first sign that you are losing your cool? Start your anxiety scene and watch for cues such as a breathing change or increased muscle tension. Your goal for this week is to identify your unique first link in the chain. You can then use your relaxation to snap that chain before the anxiety can bowl you over.

Practice your anxiety scenes to identify how the anxiety starts. Then initiate the deep breathing and feelings of muscle relaxation at the first sign of anxiety. Your practice should focus on producing your anxiety cues and then getting rid of them through deep breathing, muscle relaxation, and your relaxation scene. If your anxiety begins with dryness in your throat, practice starting to relax as soon as you get that feeling in your throat. Your daily practice routine should follow the same schedule as last's week assignment. Ten minutes to relax, then twenty to thirty minutes of experiencing the cue and reducing the anxiety.

After you have singled out the precursors of an attack of golf nerves, it is time for the second step in this week's program. Take that knowledge with you into your next match. See if you can catch the anxiety before it grows into a monster. Don't expect to succeed every time or waste your relaxation shots on anxiety that is already going full tilt. In those situations where you can pick up the first signal of anxiety, breathe deeply, feel your muscles become warm and heavy, and, if necessary, initiate your relaxation scene. The important assignment for this week is not to conquer your anxiety. This is a reconnaissance mission. Watch yourself as you play to see if you can identify the aura of oncoming anxiety and what happens when you try to slow it down. These early warning signals will give you a chance to meet the anxiety with a wall of relaxation and calm. Once you start to relax early enough, it will take a great deal to upset you.

Week 5

The final week of the program is aimed at making your relaxation training a tool for everyday use out on the course. Again, begin your sessions by getting yourself deeply relaxed through deep breathing and focus attention on feelings of relaxation in your muscles. Commence your relaxation scene as soon as your muscles feel relaxed, and continue your rhythmic breathing.

Once you have established the sensation of relaxation, begin one of your anxiety scenes. Get into it as completely as you can. Build the scene so that you experience some real tension! *Stay with the scene* but begin to breathe deeply and feel your muscles become heavy and relaxed. Feel yourself becoming calmer and more at ease. Recognize and accept those feelings. Stay with the anxiety scene, but let yourself see that you feel calm and relaxed. Say those words to yourself: "I am calm and relaxed." Practice is crucial at this point. You are trying to develop a controlled, passive, and ongoing relaxation. The practice should include a variety of tension-producing scenes. Daily sessions are once again the preferred method of practice with relaxation taking less than ten minutes, leaving thirty minutes to use deep breathing to halt the rise of anxiety as you imagine various stressful, match situations.

For many people, a week of practicing these techniques is enough to produce a sense of relaxation simply by breathing deeply in the face of any anxiety-producing situation. If you find that you require more practice before you can dispense with the relaxation scene, there is no harm in continuing for a second week.

You will probably not need a record of your anxiety to tell you that you are playing a much calmer game now that you have learned to relax. If you have not improved radically, start to record your estimate of your relaxation as you go through each round just as you did in your imagery exercise. If these records show that you are not becoming less tense, return to the full tension-relaxation program. During your home practice of the full muscular tension-relaxation program, be sure to include some relaxing mental imagery. After you have become completely relaxed, imagine in short exposures, the shots that are giving you difficulty. As soon as you feel anxious, bring back a scene of relaxation. Slowly lengthen the anxiety scene until you can go all the way through it without feeling any anxiety. This kind of gradual, relaxed exposure to greater and greater stress should overcome the anxiety so that you can return to the course feeling relaxed.

Even when you feel that the program has been completely successful, do not stop practicing! Once-a-week practice at home is probably enough to maintain your skills. Rathus and Nevid (1977) recommend a full, muscular tension-relaxation booster session once a month. We concur because it is necessary to remind yourself of just what completely relaxed muscles feel like. It is also necessary to make sure that your relaxing thoughts and deep breathing continue to produce a state of relaxation that is the equivalent of the swing-back relaxation you get by overtensing the muscles. By doing this once-a-month practice, you strengthen the bond between deep breathing and self-messages of muscle relaxation on the one hand and the feeling of relaxed muscles on the other. If you continue to follow these precepts, your deep breathing and relaxation techniques will enable you to play relaxed golf for many years to come.

10

Hypnosis and Visualization

"Never underestimate the power of suggestion in a round of golf."

JACKIE BURKE

The techniques presented in the last chapter to help you become calmer are not the only choices available. Relaxation can also be achieved by using a number of variations of those procedures. Benson's (1975) relaxation response and the autogenic training of Schultz and Luthe (1959) are similar relaxation-based training programs. Hypnosis also produces relaxation but that may not be its only function. It is because of these other potential benefits that we present instruction in hypnosis. Although the scientific study of hypnosis has not progressed to the point where any of these effects can be touted with certainty, case-study material indicates that hypnotic suggestions may be quite effective.

If you went through the full relaxation program of the last chapter, most authorities would argue that you were hypnotized by the time you finished the mental relaxation exercises. Hypnosis is not easily defined. The most frequent criteria are: (1) a feeling of relaxation; (2) hypersuggestibility or a desire to respond to suggestions; and (3) a reluctance to spontaneously initiate new activity (Udolf, 1980). If you were doing the relaxation properly you should have experienced both the first and third conditions, although there may have been no opportunity to test the second. In this chapter we will try to help you to use the hypersuggestibility of hypnosis to add further improvements to your game.

To begin to use hypnosis we have to dispel some of the myths that surround this topic. Hypnosis is not supernatural or mystical. It has no connection with Satanism or black magic. The Svengali-like image of the hypnotist bringing someone under his power is a vestige of old Bela Lugosi movies and has no basis in fact. Indeed, hypnosis works best when it is viewed as a cooperative venture between the hypnotist and the client who endeavor together to accomplish certain objectives. The client must let himself become involved in the suggestions of the hypnotist as he does when he becomes emotionally involved in a movie or a good novel (Barber, Spanos, and Chaves, 1974). The research indicates that hypnosis is not dangerous (Hilgard, 1965). It is possible to be crazy before hypnosis and just as crazy afterward, or to convince yourself that hypnosis will harm you. In eleven years of work with hypnosis the second author (Dr. O'Brien) has had only one adverse reaction. That occurred in a coed who had read a sensationalist magazine piece on the dangers of hypnosis the night before she was hypnotized. Even under these conditions the reaction wore off in less than an hour. Nevertheless, if you are afraid of hypnosis, do not attempt the procedures that we outline in this chapter.

Hypnosis is a phenomenon that follows the natural scientific laws of psychology. For this reason many of the problems that some people anticipate turn out not to be problems at all. For example, some people worry about not coming out of the "trance." In actuality, everybody comes out of hypnosis. Even if the hypnotist leaves the room, subjects wait a period of time, usually about forty-five minutes, and then simply wake of their own accord and go about their business.

Researchers, from the most skeptical like T. X. Barber (1972), to ardent advocates such as Kenneth Bowers (1976), completely agree that the reactions seen in hypnosis are real. Their disagreements revolve around how to account for these reactions. No matter what the theoretical explanation, it is clear that for some people hypnosis can produce dramatic effects that may be useful in a variety of ways in athletics.

The case history reports of professional athletes who have benefited from hypnosis have been well covered in the popular press. It would serve no purpose to recount them here except that they may be useful in illuminating the variety of methods at a hypnotist's disposal. At the simplest level is the report of the way hypnosis was used to help Cincinnati Reds centerfielder, Paul Blair, overcome his anxiety about again being hit in the head by a pitched ball. As Blair has indicated, what was called hypnosis in this instance would be more appropriately described as relaxation and probably systematic desensitization (Wolpe, 1958). As described in the last chapter, this procedure involves repeatedly imagining the anxiety-arousing situation in a relaxed state until the situation no longer gives rise to anxiety. If hypnosis was used at all in this situation, it served only to make the client more relaxed.

In addition to relaxation, hypnosis may be used to increase confidence by rehearsing upcoming events. Visualizing a successful outcome removes the unknown quantity from the situation as well as increasing one's confidence in his ability to handle the course or opponent. Boxers such as Duane Bobick and Ken Norton have successfully used hypnosis to increase self-confidence. As early as 1963, such confidence-building hypnosis was suggested for Ben Hogan's putting woes (Wood, 1963).

Eric Soderholm of the New York Yankees and Rod Carew of the California Angels are baseball players who have used hypnosis to improve concentration. It may well be that, again, this is nothing more than a relaxation effect. If you are pressing, you are not relaxed and your concentration is impaired. If you can be made to relax, you are then free to concentrate on hitting the ball. Yet, some players have reported that the ball seems larger and that they see it better than they did before being hypnotized. Direct suggestions of changes in the athletes' perceptions are another use of hypnosis in sports.

Hypnosis has been successfully used by many golfers. Its development as a technique for reducing the mental interference in a golfer's game owes much to the pioneering work of Jack Heise. Heise (1961), a follower of the great English golf instructor Ernest Jones, adopted Jones' theory that golf is a game to be played by the subconscious mind. This view of the game is similar to that held earlier by Dunn (1922) and later rephrased by Wiren, Coop, and Sheehan (1978), as we discussed in Chapter 8. Instead of separating the brain into left and right halves, Heise suggested an upper or conscious versus a lower or subconscious division. The conscious mind was responsible for setting up the shot, but the subconscious actually executed it. In one of the few golf books to do more than simply describe the game's problems, Heise advocated self-hypnosis as a way of communicating with the subconscious while turning off the conscious mind.

The self-hypnosis regimen that Heise describes has much in common with the relaxation procedures presented in the previous chapter. Some studies have even shown that relaxation training is superior to hypnosis in relaxing muscle tone. In a recent doctoral dissertation (Giacalone, 1979) under the direction of the second author, it was demonstrated that relaxation decreased the spasticity and muscle tension associated with cerebral palsy more effectively than either of two hypnotic approaches. If your goal is simply to relax, we believe that muscular relaxation training is the least complicated and most efficient way of reaching that end. Further, it does not require a trained clinical hypnotist; therefore, it is also less expensive than a hypnotic approach (Nideffer, 1976).

If your problem requires something more than relaxation, hypnosis may be worth a try. Obviously, we cannot have a trained hypnotist jump out of this page and begin to suggest that your eyes are becoming "tired, heavy, and sleepy." Any instructions that we present must therefore be a self-hypnosis procedure. But, as Desmond Tolhurst (1978), senior editor of *Golf Magazine,* observed, self-hypnosis is easier if you have first been hypnotized by a trained professional. Although our preference would be a psychologist licensed by the state, any reputable hypnotist can give you enough instruction so that you can produce self-hypnosis after a few sessions. A word of caution: If the practitioner tries to suggest that your golf problem reflects some underlying neurotic difficulty that requires further treatment, have the sophistication to request some evidence for this diagnosis. If the only evidence is the golf problem itself, find someone who will treat that problem directly, rather than trying to remake your personality without evidence that it needs to be remade.

For most people the pre-self-hypnosis trip to the hypnotist is desirable but not absolutely necessary. Hypnotic induction (placing an individual under hypnosis) can be accomplished in a number of ways. Two of these approaches are progressive muscle relaxation and imagery to block out conscious thought. If you have mastered the relaxation technique described earlier, you have learned progressive relaxation, and your relaxation scene is an image to block out conscious thought. All you need to do now is to take that relaxation a little deeper until you attain a suggestible hypnotic state.

If you feel comfortable enough to try self-hypnosis, the easiest way to do this is to use the relaxation skills you have already learned and institute a relaxation scene. Use the scene at the beach from the last chapter and just enjoy the feeling of relaxation for a couple of minutes. As you lie on your imaginary blanket, focus in on the sound of the surf. Hear the waves break against the shore. When you can clearly identify the sound of the water coming into the beach, begin to count each wave. With contact lenses removed and eyes closed, count ten waves and feel yourself going deeper and deeper into a more relaxed state. With the first wave count "one" and think to yourself "Becoming relaxed . . . Two . . . going deeper . . . three . . . deeper and deeper . . . four . . . more and more relaxed . . . five . . . feeling sleepy and heavy . . . six . . . more and more tired and sleepy . . . seven . . . more and more deeply relaxed . . . eight . . . deeper and deeper . . . nine . . . very, very deeply relaxed . . . ten . . . deeply relaxed . . . deeply hypnotized!" These thoughts should occur at a slow, unexcited pace in time to the incoming waves.

It is probably a good idea (Heise, 1961) to test yourself at this point to see how effective you have been in establishing a state of self-hypnosis. Borrowing from the standard tests of hypnotic susceptibility (Weitzenhoffer and Hilgard, 1959), we suggest a couple of hypnotic tasks. Raise your right arm straight out in front of you at shoulder level with the palm of your hand up. Now imagine that someone has just put a heavy book on your right hand. Feel your arm getting heavier, heavier, and heavier. Add two more heavy books and feel your arm coming down, farther and farther down. As your arm descends you will find yourself becoming more and more deeply hypnotized. When your arm reaches your lap, you will be at the deepest stage of hypnosis that you have yet attained. If your arm has not reached your lap, add a fourth very heavy tome. If that doesn't do the trick, just allow your arm to return to your lap. Keep your eyes closed and remove the imaginary books from your hand. See how easily you can lift your arm when they are gone. Let your arm drop back to your lap and continue to relax.

Now imagine that while you have been sitting with your eyes closed a mosquito has entered the room. You are trying to enjoy your hypnotic rest lying back with your eyes closed, but you can hear the mosquito buzzing around your head. Hear its high-pitched whine in your ear! It is flying around your body now. Feel it land on the back of your hand! Let yourself brush it away if you want to. . . . In a few seconds the mosquito flies out of the window whether you brushed it away or not, and you continue to relax feeling deeply hypnotized.

If your arm came down and you were able to feel or hear the mosquito, you have achieved excellent hypnotic depth for a first effort. But if you were not able to pass these tests, don't despair. Hypnosis is something that people get better at through practice (Sachs and Anderson, 1967). It only requires that you let yourself get involved uncritically. If you sit there and say to yourself, "Hell, I'm

140

not really on a beach," nothing will happen. Similarly, if you try to play scientist and watch everything that happens, you will have nothing to watch. You can't watch yourself do it, you have to get lost in it. Remember, there is nothing weak about the will of a good hypnotic subject. In fact, there is a tendency for brighter people to be a little better at hypnosis than those who are less intelligent. Even so, only twenty-five percent of the population are likely to be excellent subjects. Fortunately, only twenty-five percent turn out to unhypnotizable. It appears that for most of the things that we ask of hypnosis in relation to golf, only a moderate hypnotic response is necessary.

Whether you passed the tests or not, remain deeply hypnotized and enjoy the feelings of contentment. Now think about your golf game. Identify a problem and let us see if we can improve it during your next round on the course. Suppose, for example, that you hurry your downswing or fail to pause at the end of your backswing. Leave a direct suggestion that the next time you play you will automatically pause at the end of your backswing. It will be like a car shifting from reverse to forward. It simply will have to stop before the shift can be made and you will feel the pause. It will require no conscious effort. Once you have left this post-hypnotic suggestion to pause before your downswing, the pause will feel natural and occur spontaneously. It will simply happen!

It is time now to wake yourself up, but before you do, give yourself some post-hypnotic direction for your next hypnosis. Remind yourself that the next time you lean back in your chair, close your eyes and count imaginary waves hitting the beach, you will find yourself going easily into deeper and deeper stages of hypnosis. When you reach ten you will be deeply hypnotized.

When you come out of the hypnotic experience you will feel relaxed but refreshed. There will be no grogginess, headache, or dizziness, just a feeling of being well rested. Now, slowly count backward from five. At the count of one your eyes will open and you will be completely awake. Should you experience any adverse reactions, do not be upset. It will disappear quickly! If it doesn't, you are probably one of the few who should confine your hypnotic experiences to the care of an experienced clinician.

Write down the post-hypnotic suggestion that you gave yourself on your overall golf baserate chart described in Chapter 7. It is crucial that you keep records of the results of your post-hypnotic suggestions. In order to do that you must note on the chart when the suggestion was given and compare the rounds following the suggestion to your earlier rounds. In the case of pausing at the top, you might also ask some member of your foursome, who knows your swing, to watch and tell you if you were pausing appropriately. You needn't worry about becoming too mechanical by focusing on this aspect of your game. As Cochran and Stobbs (1968) note, it is possible to focus on correcting one error without messing up the rest of your swing.

It is most important to use your first attempt at self-hypnosis to lay the groundwork for condensing the induction procedure. Hypnotist Jack Halpin (Tolhurst, 1978) recommends practicing five times a day so that you can get the induction down to less than two minutes. If you have mastered the relaxation and breathing exercises described in the last chapter, that much practice is probably not necessary. All you really need is to deepen the relaxation state so that you are receptive to suggestion. As in any learning, the more you practice the suggestions, the more effectively they will be learned. If you have learned the relaxation techniques, you should be able to relax yourself, deepen it, give your-self a suggestion, and bring yourself out in less than a minute. You can do that while taking the train to work (not while driving!), before falling asleep, while cleaning the house, or while waiting for a client. Eventually, the deepening pro-cedure can be shortened to a simple three-step count of, (1) breathe slowly and relax, (2) more and more deeply relaxed, and (3) deeply hypnotized.

One of the major uses of hypnosis in sports is to provide a cue for concen-tration and relaxation. Los Angeles Dodger pitcher Burt Hooten presses his thumb and forefinger together as a post-hypnotically established signal to relax and concentrate. (Fox, 1979). In this instance hypnosis is being used to aug-ment relaxation by helping the individual to become relaxed at a signal that he can give himself. For most people this effect can be produced by taking a few deep breaths without first leaving a cue under hypnosis; but for those who can-not master this technique, hypnosis is a viable way of increasing the strength of the impulse to relax.

Post-hypnotic cues can have other purposes as well. In golf, post-hypnotic cues may be helpful in correcting some persistent error. You can touch your hand or take a deep breath on the first tee to feel yourself relax or you can leave a post-hypnotic directive that your eyes will become riveted to the ball as soon as you begin your backswing. Bobby Locke, the master putter from South Africa, was well known for his unvarying putting ritual. It is entirely possible that you can directly suggest that when it is time to putt, you will (1) line up the putt, (2) address the ball, (3) aim at a target, and (4) stroke the putt. Using a cue to ini-tiate this chain, you should be able to attempt the putt while shutting out all doubts, fears, and overanalysis. Hypnosis can be especially useful for es-tablishing a ritual that leaves no room for anxiety when the pressure increases.

Suppose, however, that your problem is a persistent mechanical error. If your pro identifies such an error, it may be possible to learn the correct action hypnot-ically. If your wrists get floppy or you rush your backswing, you can give your-self a direct post-hypnotic suggestion (as we did earlier) to slow your swing or firm up your wrists. Yet this is not likely to be particularly effective. One of the lessons to be learned from hypnosis research is that indirect suggestions are more effective than direct ones. If you want to slow your backswing, give your-self the suggestion that you are swinging behind an imaginary swinging door as in the accompanying illustration. As you make your backswing, the door swings toward you following your club. Before you can begin your downswing, you must wait until the door starts to swing back in the other direction. If you start the downswing too early, you will bang into the door before it has swung out of the way. The pendulum motion of the door stopping and then swinging back forces you to pause briefly at the top and wait for the door to swing back past the ball.

Similarly, if you want to keep your wrists firm or your head steady, don't give yourself a command as in "I must keep my wrists firm!" Instead, imagine that there is a cast on your wrists. Feel the cast! Feel your wrists becoming firm as you feel the cast hardening. Feel the neck brace that keeps your head from turn-

If you want to slow your backswing, give yourself the suggestion that you are swinging behind an imaginary door.

ing. You will find that indirect post-hypnotic suggestions put you in a position where the correct action occurs naturally as a function of the situation. This is much more effective than direct suggestions to control your reactions.

HYPNOSIS AND THE PSYCHOLOGICAL ASPECTS OF GOLF

The mental handicaps of golf that may be susceptible to hypnotic interventions include problems with concentration, confidence, and motivation, in addition to the all-important area of relaxation discussed previously. Concentration is best gained by learning relaxation and providing a cue or thought that shuts out all other concerns. The obvious post-hypnotic cue in golf is the ball. In your post-hypnotic suggestion, repeat to yourself that as soon as you focus on the ball at address, your attention will be completely attached to it. It will be as if you are alone on the practice tee or green at the end of the day. It will be lonely and desolate. You will feel as if you were hitting just another practice ball and your concentration will adhere completely and unwaveringly to that white, dimpled surface. In this way you leave a cue for concentration and wall out all interfering thoughts. The positive effects often attributed to visualization may be a result of just this type of focused attention.

Hypnotic attempts to increase confidence and relaxation are not quite as simple as cuing for concentration. There are various approaches that have been used to increase self-confidence. Nideffer (1976) recommends hypnotic rehearsal, in which the subject is hypnotized and imagines successfully going through a tournament or mastering a particular shot. This technique may be superior to nonhypnotic fantasy rehearsal as recommended by former LPGA Rookie of the Year, Sharron Moran (1978) because the client experiences the hypnotic images as more vivid than a simple daydream. If this technique works, it does so because repeatedly conquering the feared situation in fantasy robs it of its unknown quality, thus allowing the individual to feel the contempt that comes with familiarity. Whether or not the fantasy is hypnotic, the reader should keep in mind that there is no evidence that rehearsal of images or daydreams can actually improve the way that you hit the ball. As will be discussed at the end of this chapter, if visualization has any positive effect at all, it is by making the golfer more relaxed and confident, not by improving his physical skills.

Hypnotic fantasy techniques to build confidence can be augmented by post-hypnotic suggestions to dream about superior play at night while one is asleep. Many subjects report that they experience nocturnal dreams that are hypnotically suggested to them (O'Brien and Rabuck, 1977). Recent research by the second author (O'Brien, Cooley, Ciotti and Henninger, in press) indicates that the suggestion of positive experiences with feared objects can effectively reduce that fear. The vivid experience of a nocturnal dream in which you sink all the putts and win the tournament is likely to be a confidence builder of some import.

While you may be able to manipulate your own hypnotic fantasies and rehearsals and even suggest your own dreams, the other methods of expanding your confidence are best carried out under the direction of someone experienced in hypnosis. In rehearsal one prepares to successfully overcome the obstacle and gains confidence from repeatedly experiencing the feeling of accomplishing one's goal. It is also possible to gain confidence by attacking the memories of past failures that have eroded that confidence. In theory at least, the hpynotist can produce amnesia for a particular golf disaster. This takes a good subject. But suppose, for instance, that Ed Sneed were such a subject and were having doubts about his ability because of problems at the end of the 1979 Masters. It might be possible simply to eliminate his memory of those holes. It would be even easier to eradicate the memory of a ten on a particular hole or early difficulties with traps or water hazards. Nideffer (1976) reports that amnesia-producing suggestions can be effective in helping athletes overcome anxiety-inducing failures. Although we have not tried this technique, it is theoretically sound.

Memory can also be heightened through hypnosis. It is possible to increase a client's confidence by having him relive his past triumphs. In this technique every effort is made to make the situation as vivid and dramatic as possible. The client is given the chance to relive his best moments in the sport. In addition to building confidence, this hypnotic experience can help the individual to identify differences that may have developed between his previously successful performance and his current difficulties. He may find at address that his hands are out of position or that his shoulder is out of alignment. Variations in grip or even attitude may show up as he hypnotically relives the experience.

Suinn (1977) has reported considerable success using nonhypnotic visualization of failures in skiing to identify errors. He then presents a chaining instruction to correct the skiing fault in a similar manner to the teaching method that we used to groove your golf swing. It may be possible to shorten Suinn's procedure through hypnosis, although the research on how much hypnosis actually improves memory is inconclusive (Udolf, 1980). At the very least, hypnosis allows the individual to concentrate on his past experience in a relaxed way without having his memories distorted by anxiety or the need to avoid recalling a painful event.

It is also possible to relive bad experiences while adding a happy ending. We have had good success in some cases with this approach, particularly when a fluke situation was involved. It is not possible to change the outcome of a sporting event but it may be possible to inhibit the "agony of defeat" by having the individual experience the loss as a victory in hypnotic fantasy. A missed putt cannot ruin your next tournament. If you exaggerate the importance of that putt into an overly emotional view of yourself as a choker, however, it may foul you up for months. Turning the real failure into a fantasy of success can be helpful in arresting that emotional reaction.

The most all-encompassing way of using the past to build confidence is age-regression. The second author has used this technique on older athletes who seem to have lost the confidence that they had in their youth. The subject is told that he will feel that he is twenty-two and play accordingly. As in all post-hypnotic suggestions, the instruction is limited to a specific action in a particular place. Our client would certainly not wish to respond as if he were twenty-two during salary negotiations so you limit the suggestion to the golf course during the round.

As the well-known Los Angeles hypnotist, Arthur Ellen (Fox, 1979), observed, hypnosis does not change the athletic ability of the client. When we regress someone to age twenty-two, it does not mean that he can run as fast as he did in his early twenties. It only means that he may resurrect some of the naive, ebullient confidence that his experience has destroyed. Hypnotic age-regression has resulted in adults writing the Lord's Prayer in typically six-year-old fashion: e.g., "Our Father who art in heaven, Harold is thy name," (Reiff and Scheerer, 1959). It has enabled adults to achieve the more accurate perception typical of children (Parish, Lundy and Leibowitz, 1969) and reduced college students to the philosophical level of eight-year-olds (O'Brien, Kramer, Chiglinsky, Stevens, Nunan, and Fritzo, 1977). Although we remain skeptical, age-regression has even been demonstrated to increase the size of a woman's breasts through having subjects experience puberty a second time (Williams, 1974; Staib and Logan, 1977). Although your golf game may not be a bust (sorry about that!), if you feel that it is and you didn't always feel that way, age-regression may help you to recover your confidence.

The simplest confidence builder in hypnosis is to belittle the opponent or, in the case of golf, the course. The fear of playing Pebble Beach may be reduced by the hypnotic suggestion that it is a Mickey Mouse course. The most effective suggestion is to convince yourself that you are really only playing a practice round on the easiest course you have ever played. The well-known baseball hypnotist, Harvey Misel, once told Eric Soderholm that the great curve-baller Burt Blyleven was just a batting practice pitcher. Soderholm had a three-hit night against Blyleven who usually gave him fits (Fox, 1979).

MOTIVATIONAL SUGGESTIONS

Hypnotic effects on motivation fall into two categories. First, there are those that remove pain so that the performer can respond to the demands of the sport. The second are those post-hypnotic suggestions that increase the player's commitment to the match.

Hypnotic anesthesia is well documented and the literature includes some very impressive reports (Udolf, 1980). Methods vary from numbing the painful area to suggestions that the pain drains from the body into a balloon which is then cut loose. Perhaps the most common technique is to suggest that the right hand is becoming cold or filled with novocaine so that it has no feeling. One then tells the subject that he can transfer the numb, painless feeling to any part of his body simply by touching it with his right hand. These methods often result in a very substantial reduction in the amount of pain reported by the client.

The difficulty with hypnotically reducing pain in sports is not that it is ineffective but rather that it may not be such a good idea. Since pain is usually viewed as a warning from the body that something is amiss, many physicians would object to helping an athlete to ignore this signal. As behavior change is the province of the psychologist, the decision as to whether a client should be helped to become insensitive to pain requires the expertise of a medical specialist.

Post-hypnotic suggestions to motivate a client have little general applicability to golf. They are often used to increase the emotion that a player brings to his sport, but golf is a cool, controlled game in which emotion is usually a liability. Under the appropriate conditions, however, it would be possible to increase a player's emotional involvement in any sport. As an example of this approach, the second author recently hypnotized a member of the women's fencing team at a major university who had a problem following through on her attacks. Her coach described her as not being aggressive enough in meets. Before the national championship she was given the post-hypnotic suggestion that every opponent would bear a striking resemblance to her current rival for her boyfriend and that this was her chance to really show her rival up. Although she was the poorest of the four varsity fencers, she had been fencing in the number one slot in order give her team an advantage in the other three matches. In the sectionals she had won only two of twelve matches. In the nationals, following the post-hypnotic suggestions, she won eleven of twenty-four encounters, including victories over two opponents whom she had never beaten in four years of competition.

As we noted in the beginning of this chapter, hypnosis is a potentially useful but largely unresearched field. To our knowledge there are no sound scientific research studies to document the benefits of hypnosis in sports. There are, however, numerous case studies that warrant further investigation of this technique. For the golfer who has tried everything, post-hypnotic suggestion may provide answers to the mental blocks that keep him from playing his best game. Whether the effects are greater than those produced through simple relaxation remains an unanswered question, yet hypnosis has been endorsed by many of the athletes who have tried it.

VISUALIZATION

If the psychology of golf has a sacred cow it is visualization. Over the last fifteen years the act of imagining the perfect shot has been credited with improving every aspect of a golfer's skills. Whether your problem is inadequate club selection, tension, or a persistent mechanical error, someone is sure to recommend that you spend your time visualizing the correct swing movements or the ideal flight of the ball. In fact, the practice of visualizing the result that you wish to produce, actually can have beneficial effects, but many of the claims that are frequently made for imagining good performance lack even the most meager supporting evidence.

Jack Nicklaus, (1978) describes the realistic use of visualization, when he suggests that you picture the ideal shot to give yourself a goal. You identify what you want to accomplish. As Johnny Miller (Miller and Shankland, 1976) suggests, visualizing your shot is a key to club selection and strategy. Further, it is probably impossible to aim a shot adequately without picturing where you want that shot to land (Middlecoff, 1968). There can be no denying that visualization has a major role in shot preparation. The validity of the claims for visualization becomes hazier when it comes to actually executing the shot.

Bob Toski (1971) has been an outspoken proponent of visualization as a means of getting the "feel" of a good shot. As he suggests, this feel comes from having practiced and previously executed good shots. In this instance visualization is used to cue the appropriate bodily reaction. It serves as a signal to engage the swing that was effective the last time that you had to make this kind of a shot. Toski suggests a very successful way of picking out the properly grooved swing while avoiding overanalysis and thinking about swing mechanics. Whether you call this plugging into your subconscious (Heise, 1961) or your right hemisphere (Wiren, Coop, and Sheehan, 1978) is not really relevant, as long as you remember that analysis leads to paralysis (Blalock and Netland, 1977) and that thinking about swing mechanics will destroy any possibility of a fluid swing. As Jack Nicklaus points out, "You can't govern the swing segment by segment" (Nicklaus and Wind, 1969). Like the centipede that was unable to walk when it tried to think about moving each of its one hundred legs, the golfer who tries to think through each aspect of his swing will never be able to get it together successfully. If your visualization helps you avoid dissecting your swing or keeps you from being mechanical by giving you the "feel" of the swing, it is most certainly useful. But as Jack Nicklaus has so succinctly put it, "Feel only becomes the critical factor once your mechanics are reasonably sound" (Nicklaus, 1979).

Visualizing a positive outcome for each shot is very likely to give you more confidence and make you more relaxed, as we pointed out earlier. This is the logical and rational way to allow your imagination to help your game. Your score may improve because you are more relaxed, but simply imagining the proper action is not likely to improve your golf skills or your swing mechanics. Yet there are many who claim that such imagined rehearsals can effectively remove mechanical faults and provide even more magical wonders. A recent article in a popular golf periodical suggests, for example, that "One of the best ways to practice at home is to simply visualize the swing of a great player such as Sam Snead" (Harrison and Mitchell, 1978). Mickey Wright (1966) recommends picturing the swing of Snead or Louise Suggs in order to get the proper tempo, and a recent *Golf Magazine* listed a group of "mental" schools, many of which teach visualization to improve mechanics (Tolhurst, 1979). Unfortunately, sitting in your armchair fantasizing about Sam Snead's lovely swing is simply not very likely to produce any change in your own swing. The golf swing is a muscle-memory reaction. You learn it by practicing it, not by practicing thinking about it. You can vividly imagine the "swoosh" and "click" (Harrison and Mitchell, 1978) of Snead's blasts off the tee all you like. The fact remains that there is precious little evidence to indicate that your game will improve except as you gain confidence from these mental exercises.

About every two months or so the national golf magazines carry some article on pop-psychology to enhance your game. As often as not such mystical approaches are said to be firmly grounded in "humanistic psychology," Eastern meditation, or Zen. The truth is that none of these approaches has any serious commitment to scientifically validating what they preach. It may be very pleasant to believe that you can increase your distance off the tee by imagining an energizing power that enters your body through a spot near the belly button (Merklingar, 1977), but as yet we know of no impartial study that shows that golfers who engage in such meditation actually have "The Force" with them.

Each time you read such a claim you should ask, "Seriously, fellas, have you any data to show that this works?"

Many professional golfers swear by visualization. They report that when they hit it well, they were visualizing a perfect shot. They probably were doing just what they describe but this doesn't necessarily mean that because two things occurred at the same time that one must have caused the other. Golf is not an intellectual exercise, yet when your body hits a good shot something has to be going on in your thoughts. That does not mean that those thoughts caused the good shot but only that they occurred at the same time as the good shot. Charlie Coody wears red socks to tournaments because he thinks they will help him win (Schapp, 1970). His belief is superstition because the color of his socks cannot help him score better any more than your picturing of the ball six inches from the pin when you swing can magically make it land on that spot. At one time or another Coody probably won a tournament while wearing red socks, so he believes he should always wear them. Similarly, the professionals who advise visualization of a positive outcome during your swing are doing so because that is what they remember doing on their good shots. In all likelihood their visualization served only to block out other thoughts so that a reflex swing could occur naturally.

The idea that mental practice, that is, imagining good shots, can improve motor performance dates back to Washburn (1916) and Alex Morrison (1940). A considerable number of research attempts have failed to document the efficacy of this approach (Corbin, 1972; Richardson, 1967). Even such forthright advocates of mental practice as Michael Murphy and Rhea White (1978) admit the limitations of this technique by saying, "Merely imagining a good round of golf . . . is ineffective without hitting shots . . ." (p. 156).

Although many golf authorities would dispute the efficacy of mental practice, they would still endorse the idea that you should picture the perfect shot in your mind as you begin your swing. But how could such visualization actually affect your shot? In by far the most scientific study of golf mechanics yet reported, Cochran and Stobbs (1968) demonstrated that the golf swing is set in one motion shortly after the golfer begins to take the club back. The swing is a "reflex" that occurs as a single unit once the signal has been given to execute the act. Nonetheless, they recommend that the golfer concentrate on one positive thought during the swing. This positive thought could well be a visualization of the perfect shot. This does not mean that visualizing that shot helps you produce it. As Cochran and Stobbs, Johnny Miller, and others have noted, the positive thought should be kept in mind since it serves to block out negative thoughts. According to Cochran and Stobbs: "These positive thoughts can be almost anything. Interpreted literally they may even be quite nonsensical." Sam Snead (Snead and Stump, 1962) reports that he thinks about cows in a pasture while taking a shot. This thought relaxes Snead and keeps any dire predictions and fears of a negative outcome out of his mind. This is the real advantage to be gained from visualization!

If visualizing the perfect shot only serves to occupy one's thoughts so that negative images do not increase anxiety, it seems logical to assume that thinking about calming images such as trees and clouds could have the same effect. Research recently completed by the first author (Simek, Miller, and O'Brien, 1980) confirms this conclusion. Golfers trained to visualize trees and clouds while swinging improved as much as those who visualized the perfect shot. In comparison with a group given relaxation training, the relaxation group improved the most, almost three strokes per round, while the groups which imagined golf or nature images both improved less than one and a half strokes per round.

Once you have decided what it is that you have to do on a given shot and have identified how you want to do it, the key concept in golf is to get your head out of the shot. If while you are swinging you think in detail about what you have to do, your swing will deteriorate. Perhaps Harry Pressler, the noted women's golf teacher, said it best when asked about a particular woman's swing problem: "She was trying to think about too many things. Like everybody," he answered (Seitz, 1974). Hypnosis and visualization can provide positive thoughts that effectively occupy the overactive mind. In this way these techniques can help the golfer build confidence and feel more relaxed (Wells, 1962). In addition, it is possible that hypnosis can provide even greater benefits to your play.

11

Brief Behavioral Techniques for Combating Negative Emotions

> *"Golf is a game that tests you as a person far more than it tests you as an athlete."*
>
> TOMMY BOLT

Maybe you do not feel that your problems with either anxiety or frustration require a full program of relaxation training or hypnosis. What you are really looking for are techniques to control your negative emotions when they begin to ruin your round. There are few psychological or physical golf skills that can be mastered without practice but some do take longer than others. The techniques that we present in this chapter are designed to be implemented quickly. They will give you a set of weapons to use against your overreactions as they occur on the course.

NEGATIVE PRACTICE

You may recall that when we first described golf anxiety we said that the first response that most people make is to try to get a grip on themselves. They mobilize their resources in an attempt to suppress their emotions. You can almost see their muscles tighten as they force themselves to become "relaxed." As the tension continues to mount and their swing begins to come apart, they usually feel a sense of frustration that compounds the anxiety. They may become embarrassed over their nerves and feel that everyone is watching them choke. All of these feelings serve to increase their fear to a fever pitch. There is only one way to end their discomfort and they take it; a ninety-mile-an-hour swing. At this point they have completely forgotten the goal of the shot. All that they want to do is to get out of the spotlight and end the dread. As everyone knows, fast swings are very unlikely to produce good shots but these players continue to react in this way each time that they encounter stress.

These rushed swings obviously do not produce favorable results on the scorecard, so why does the anxious golfer continue to engage in this maladaptive behavior? The reason is that this behavior reduces the tension of having to take the shot. You can't fear something that has already occurred, so that once you get the shot over with you feel better, no matter how badly you butchered the swing. Any action that makes you feel better is likely to be repeated when you get into a similar situation. The fast swing doesn't produce competent shots but at least it gets you out of the tension-producing situation.

But, suppose that you didn't try to get control of yourself? Suppose that you didn't get mad at yourself for being tense and suppose that you didn't make things worse by feeling guilty over your "weak nerves" and "poor self-control"? Anxiety can only go one of three ways: it can increase, decrease, or stay the same. In the face of stress you can grit your teeth and try to make yourself less anxious, or you can say the hell with it and try to ignore the anxiety, or you can try to make yourself more anxious. As we noted earlier, the first of these alternatives doesn't work and the second leaves you no better off than you were before but surely the third sounds ridiculous. It is one thing to intentionally tense up your muscles so that they will relax, but to intentionally try to make yourself more nervous certainly sounds self-defeating. But is it?

Let's take a hypothetical example. Imagine that sand has been your nemesis since you waggled over your first wedge. You may substitute rough, water, short putts, or long irons in this example as befits your individual tastes. See yourself in the middle of an important match. You are having a pretty good round when suddenly you catch a deep trap on your approach to the eighth green. As you walk up the fairway you remember all of the failures that you have had in sand and you feel yourself beginning to get anxious. You tell yourself not to worry about it. You urge your body to relax but you actually feel yourself getting more and more tense. By the time you get up to the pit your anxiety is really rolling. In exasperation you say to yourself, "Well if I'm going to be anxious, I might just as well make myself as nervous as I can. I'll be so tight on this swing that I'll look like a robot, a regular man of steel." You try to make yourself more anxious and you try to make yourself tighter but it isn't so easy. In fact, it seems almost laughable and instead of getting more anxious you find yourself beginning to relax. By trying to increase your anxiety you have actually made yourself less tense.

Psychologists call this technique Negative Practice (Dunlap, 1930, 1932) —intentionally trying to produce the reaction that you want to avoid. When anxiety is at issue, it means trying to make yourself more afraid so that you become completely bored with the things that used to make you nervous. This approach to anxiety is based on the same principles as a number of other psychological procedures such as flooding (Polin, 1959), implosive therapy (Stampfl and Levis, 1967), and paradoxical intention (Frankl, 1960). Part of the theory that underlies these techniques is the understanding that some of your anxiety comes from your extreme efforts not to be anxious. When you try to become more anxious you remove the feeling of panic or loss of control that increases your fear. At the same time you are demonstrating that you are not helpless and that, in fact, you can get rid of your tension. This version of "reverse psychology" actually leads to feeling more loose when you try to make yourself feel more nervous than when you try to make yourself relax.

Lessening the feelings of being out of control is only part of the explanation for why negative practice works. Anxiety is just like any other bodily reaction. It can only go on for so long before fatigue sets in. Eventually you simply become too tired to be afraid. This fatigue is specific, not general. If you swing a club for a long period of time your arms become tired but your thoughts may be as active as ever. On the other hand, if you spend ten minutes being terribly anxious your arms aren't tired but the systems of your body that react to make you feel nervous are worn out.

Negative practice has been used to remove a wide variety of undesirable behaviors including stage fright (Dunlap, 1932), nervous tics (Yates, 1958), test anxiety (O'Brien, 1976), spelling errors (Holsopple and Vanouse, 1929), stuttering (Case, 1960), mathematics anxiety (Streim, 1979), cigarette smoking (O'Brien and Dickinson, 1977), and piano errors (Wakeman, 1928). Theoretically it should be useful in decreasing golf anxiety as well, but as yet, that has not been demonstrated. The reader is cautioned therefore, that this represents an experimental technique.

When it comes to anxiety the simplest way to use negative practice is the method that we outlined earlier. Simply try to make yourself feel more anxious as soon as you first feel up-tight. Try to make your hands sweat! Try to make yourself tighter! Try to make yourself more nervous! See if you can do it! This is the most direct use of intentional overpractice for anxiety. It requires no home practice and can be used as a rapid intervention on the course.

If you feel anxiety on every water hole, sand shot, or short putt, you may want to attempt home negative practice to rid yourself of this tension. If, for example, you are a golf professional who repeatedly yips short putts you might want to introduce the following program of negative practice to overcome your shaky green play:

Negative Practice Homework Program for Putting Yips

1. For three days spend the first ten minutes of every waking hour imagining a two-footer to win a major title. Make yourself as anxious and uncomfortable as you can.

2. For the next two days decrease the practice to every other hour.

3. For the last two days of the week practice only three times a day.

4. During this week of home practice, play one round a day by yourself. If you spontaneously become anxious over a putt, stop immediately and negative practice the anxiety for ten minutes or as long as you can without making people wait. Try the putt only after having negative practiced the anxiety. Try to imagine tournament play during your daily rounds so that you have some reason to feel anxious.

5. For the second week of the program negative practice the anxiety once a day for ten minutes, and whenever you feel any unintentional anxiety about a putt for as long as you can up to ten minutes.

6. After the second week you should only practice if you experience spontaneous, unintentional anxiety.

This treatment is recommended for golf professionals only because they are the only ones who can give it the time that it demands. Do not try to short-cut the home negative practice program. If you haven't got the time for the whole thing don't do it at all! Your anxiety could get worse if you try to take half a dose! It could also get worse if you ignore one last caution about the use of home negative practice. This treatment assumes a bad case of golf nerves. It requires that the individual already be very anxious so that overpractice brings him to the point where his body can't make the anxiety response anymore. If you are not very anxious these anxiety directions will increase rather than decrease your nervousness because you won't reach the limit at which the body can't react.

Negative practice is a useful therapeutic intervention. It is perfectly reasonable for you to experiment with it on your golf anxiety. However, if stuttering, tics, or some other nongolf behavior represents a significant problem for you, you should not, under any circumstances, attempt this procedure without supervision by a behavioral psychologist. As Dunlap (1932) observed, the therapist must be sophisticated in learning theory and massed practice approaches. Be warned! If done incorrectly this treatment could make your stutter or tic worse rather than better.

THOUGHT STOPPAGE

Of all the techniques that we will present in this book, thought stoppage is the simplest. That is definitely a point in its favor since psychological explanations and treatments are all too often more complex than they need to be. To get some idea of how this approach works, picture yourself hitting a beautiful tee shot straight down the fairway. Now imagine that on the second bounce your ball hits a rock and darts dead left into a creek. Feel the anger starting to well up inside you! Listen to your self-messages:

> *"What the hell was that! I hit that ball perfectly! That SOB will slop the ball all over the course for par, I hit it dead straight and it winds up in a creek: that's not fair! Okay, if that's the way it's going to be today then I'll get that ball out of that creek one way or another or throw the bag in after it!"*

You are well on your way to following Tommy Bolt's first rule of temperamental golf: "One bad shot deserves another" (Bolt and Griffith, 1969). For many golfers the rage will be even greater if the ball wound up in the creek because that was the way they hit it rather than because of a rock in the fairway. Their overreactions are likely to color at least the next couple of shots if not the whole round.

Suppose you could interrupt the chain of thoughts above so that you don't completely blow your cool. As you feel your temper beginning to unravel you can say to yourself, quite emphatically, STOP! Picture a big red stop sign and put the brakes on your temper outburst. Saying STOP! to yourself temporarily disrupts your series of emotional thoughts. They will momentarily stop and then begin again so you must repeat the stop signal to interrupt them.

This procedure is applicable to any kind of temper outburst as well as to anxiety. You can disrupt your chain of tension-provoking ideas by saying STOP! when you start to tell yourself how nervous you feel or what awful things will happen if you botch the shot. Yet, this technique requires some practice before it begins to disrupt your emotional thoughts. It is not quite as easy as it sounds. The best way to begin thought stoppage is to rehearse it with someone else. Take a typical example of when you become nervous or lose your self-control out on the course. Tell somebody the thoughts that go through your mind as you come apart. Let them hear all of your self-messages right up to taking the club back for the shot. If you are sitting with your spouse, roommate, or parents, as you read this, try it right now. After you finish, tell them you are going to go through it again but this time you want them to shout STOP! early in the sequence. After your emotional reaction has been interrupted in this way, try it again from the beginning but now have your partner yell STOP! several times throughout your tale of anxiety or rage. In these trials each time he or she says STOP! you should pause until you feel the fear or anger begin to build again. Then you should continue from where you left off.

After you have done a couple of fifteen- to twenty-minute practice sessions, try to dispense with the partner. Start to say STOP! to yourself, LOUDLY and FORCEFULLY!!! Do two actual practice sessions saying the word out loud before proceeding to the final step of just thinking the word. By this time you will have become accustomed to having your negative thoughts blocked by hearing the word stop. In the last phase of treatment simply thinking STOP! serves to break up your maladaptive self-messages.

This technique should not be expected to work miracles. It will take some time before you can bring your overreactions to a halt on command. Yet, each time you try this it should come more easily. You are likely to find that as you practice, each trial of saying STOP! produces longer and longer periods of quiet before your emotions begin to churn again. It is often helpful if you pick out one key thought, such as keep your head steady, to go back to once you have used thought stoppage to break the litany of emotional thoughts.

Thought stoppage was popularized by Joseph Wolpe (1958, 1969), who reported significant success in reducing fears and obsessive thoughts. The technique has proven effective in dealing with a wide variety of problems involving emotional interference with adequate performance (Rimm and Masters, 1979), and we believe that many golfers can benefit from it. Our preliminary investigations suggest that some anxious and temperamental golfers can rapidly bring their emotions under control through this simple intervention. For others, stopping the emotional thoughts once they have begun appears to be too difficult. These golfers require a system that provides incompatible ideas that they can substitute for their emotionally distressing self-messages. This is the goal of stress inoculation training.

STRESS INOCULATION TRAINING

It really is not predetermined that you must overreact to every provocation on the golf course. It is possible to tell yourself constructive messages that will help your play instead of cursing yourself or making things worse than they are. The idea behind Stress Inoculation Training is to provide you with positive self-messages to use when you are faced with stress. This system was developed by Meichenbaum and Turk (1976) for the treatment of fears and other overly emotional reactions but it has obvious applications for sports in general and golf in particular. The fact that Meichenbaum (1977) begins the chapter on stress inoculation training in his book with a quote from Satchell Paige, the venerable relief pitcher, suggests that he has not missed the sports potential of this approach.

There are two key concepts in stress inoculation training. The first is rehearsal to anticipate stressful situations so that you are not taken by surprise. The second is to prepare thoughts you can use to cope with the expected tension. In this system anger and fear are treated identically since both are maintained and exacerbated only because we say things to ourselves to increase our arousal. For example, the temperamental golfer may respond with a barrage of self-accusations if he slices his tee shot off the first tee. The golfer calls himself names, questions his parentage, and wonders why he can't keep it straight at the top just once! He sarcastically thinks to himself, "Nice going jerk! Way to start it off!" etc.

The anxious golfer faced with a short putt responds in different but similarly maladaptive fashion. "Oh no! A two-footer, I'm going to choke on this. Look at yourself, you're shaking already! The damn thing breaks three different ways! If I could only sink this for a birdie but I won't . . . ," etc. Of course the more he thinks about how emotional he is becoming, the more emotional he becomes.

Instead of these tension-increasing statements, you can substitute statements that minimize your negative emotions. Combining elements from the work of Meichenbaum (1977), Novaco (1975), and Desiderato and Miller (1979) we suggest four kinds of positive statements to be learned to control your emotions. First are messages that prepare for stress. Second are those that encourage you in the face of tension. Third are task-relevant directions that tell you how to respond constructively to the stressful situation. Fourth, and last, is a positive statement about the way that you reacted to the tension.

To give you an example of how this system is applied, go back to the temperamental golfer on the first tee that we discussed earlier. In order to control his emotions this golfer might begin by changing the things that he says to himself before he hits his drive. Instead of arousing his emotions by exaggerating the importance of the shot he might say things like the following:

I can handle a bad shot; there is no reason to get up-tight.

I'm not going to let a bad drive ruin my next shot.

If I find myself getting upset I'll know how to handle it.

It really doesn't matter too much what I do with this first shot because I've always been able to get out of trouble.

If he does hook the drive, his thoughts should include both task improvement and encouraging statements. In the latter category he can tell himself one of the following:

You hooked the first drive, so what? You have a chance to recover from there.

It's okay, no sense getting upset!

That's one bad shot out of your system, now let's hit some good ones!

Getting upset won't make that drive any better.

You parred many a hole with worse drives than that.

Relax! Let somebody else make a fool of himself for a change.

He should also give direct instructions to himself about what he wants to do with his next shot. These are the task-relevant messages that we referred to. They will help the golfer avoid emotionally hacking away in disgust. His task-relevant thought to maintain concentration might be one, and only one, of those listed on the next page:

Make a nice slow swing!

Keep it parallel at the top!

Keep your head steady!

Get your target lined up!

Stay cool and concentrate!

Relax and watch your breathing!

Finally, he should prepare a series of coping statements to reward himself for not allowing fear or frustration to get the better of him. As he gains control of his emotions he can say such things as:

Hey, you're not getting nearly as upset as you used to. Great!

That's the way to keep your cool!

Good! You didn't tighten yourself up with silly emotions!

There's hope for you yet. You didn't let yourself panic into a bad swing!

We have not exhausted the list of positive alternative thoughts in each of these categories. If anxiety is your major problem the self-messages in the first three categories are likely to be somewhat different. Meichenbaum has provided an excellent list of thoughts to control anxiety which can be easily adapted for golf. If your problem is fear in the face of a water hazard or a short putt you might employ one of the coping statements below before you try to make one of these shots.

Okay, psych yourself up! You can handle this putt!

The anxiety that I'm feeling is natural. All I have to do is use my coping statements and it can be managed.

Stay current! Stop worrying about fears that you used to have!
  Just think about what you have to do!

What are you worrying about? Worry can't help you carry that water!

So you feel a little tense? Pause for a couple of seconds! Now relax! You're in control!

Let's start to enjoy the challenge of this game again! Some architect went through hell to make this hole tough. Let's beat him at his own game!

Stop telling yourself to be afraid! You can make this putt!

Don't worry about your hands, just focus on one thing: Keep your head steady!

You needn't confine your positive self-messages to the ones that we have given you. Feel free to invent your own coping statements. The important thing to remember is that you must prepare yourself for any stress that you are likely to encounter on the course. Before the match you should look forward to possible stressful situations and have a set coping statement already prepared for any negative emotion. Neither fear nor anger should overwhelm you because you will have planned self-messages to prevent any adverse reaction.

In our review of the literature we were able to find only one attempt to test Stress Inoculation Training on a sports problem. Desiderato and Miller (1979) employed coping statements to modify the second author's deuce point tennis play. In the three weeks prior to treatment she won only twenty-nine percent of her tournament deuce points. For the three weeks following Stress Inoculation Training this figure rose to sixty percent. The authors make the point that this startling improvement after two weeks of treatment cannot be attributed to changes in coping statements alone because they also used relaxation training. For our purposes this may be an ideal combination for the overly emotional golfer.

SUMMARY

All of the techniques that we have presented in this chapter require both practice and perseverance. They are least likely to work for you if you give up on them after a brief trial. Since thought stoppage is the simplest procedure, it may be best to start there and then add coping statements as they become necessary and you become more skilled in controlling your thoughts. If this combination of techniques fails after an adequate effort you may want to try a routine of negative practice. We suggest saving this as the method of last resort because it is the least pleasant and most difficult to do.

The final method of gaining emotional control of your game is to change your philosophical approach to golf. We present a plan of action to achieve that goal in Chapter 12.

12

The New Logic of the Links: Emotional Control Through Rational Self-Messages

"I don't get nervous at the Masters or Open anymore but I do get more interested."

HALE IRWIN

Earlier we told you that once you begin to feel anxious you cannot just put the thought out of your mind or get rid of it by trying to forget about it. It is impossible to replace something (a thought) with nothing (not thinking about it). But you *can* think about something else! Better yet, you can think about things in such a way that the anxiety never develops in the first place. You can think of the mistakes that you make on the golf course without being tempted to throw your clubs down a ravine.

Unfortunately, relatively few golfers ever learn the secret of enjoying the game. To quote once again the great teacher Alex Morrison (1946), "As played by ninety-nine out of one hundred people, it (golf) results in mental strain, nerve-racking and actual physical suffering." The average golfer loves the game but "hates himself for the way he plays it" (Morrison, 1946). Yet, some golfers are able to see the game for what it is and avoid the psychological trap of having their entire self-worth at stake with every shot. Walter Hagen, who many feel first brought "star" status to the professional golfer, was always able to keep the game in perspective. His oft stated motto of "Don't hurry, don't worry and don't forget to smell the flowers along the way" (Scott and Cousins, 1969) was the heart of a philosophy that allowed him to accept himself even if he did not play well.

Once you begin to accept a less self-evaluative approach to golf, you will find that such a philosophy can also be beneficial to other aspects of your life. One of the greats of women's golf, Louise Suggs (1953) suggests that "the zealous golfer develops a philosophy which enables her to rise above the 'hazards' and 'penalties' which occur in her everyday life." In her view, "the greatest single lesson to be learned from playing golf . . . is that of controlling one's thinking and emotions." In this chapter we will help you to develop a philosophy that enables you to achieve those goals.

Why do you get so upset when you play golf? It is not because you hit the ball into the rough. Between hitting the ball into the rough and getting upset something else occurs. You evaluate what has happened as *terrible, unfair, disastrous,* something *more than you can stand,* and something that *should never happen* to you. When you start playing golf you hit plenty of balls off the fairway without getting upset. Emotional reactions are, therefore, not caused by poor shots. They are caused by our irrational ideas about those poor shots.

Golfers seem particularly prone to such irrational thoughts. Perhaps the time provided between shots and the quiet, pastoral surroundings offer too great an opportunity for contemplation. Golfers spend most of a round listening to their inner voice. More often than most of us would like to admit these inner conversations become self-condemnations or forecasts of failure.

In their superb book *A New Guide to Rational Living,* Albert Ellis and Robert Harper analyze the effects of self-messages in terms of *A*ctivating events, *Be*liefs, and emotional *C*onsequences. While it does not appear that they had the golfer in mind for their ABC model, the distinction they make between the effects of rational and irrational beliefs could save the sanity of duffer and professional alike. In this chapter, with apologies to Dr. Ellis, we will present a list of golf's most common irrational beliefs and a system for combating them. Based on Rational Emotive Counseling, this system requires some work. Learning how to rethink your golf game means spending some time rehearsing appropriate thoughts. If you take the time to dispute irrational ideas you will be less emotional on the course, make golf more enjoyable, and score better.

Let us begin with the golfer's #1 Irrational Belief, i.e., THE IDEA THAT IT IS TERRIBLE AND UNBEARABLE WHEN YOUR GAME IS NOT THE WAY YOU WANT IT TO BE.

You are being irrational each time you find yourself saying things like "I *should* be playing better." "I *ought* to make this putt," or "I *must* win this tournament."

When you say that something *must* happen, you really mean that it will be *awful* if it does not happen. Come now, is it really *awful* to miss a four-foot putt? Inconvenient, maybe even unpleasant, but *awful* or *beyond endurance,* no! To say that you *ought* to be playing better actually means that you *ought* to be playing better than you are. That is, that reality is wrong and should not exist as it actually does. It does not take an expert in logistics to identify that statement as nonsense. If you say that you *should* make the four-foot putt, you are actually saying that somewhere on that great scorecard in the sky it is written that Joe Duffer or Joan Hacker will never miss a four-foot putt. Everyone else in golf has missed four-foot putts but you *should* sink every one of them. You have somehow decided that it is *terrible* that you have the same problems as every other golfer.

A common example of irrational belief number one is first tee jitters. How many times have you heard someone in your foursome say, "If I can't get through the first hole I'm dead," or "If I don't get a good shot off the first tee it ruins my whole round"? This self-dooming philosophy is endorsed by everyone from the duffer who can't break 100 to the reigning professional champions such as Johnny Miller and Tom Watson (*Golf Magazine,* 1977). One golfer of our acquaintance normally shoots around 85. That means in a complete round he has eighty-four additional swings that on his scorecard are of equal importance to the first one. As Hale Irwin (1978) suggests, the problem with first tee jitters is not the effect one bad shot will have on your total score. It is what you tell yourself about that one bad drive that causes the problems.

If you believe that you *must* get off the first tee in good shape it is time for you to start learning just how much nonsense you have been telling yourself. Jack Nicklaus is known for hitting a duck-hook on the first hole of the Master's nearly every year. Arnold Palmer once began the Eastern Open by hitting his tee shot out of bounds, yet he won the tournament. Ah, but you're no Arnold Palmer, are you? Well, maybe your approach to the game is closer to Palmer's than you think. The truth is that Palmer was ready to give up after that shot but his playing partner Doug Ford, pointed out that the way Palmer was playing he could spot the field two strokes and still win by six. Palmer was telling himself the same negative emotional things that you tell yourself, but fortunately he had someone to contradict his irrational messages.

Your emotional problem, your anxiety on the first tee, comes from repeating to yourself the thought that hitting a bad drive is *intolerable.* It only becomes intolerable if you believe that you *must* hit a good drive because every competent golfer gets off the first tee in good shape. If that is your assumption and you slice the drive off the first tee, you will quite logically conclude that you are not a competent golfer. Such a conclusion would be logical only if the assumption were correct, which it is not.

If every competent golfer hit a perfect drive off the first tee they would start championship tournaments with a second shot two hundred fifty yards down the fairway. It is fine to want to get a good drive off the first tee. If your view is that you would like to get off well we have no quarrel with your logic and you probably do not have a problem with first tee jitters. You knot yourself up only when you make it *horrible, disastrous,* and *beyond human endurance* when your desires are not granted.

When you look at your golf thoughts in this light they sound pretty silly, don't they? A bad shot really is not *awful, terrible,* or *tragic.* It will not leave you in constant pain, or crippled. It will not decrease your sales or leave you unable to make love. It leaves you able to enjoy all the things that make life worthwhile away from the golf course and it certainly doesn't make you less of a human being. In fact, one shot won't even ruin your chances for a decent score—unless you *think* it will!

No one is suggesting that you can have any fun at this game if you no longer care how you play it. What we are suggesting is that there is no reason that you *must* play well or that it is *unbearable* when you don't. As George Archer once said, "You learn over the years that nobody is going to strike you dead over a shot" (Kemp, 1978). Golf is meant to be a sport. Even the professional who earns his living on the course needs outside interests in order to keep the game in perspective. It will be very difficult to develop a philosophy of golf that does not overemphasize its importance if all you talk about is your game. Mary Mills (1973) stated that the LPGA tour players "have to keep themselves up all the while we are out here." Given what tension does to one's game, that philosophy is not likely to be productive. You will be much better off if you follow the lead of golfers like Walter Hagen and Lee Trevino who remember that they are more than just golfers even when they are out on the course. Joanne Carner has suggested that one of the things that makes Nancy Lopez such a great golfer is that "she has a life beyond golf" (Bartlett, 1978).

You probably keep a running discourse going in your head throughout each round. Why not use those thoughts to your advantage. Take the time between shots to ask yourself, "What is the worse thing that can happen if I don't do what I want to do on this next shot?" You are likely to find that the worse thing that can happen is something that you have survived many times before. Therefore, it is something that is not worth worrying about. Golf is fun! Despite what some golf authorities say (Toski, 1971), don't try to make it your proving ground, unless you want to make yourself nervous. If you feel that you have something to prove you are going to feel that you *must* play very well. Remember, *oughts, shoulds,* and *musts* are best left at home when you go to play golf. In fact, if you would like to live more pleasantly, you might kick them out of your house as well.

The second irrational belief that golfers often fall prey to also crops up on the first tee. If you worry about driving in front of a gallery, you have encountered Irrational Belief #2: THE IDEA THAT YOU MUST WIN THE APPROVAL OF OTHERS AND IMPRESS EVERYONE WHO SEES YOU PLAY.

Everyone wants attention and approval from others. We all want our fellow golfers to respect our skills. But, when you believe that you *must* play so well that you impress all comers, you are asking for emotional problems. If you tell yourself that you *should* sink every putt within four feet, what you mean is that if you were a "class" player you would sink those short ones. Since you do not always sink them, you are not the golfer that you want everyone to think you are. You then decide that it is *awful* or *unbearable* that you are not everyone's ideal golfer.

These self-messages are pure garbage. Even if you did destroy your golf image with the entire membership of your club it wouldn't make any difference. The only one that you have to please is you! People could discuss your missed four-footers for the next ten years without producing one inch of damage to your flesh, so why are you worrying about it? You worry because you believe that you *have to* impress these people. When you begin to impress yourself with the fun you have playing golf, you will stop worrying about judging yourself against others' standards.

What other people say about your game cannot hurt you unless you decide that it is a *terrible tragedy* that anyone should think you play badly or conclude that they are probably right in saying that you *should* play much better. The surest way to ruin your game is to tour the links trying to gain the approval of everyone you see. As sure as one person will think your form is excellent the next person will criticize your hand position or your address. It is impossible to play a game that everyone will agree is perfect.

On the four lines below we would like you to put together a hypothetical foursome of the game's greatest players. Make it a mixed foursome with one female and three males. Since women's golf has a somewhat shorter history and has received considerably less publicity and television coverage than the men's tour, the reader is entitled to be more familiar with the male pros.

1. _____   3. _____
2. _____   4. _____

The ideal list in answer to our request could be: (1) Nancy Lopez, (2) Arnold Palmer, (3) Tom Watson, and (4) Harry Vardon. That is a pretty fair foursome but why not, (1) Mickey Wright, (2) Billy Casper, (3) Ben Hogan, and (4) Sam Snead? Then there is (1) Babe Zaharias, (2) Bobby Jones, (3) Jack Nicklaus, and (4) Gary Player. Or (1) Kathy Whitworth, (2) Jimmy Demaret, (3) Walter Hagen, and (4) Byron Nelson. All of these lists seem to be beyond criticism. Yet, if you asked people to defend their choices they would begin to find flaws in the golf played by even these legends of the game. If people cannot universally approve of the shots played by the game's superstars isn't it absurd for you to try to impress them with your skills? When you start to accept honestly the notion that what others think of your game cannot hurt you, you will start to relax and play better golf.

Irrational beliefs one and two account for a great deal of golf anxiety, but number three is the real "bogey" man. Irrational Belief ✕3: THE IDEA THAT YOU SHOULD BE THOROUGHLY COMPETENT IN EVERY ASPECT OF THE GAME AT ALL TIMES.

If you believe that you must be competent in every aspect of the game you do not need to worry about what others think, you can make yourself miserable without them. You are going to miss shots! If you believe that such imperfection is unendurable you must end up in a rage or a massive anxiety reaction. The basic cure for your golf nerves is to stop dumping on yourself because you do not play the game perfectly. Ben Hogan and Bobby Jones have both noted that only two or three shots in a round are hit perfectly (Scott and Cousins, 1969).

From a psychological perspective, the most adaptive golf philosophy that we have read belonged to Walter Hagen. Hagen seems to have accepted the game for what it is without turning it into a life or death struggle. He stated many times that he expected five or six bad shots in every round. Since he wisely expected some bad shots, he did not panic when they occurred. Hagen seems to have taken the view that the chance to recover from a bad shot made the game more interesting. The key thought is to become interested in your results rather than emotional about them.

Perhaps you find it hard to believe that in a sport as difficult as golf anyone would be foolish enough to adopt rigid standards for judging the adequacy of his play. You probably recognize that as a human being you are fallible and therefore you refuse to buy into many of the perfectionistic guidelines that other golfers have developed. We would like you to go through the golf ideas listed below and see how many of them you believe. Be honest now! Think about the last time you faced the situation in question on the course and answer our survey based on what you remember of your reactions at that time.

GOLF ATTITUDE SURVEY

Instructions: Circle the number that represents your honest feelings about each question according to the following scale.

1. Strongly Disagree 2. Mildly Disagree 3. No Opinion
4. Mildly Agree 5. Strongly Agree

1. A competent golfer should never three-putt. 1 2 3 4 5

2. It is much worse to bogey a par five than a par four, therefore, one should never bogey one of the par fives. 1 2 3 4 5

3. A chip to the green should always be close enough to hole out in one putt. 1 2 3 4 5

4. If you have just had a lesson you should see great improvement in your game. 1 2 3 4 5

5. One should always hit one's drive so that it lands on the side of the fairway away from the sand trap guarding the green. 1 2 3 4 5

6. One should never take more than two putts from within twelve feet. 1 2 3 4 5

7. A good golfer always reaches a par three in one. 1 2 3 4 5

8. Putts should never be left short or "never up, never in." 1 2 3 4 5

9. One should never miss the ball. 1 2 3 4 5

10. A competent golfer should make 80% of his ten-foot putts. 1 2 3 4 5

11. One should never make the same mistake twice in a row. 1 2 3 4 5

12. One should never dunk a ball in the water. 1 2 3 4 5

Total the numbers you have circled and put your score here _____

If you scored between 12 and 24 you are very much at home with your golf imperfections or you are beginning to grasp the message that we hoped to impart in this chapter. If you were telling the truth, congratulations. (If you fibbed a little that isn't terrible either.)

A total between 25 and 36 suggests that your golf mind is in pretty good shape. You seem to be resisting some of the traditional golf commandments that can lead to a shaky round.

A score between 37 and 48 indicates that you have some irrational cobwebs in your golf psychology. You probably experience a considerable amount of emotional interference in how you play the game. If you take the time to examine those beliefs with us and throw out those that do not pass muster, you will probably become a calmer and lower handicapped golfer.

If your score was over 48 you had better pay strict attention to our lessons on disputing these beliefs. It is very likely that your feeling that you *must* adhere to these rigid standards is causing you to relive your shots in agony every time that you fail to live up to your expectations. There can be no questioning the fact that if you can give up these irrational beliefs golf will become a much more enjoyable game for you.

On the slim chance that one of our readers would score a 60 we wanted to hide a telephone number on the back flap of this book that would put you in touch with our emergency hotline. Failing that, we would suggest that you find a place to sell your clubs because it is unlikely that you will be able to have any fun at this game if you continue to hold onto these irrational rules.

And irrational they certainly are. Once you have accepted them you become their psychological whipping boy. Why shouldn't you three-putt? Everybody else three-putts. Pros three-putt, but for some reason you are not allowed to. Admittedly it is inconvenient to three-putt but it is not a sin. If Jack Nicklaus three-putts a green you do not brand him as a lifelong loser or a hack, so why do it to yourself? The same logic applies to bogeying a par five, having to hit a par three in one or having to chip within the range of one putt. If someone were to invent a robot that played perfect golf, no doubt named Double Eagle One, you might expect that it would never make any of the mistakes that are listed above. Unless you are a robot, however, you are going to make those errors.

The things we have talked about are really not disturbing enough to let yourself become anxious, but it is frustrating to take lessons and show no improvement or to continue to make the same mistake over and over again. It is frustrating but that does not mean you *have to* blow up. It is not written anywhere that when you are frustrated you must lose your cool. It is quite likely that Irrational Belief ※1 appears in between the frustration and the emotional response. You say to yourself that your game *should* be better and that you *should not have to endure* such frustration. You conclude that you *can't stand* being frustrated like this. If you were eight years old you might well be right, but as an adult you no doubt recognize that there is no sacred tattoo on your bottom which says, "This person must have everything go exactly the way he wants it to and never be frustrated." When you lose your temper it usually means that you are taking the frustration as a personal insult, an attitude that only does more damage to your own cause. You add to the problems and make life more inconvenient.

If you have a temper problem, start by recognizing that the missed shot, repeated error, and lack of transfer from lesson to play are normal parts of the game. They come in the package you get when you decide to pick up a club. Your temper tantrum is not part of the game but an obstacle that you add to make it more difficult to play successfully. When you work to convince yourself that it is not a *horrible disaster* to play badly you will be able to play without becoming a childish brat.

The following exercise will demonstrate how important it is for you to gain control over your temper. During your next round, mark an "X" over the number of each hole that you respond to emotionally. When you finish the round compare the scores on the two holes following each X to the holes that preceded the X. If your scores are worse on the holes that follow the X, your temper is adding to your handicap.

The perfection that many golfers demand of their game is best evidenced in question ✕10: "A competent golfer should make 80% of his ten-foot putts." The pros, in fact, make less than half of those putts (Cochran and Stobbs, 1968), but if you accept this notion you will be coming down on yourself if you don't make eight out of ten. To make matters worse you have probably never missed a ten-footer and said, "well, that was one of the twenty percent that I am not supposed to make." Deep down inside you expect to make all of them so it becomes awfully disappointing when you don't. Obviously, it would be nicer if you did make those putts but there is nothing terrible about not making them.

By now you may be starting to get the idea of how to dispute your irrational beliefs. Let's see if you can do one yourself. Try number five, "One should always hit one's drive so that it lands on the side of the fairway away from the sand trap guarding the green." Is this statement true? If it is, why? If not, why not?

If you said, "no because, although it would be nice to be on that side, it is not a dire necessity," you are on the right track. If you went on to suggest that you "can recover from the other side and still birdie the hole," and that "nobody always hits the open side," you are beginning to grasp a more rational approach. Now try this one which is a little bit harder. "One should never hit the ball out of bounds."

If you said that this is false "because everyone is going to hit OB eventually so you have to accept it as part of the game," you are off to a good start. You might have continued by pointing out that taking a stoke and distance penalty is only inconvenient not *terrible* or *disastrous*. If you concluded with something like, "after all, a stoke and distance penalty doesn't leave me paralyzed from the waist down," you are on the road to knowing that you can stand a bad shot, that a bad shot is not *awful,* and that there is nothing to get anxious about.

The first three irrational beliefs are probably the most pervasive and generally damaging to one's game but they have plenty of company in the average golfer's head. Irrational Belief ✕4 is the idea that BECAUSE SOMETHING ONCE PRESENTED A PROBLEM FOR YOUR GAME, IT MUST CONTINUE TO DO SO. Below are some typical examples of this fallacy that may sound vaguely familiar to you:

At least a couple of those are among the ten commandments of your golf game, are they not? Well, you are not alone. The first author of this book has sworn that on one particularly blustery day, on a tee where he had a history of duck-hooking his drives, he could actually hear the wind instructing him to "Hooook, Hooook!" as it whistled through the trees. While most of you will probably never get to the point where your self-messages turn into voices in the wind during your address, your unspoken prophecies can be just as damaging. To be blunt about it, there is no reason to believe that because you once lost thirteen balls in the lake you must forever after have trouble with water holes. There is no relationship between this water hazard and the last one except the connection that you make in your head. Each time you tee off is a new beginning, or as Sam Snead (1961) once said, "The most important shot in golf is the next one."

Behavioral psychology has demonstrated that past experience influences present behavior. But that does not mean that you are *bound* to repeat the errors of the past. So you took a 13 on the first water hole that you ever played. That can influence you to freeze up every time you play a water hole, or it can influence you to recognize that you had better relax and become less concerned about the water hazard. In the first instance you will continue to play badly. In the second your play will improve. It depends on the use that you make of your past experience.

Part of your past experience now includes having read about the negative effect that your thoughts can have on your performance. Now maybe you can stop cursing yourself as a loser who always misses pressure putts and start to correct the problem and break away from your past. Instead of looking at the six-footer for par and the match as a sure disaster, it is possible to say to yourself that "I have always choked on putts like this but this one is going to be different because I am not playing yesterday I am playing now!" YOU DO NOT HAVE TO CONTINUE MAKING THE SAME MISTAKES! Unemotionally accept the failures of the past and try to improve the present, keeping in mind that there are no *disasters*. It would be more convenient if your ball carried the water or if you made the putt but you will not suffer everlasting damnation if that doesn't happen. You can find it interesting or even amusing that you had such a hard time in the sand trap but do not make it into a rule that you always have trouble in sand. If you keep reminding yourself to play the water hole badly, your body will do what it is told. As Johnny Miller points out you have to learn from the past, not live in it (Miller and Shankland, 1976).

If you have experienced the clutch that grasps the sand-phobic golfer as he steps into the trap you may feel that you already know many of the things that we have been telling you, but that by the time you think about it rationally your emotions are completely out of control. Everybody knows that you cannot help but feel angry, depressed, or frightened, right? Irrational Belief ⌖5 is THE IDEA THAT YOUR EMOTIONS ARE COMPLETELY BEYOND YOUR CONTROL.

Technically this idea is partially correct. You cannot directly control your emotions. If missing a putt automatically led to anger we could not tell you how to stop that from happening. Fortunately, however, you can control the thoughts that lead to emotions and, as we stated earlier, it is your thoughts about how awful it is to have missed that putt that cause you to respond emotionally. If you have been playing competitive golf for any length of time these irrational thoughts occur quickly. You have been practicing them for many years. You do not need much time to develop your negative, emotional self-messages. They are in your head just waiting to be selected at the appropriate, or perhaps inappropriate, moment.

The idea that you cannot control your emotions usually goes hand in hand with Irrational Belief ⌖4, that you are a prisoner of your past. The temperamental golfer often takes the view that his tantrums and emotional explosions are just the way he is. He believes that he has always been this way and that he cannot help doing these things. Tom Weiskopf, who is sometimes referred to as Terrible Tom II (the first was Tommy Bolt), stated this point of view very succinctly in a 1977 *Golf Magazine* piece. When he was asked if his notorious temper hurt his game or would shorten his career, Weiskopf said that he believed it kept him going. He went on to suggest that he could become controlled "but that wouldn't be me. . . . God, sports would be pretty boring without Woody Hayes . . . and Ilie Nastase . . . Maybe I'd be a better player if I had a different approach. But that's me" (Barkow, 1977). The answer to these contentions is that the tantrums are neither uncontrollable nor the "real" Tom Weiskopf. However, as long as you tell yourself that the "real" you is an eight-year-old who throws clubs when things do not go your way, you are a candidate for laying down and kicking your feet in the middle of the fairway. Weiskopf has made the mistake of deciding that because he has blown his cool a couple of times he will always lack emotional control and that this is his "true inner self." In fact, in recent years, it appears that he is beginning to define himself as someone who can control his emotions. As a result he is becoming less of a temperamental terror.

Believing that your emotions are uncontrollable is a major factor in failing to control them. Once you accept the false idea that they are uncontrollable, you can rationalize the knowledge that your emotions are hurting your game. The rage and resulting poor play are accepted as givens so you don't do anything about them. If you had a partner who was losing several strokes a match because he did not own a sand wedge, you would think it very self-defeating if he failed to buy one at the next opportunity. Unless, of course, he told you that they weren't available anywhere so it was impossible for him to get one. The player whose emotions resemble a runaway truck is telling himself that there are no brakes available. He does not want to face the reality that he could control his behavior if only he would change the thoughts that key his outbursts. Bobby Jones faced just this temper problem before going on to greatness. He simply decided to control his temper.

Many of the thoughts that lead to club throwing and putter snapping were reviewed earlier. The rage reaction usually comes from feeling that your game *should* be different and an exaggeration of each negative outcome into a tragedy. Terrible Tommy Bolt can be credited with describing the mental attitude that is most likely to turn you into an emotional powder keg on the links. In *The Hole Truth* (Bolt and Mann, 1971), his view of golf is summarized in the following way: "To fail, to Tommy Bolt, is to die a little." He said, "If you die a little many times, sooner or later you will die for good." If you make every shot a life or death issue, missing a shot is indeed terrible and it is no wonder you lose your temper. On the other hand, do you really think that you die more quickly when you miss than when you hole-out? We doubt it! It really is only unpleasant, not awful, to miss a shot and that difference is more than semantic. Once you understand that you do not become the club zombie when you miss a shot there is no longer anything to get emotional about. If you have really grasped the thought that your worth as a human being does not rise and fall with each swing, you will stop being at the emotional mercy of the course. You have to work at it though. You can't kid yourself along or hope that pretending it doesn't matter will make you able to calmly show how great you are.

Part of the reason that golfers so often lose their tempers is that many of them endorse Irrational Belief ⚡6 THE IDEA THAT GOLF SHOULD BE FAIR AND THAT IF YOU DILIGENTLY WORK AT YOUR GAME YOU MUST SCORE WELL. Golf is not fair. Say it again to yourself! GOLF IS NOT FAIR!!! You knew that, of course, so why do you explode every time you hit a good shot that has a bad result? You can either adjust to the reality of the unfair game that is played in this world or you can put your clubs away until you get to the perfectly fair game in the next world.

How many times have you hit four nearly perfect shots to get a par four and watched in dismay as your opponent went from rough, to trap, to fringe, to sinking a long putt for the same par four. He did not hit it well, yet he got the same score you did. That certainly is not fair. Unfortunately, if you make an emotional zinger out of it, he is also going to win the next two holes. You cannot transform the game into something it is not. Nobody promised you that life would be fair, so stop wasting your emotions in reaction to the thought that you should have won that hole. When you think that way you are not dealing with reality.

The same can be said of some of the other truisms of golf. It would be nice if your game improved every time you practiced or took a lesson but it simply doesn't. You have no right to feel cheated. You are just sabotaging your game with those expectations. Be aware that your emotional reaction does not stem from the fact that you practiced and did not improve. You are frustrated because you believe that you *should* have improved; that you *deserved* a better score. It is almost as if the fates cheated you of the good score that you earned through your diligent practice. This belief is sometimes referred to as the "Door-Knob Polisher

Philosophy" from the Gilbert and Sullivan operetta *H.M.S. Pinafore,* but it has its roots in the religious philosophy of John Calvin. Calvin preached that if you worked hard enough you would get your just rewards. Well, if you believe that, we have some bad news for you. There will be times when you work at the game of golf as hard as you can and the only reward you will get is the part of the club between the grip and the blade. That is not fair or particularly Calvinist but then Calvin expected the rewards to come in the next world, not on the next tee. Once you give up the notion that golf *should* be fair and that certain things *should* have happened, you will be able to adjust to the things that actually do happen without becoming a golfing basket case.

While it is obviously illogical to expect a hook on hole six because you hooked your tee shot on hole six the last time and illogical to get upset at the unfairness of a bad lie after a good shot, Irrational Belief ⋕7 may be the most nonsensical piece of links logic. THE IDEA THAT THE BEHAVIOR AND SCORES OF OTHER GOLFERS ARE EXTREMELY IMPORTANT TO YOU AND CAN DESTROY YOUR GAME.

This fallacy takes many forms but it is always irrational. Golf is played against the course! The opposition is par, not the other golfer. If you beat par you are also likely to win the match, but your goal has to be to improve and enjoy your game not to beat the opponent. As Kemp documents, this point has been made repeatedly by the greats of the game including Harry Vardon, Arnold Palmer, Cary Middlecoff, Don January, Al Geiberger, and Lee Trevino. In match play you do have to plan strategy based on your rival's shot but at no time can your opponent's shot directly affect your own. Even those legends of the halcyon days of match play, Bobby Jones and Joyce Wethered, emphasized playing against par no matter who the opponent was (Jones, 1960; Scott and Cousins, 1969). Often players seem to tighten up in response to a good drive by their opponent. Try to remember that his shot and your shot are also independent events. One cannot influence the other but your thoughts about his shots can affect your game if you let them. When you start to believe that your opponent's good drive means that you must hit a better one, you are on your way to tension rather than relaxation, and jerking the club rather than making a smooth swing. Feel free to admire his shot, to aim to do as well, and to be intensely involved in doing so, but do not fall into thinking that it will be marvelous if you do or terrible if you don't.

If an opponent makes a long putt, it is not unusual to see a player react as if the cup were full. These putts are also independent events that are not logically connected. In terms of your score the meaning of your four-footer has not changed. It is still better to make it than to miss it, but his success does not mean that you *must* make it. His shot does not put pressure on you, your thoughts do.

Another kind of illogical relationship is sometimes drawn between these putts. When the opponent makes a long one it may produce a feeling of insignificance for the golfer playing the four-footer. The rewards for sinking the short putt are simply not as great as the "oohs" and "aahs" that follow a breaking, roller-coaster ride into the cup from the fringe. The short putt is not a rewarding situation at all because most golfers take it for granted that they are going to make it and castigate themselves if they miss. Thus, it is no big deal and nothing to feel good about if they succeed but it is "something *awful*" if they fail. No wonder the yips are most frequent on the short ones. It is a no-win situation. Nevertheless, if you are playing your game, rather than the other fellow's, it will not tighten you up into hitting a dub.

In match play, when your opponent collects a birdie in front of you, it is absolutely necessary for you to make your putt in order to halve the hole. Right? Wrong! There are seventeen other holes but even if it is the last hole, there are many other matches. If you were playing some sort of gladiatorial golf in which the loser actually was killed, it might be an absolute necessity to equal his shot. Fortunately, that is not the case. Even if it were, you would only lessen your chances if you told yourself that you *must* make it.

There are other myths that fall into the category of overreacting to the antagonist but they are of a somewhat different nature. The opponent's shots are not the only things that emotional golfers allow to influence their game. For instance, some golfers believe that they cannot possibly lose to someone wearing jeans, or to someone playing with mismatched clubs. Such beliefs are totally unreasonable. If you continue to accept those ideas you are priming yourself for increasing stress as you recognize that the opponent plays a better game than you do even if he doesn't dress like Johnny Miller. What you have done is to establish an arbitrary rule, "I *should* always beat anyone wearing jeans." It becomes upsetting when someone forces you to see that the world just does not turn that way. The simplest solution is to give up your superstitious rigidity. If your thinking is irrational, however, you will cling to your rules and blame yourself for not being able to fulfill their demands. Since people in jeans are bad golfers and you are losing to such a person, you must be a terrible golfer. Of course, you are not a terrible golfer although you do make some pretty silly rules.

A related and more common phenomenon is the "I can play well with anybody but _____" reaction. The blank is usually filled in with the name of a spouse, parent, sibling, close friend, teacher, boss, club pro, or local rival. You could play well with these individuals and perhaps even beat your husband or father, if you would let yourself. Your self-messages are your undoing in two ways. First, you tell yourself that you *have to* play well in front of that person. It would be *awful* if you did not make a good showing. You will even hear people openly state this position as "I don't care if I win or not, just so I don't look bad." If you are not out there to have fun but rather just to avoid making yourself look bad, you are going to be swinging with anxiety on every shot. On the other hand, if you believe that you must beat your boss to show him how great you are, you are probably carrying many years of frustration and anger on your back as you walk the eighteen holes. It is pretty hard to swing a wood lugging all that emotional weight. It gets a lot easier when you go out only to enjoy the game. All of these superstitious beliefs would not be too harmful if it were not for the fact that Irrational Belief #4 is usually added as the second part of this equation. The convoluted thought pattern then becomes "Because I did not play well against Dad last time and the time before that, I must continue to play badly against Dad." As we discussed earlier you are not a prisoner of your past and there is no logical basis for that belief. So, give it up! It is okay to find it

173

very interesting that you have never beaten your father. Unless he is significantly better than you that fact is likely to change. You can only keep yourself superstitiously incapable of beating him if you feel that you *must* beat him or continue to be convinced that you can never beat him.

Irrational Belief #8 takes its name from the old Ink Spots song of the late 1940s "Into Each Life Some Rain Must Fall" or I'VE HAD THREE GOOD HOLES IN A ROW SO IT IS TIME FOR SOMETHING TO GO WRONG.

As a child you were taught to take the good with the bad in order to cushion life's agonies. If you reasoned in a normally childish and illogical manner, you turned that idea around to the supposition that "if you are getting good things something bad is sure to follow." Picture the irrational fifteen handicapper who is one under walking toward the fourth tee. His head will be ablaze with messages about his impending doom. He has had three good holes in a row. Disaster must be just around the corner. He feels due for a bad shot. He convinces himself that something is about to go wrong and he is seldom disappointed. Yet, his tee shot on the fourth hole is independent of his play on the three earlier holes. Only his self-defeating thoughts connect these two unrelated events. His belief that he is overdue for a bad shot will get him one.

The longer he continues to play "one under," the stronger his belief in the eventual disaster will become. If he was still playing well after nine he would be sure that the other shoe would drop after he had made the turn. This view can even be carried across days. At the 1979 Colgate-Hall of Fame Classic, Dana Quigley opened with rounds of 63 and 74. He explained his poor second round by pointing out that he "owed the course something" (the New York *Times,* August 25, 1979). The greatest absurdity in this kind of thinking was recently facetiously expressed by Jerry McGee when he said that he was very relaxed at the beginning of the Kemper Open in Charlotte because he had been seventeen over at the last tournament and was happy to be back at par (*Golf World,* June 8, 1979). These feelings are so strong because the golfer did not play this well in the past and, therefore, quite illogically, believes that he should not play this well in the present, and because, "everyone knows that good things are followed by bad things and vice versa." He sees bad breaks follow good breaks every day. But his perception is selective. He does not notice the strings of good things that he sees happen every day nor the series of bad things that he sees happen every day.

If you watch the professional tour you will see a golfer put together three or four superior rounds each week. Based on irrational reasoning the golfer's good Thursday round should have been a cue for a Friday disaster, but it wasn't. Only some of the more anxious pros seem to play according to this "rainy" philosophy. It occurs to them not because it has to but because once they have the bad round they no longer have to worry about winning the tournament so their anxiety lessens and there is nothing to stop them from playing well. Certainly strings of good things happen without some nasty kicker being attached and anyone familiar with sports can cite numerous examples in which a succession of bad outcomes did not end in something wonderful happening. If you do not believe us ask the baseball fans who follow the Chicago Cubs or the football supporters of Texas Christian University. If you are still unconvinced, review the success records compiled by basketball players drafted by the New York Knickerbockers or the list of professional golfers who have never won on the tour. As a child we were all taught to expect the bad with the good so that we would be able to adjust to the bad when it came. That does not mean that it *must* come. It only means that it *sometimes* comes. There is no great score-keeper in the sky saying, "Uh-oh that duffer is one under after four. It is time for a hook!"

The next time that you are in this position and you decide that something must go wrong ask yourself, why? If the answer is because you did well on the three holes before, remind yourself that you are playing against the par for this hole. Your score on the hole before can neither help you nor hurt you. As Kathy Whitworth (1973) said, "Golf is really eighteen separate games." The only way that the score on hole three can affect your score on hole four is if you nonsensically connect these two unrelated events. If you insist on being illogical you can talk yourself into botching the fourth hole. Be aware that it was not because it was bound to happen. It was because you talked yourself into it.

There is a well-known demonstration of this truth that psychologists often use in the classroom. The instructor flips a coin five times. Each time he tells the class that the coin comes up tails. Before the sixth coin toss, the instructor asks the students what they think the chances are that the coin will again come up tails . . . The chances are fifty-fifty, as they are on every flip of any undoctored coin, because this coin toss is independent of the five that went before it. The chances of throwing six consecutive tails may be quite small when considered as a group, but tails is always a fifty-fifty chance on any one toss of the coin. Like coin tosses, your golf shots are independent events. While the chances of your shooting a 65 may be quite remote, that provides no information at all about your chances of making any particular shot. If you work at keeping this fallacy out of your mind you will find yourself a lot less likely to kiss off a whole round because of a few bad shots.

Perhaps the most tempting of all Irrational Beliefs is ⚹9. THE IDEA THAT IT IS EASIER TO AVOID ANYTHING ON THE COURSE THAT CAUSES YOU ANXIETY THAN IT IS TO FACE IT AND OVERCOME YOUR FEAR.

The easiest way to demonstrate this belief for most golfers is to ask them about their two-iron. You know the club that we mean, it's the one that still looks brand new. It looks unused because it is. Since you feel anxious about using it, you avoid using it. Indeed, some people avoid their three- and four-irons as well. The difficulty with that decision is that you cannot improve your long-iron play unless you use your long irons. You have given up any hope of achieving better scores in order to avoid the stress that you feel when you approach a difficult shot with the feared club.

This would be a relatively minor problem if it occurred with just one or two clubs, but this fallacy has much broader implications for your game. Suppose that you are facing a par five, dog-leg left. You hook your tee shot and are faced with the choice of trying the spectacular shot over the trees or playing two safe shots; back to the fairway and then on to the green. Your partner yells over to remind you that if you play back to the fairway you *"should* make an easy par." So you try to hit it over the trees. A sucker shot that at your level of play you have one chance in five of making. Why did you do that? Because your partner said that you *should* make par if you play it safe. Once that has been said it raises all of your anxieties about not making par even if you do play it safe. If you go for broke and miss, nobody really blames you; after all it was a tough shot! You become a courageous gambler with a double bogey 7. If you take the safe route and do not make your par, you label yourself a klutz who blows even easy safe pars and winds up with a 6. Once somebody decides that you *should* make it you really whip yourself if you don't. It is easier to go for broke where nobody blames you if you miss. Naturally, giving in to anxiety in this way will cost you a couple of strokes. You could save those strokes by attacking the fears directly rather than avoiding the anxiety arousing situation.

Why *should* you make par if you play it safe? Where is it written that all fifteen handicappers who hit the safe, back to the fairway, shot from that spot, *must* end up with a par? Remember that every time you tell yourself a *"should"* or a *"must"* you set up a situation for anxiety in case you don't.

Your negative self-appraisal makes you anxious. Your belief, that the easiest way to handle that anxiety is to run away from it, keeps you anxious. If you start to realize that there is no reason that you *should* make the safe par, or that you *must* be competent with your long irons, you will stop worrying about looking bad if you do not accomplish these ends.

Irrational beliefs ten and eleven are both closely related to irrational belief nine. All of these irrational ideas involve the notion that you can improve your game without working at it or by avoiding certain aspects of it. Irrational Belief ⚹10 is the fantasy that ONE CAN IMPROVE ONE'S GAME THROUGH INACTIVITY OR SIMPLY BY THE PASSAGE OF TIME.

Wishing will not make it so. The only way that you can improve your swing is by working at it. Grousing, bitching, and endless discussions at the nineteenth hole have no curative properties for a sick swing. You have to actively do something about it. The notion that you can solve the problem through inaction is a fallacy.

We all know golfers who have been hitting the same bad shots for ten years. If this is as much as they want to put into the game and they are content with the way they play, we have nothing but respect for them. However, some of these individuals are not content. They are normally rational people who, for some reason, expect their slice to disappear by itself, even though they swing the club exactly the same way they always did. One golfer of our acquaintance, a very bright young man who is now attending Yale, would play until he developed a shank. When that happened his clubs headed for the attic and he headed for the tennis courts. After a lay-off of a couple of months, he would try again to see if the shank had disappeared. If it had he would play until it came back, which usually did not take very long. It had to come back because he had not done anything to get rid of it.

There is a magical nature to thinking that a swing problem will go away by it-self. It is as if your hook or slice had a life of its own. If you listen carefully on the course you can hear people talking to their "slice spirit" and "hook goblin." They beg it to go away, entreat it not to return, and curse it when it appears. One almost gets the feeling that they are talking about some sort of black-sheep relative that visits them on the tee. The point to keep in mind is that your crooked drive is the result of something that you do with your driver, not a spirit that whimsically comes and goes amongst the woods in your bag. If you assume that your hook comes and goes of its own accord you will traverse the course in fear that something will summon up the demon and your hook will return. Some golfers take this thought so far that if they hit a slight draw on the first hole they expect to be hitting duck-hooks off the tee by the back nine. These golfers have reached a new height in the art of making a mythological creature out of the way that their driver intersects with the little dimpled ball. They have actually created a demon that grows up as they proceed through the round.

To get rid of the "goblins of the link" requires practice and hard work. The hook has no life of its own. It does not come and go by itself but only as a result of what you do. The same can be said of all other golf problems. Sitting around and wishing that they weren't there will not chase them away. You can improve your chipping by learning how to do it correctly and practicing what you have learned. You can get rid of your tension on the course by developing a new golf philosophy but for that to be effective you must practice it until it is mastered. In Chapter 13 we will provide more help with overcoming your inertia and teach you some techniques for developing good programs of mental and physical practice.

The poltergeist of the hook is not the only black magic that golfers conceal on their carts. Irrational Belief #11 is THE NOTION THAT ONE CAN IMPROVE ONE'S GAME THROUGH MAGICAL INSTANT CURES OR GIMMICKS. The secret technique, that will overcome all of the flaws in your golf game overnight, just does not exist; so stop searching for it. You may get a tip that helps you for a round or two but unless you groove your swing and change your psychological habits of brow-beating and *catastrophizing,* you will not show lasting improvement. The book you are currently reading will help you if you work with it, but it is not a panacea that will pull your game together with one application.

If you read through the back pages of any golf magazine you will find a large number of quick cures for the ailing game. We suspect that your golf may benefit from some of these things but nonetheless they represent an irrationality trap. Once you buy one of these things and begin to use it, you believe that your game should get better, a lot better! When that does not happen, you get down on yourself. The self-messages go something like this, "Gee, this is *supposed to* work for everybody but I'm such a rotten golfer even this special magic new putter doesn't help. I must really be *awful!*" You have made another disaster for yourself and proven once again that you are not half the golfer that you think you *should* be.

If you believe that your special black putter guarantees that the ball will go into the hole as often as possible or think that without legend or graphite shafts you cannot possibly play well, you had better ask yourself why. There are no magic clubs to make your game better, nor are there lucky balls that always go into the hole under par. You are an adult now! Give up the superstitions and start working to achieve your goals. The more time you spend looking for the cure-all for your swing, the more time you could spend enjoying the game and improving that swing. There can be no questioning the fact that the right equipment can help your game. We recommend buying your clubs from your local golf professional who knows your game and can help you select clubs to match your stature and ability. There is nothing irrational about getting the best equipment unless you demand perfect play once you obtain it.

Our last irrational idea deals with how you handle the other eleven. Irrational Belief ✗12 is THE IDEA THAT YOU CAN EASILY DEVELOP A TOTALLY RATIONAL APPROACH TO GOLF AND THAT YOU SHOULD FEEL TERRIBLY GUILTY EACH TIME YOU THINK IRRATIONALLY ABOUT YOUR GAME.

Your goal in changing your golf philosophy is to eliminate self-messages that give rise to negative emotions. The three negative emotions that can ruin your game are anxiety, rage, and guilt. If you find yourself thinking that you *should* spend more time getting rid of your irrational beliefs or that you *must* stop worrying about some aspect of your game, you have missed the point. True, it would be more convenient, more pleasant, and more productive if you made the changes in your golf psychology that we suggest. But saying that you *should* be thinking more rationally or *must* conquer your irrational ideas is just adding more irrational self-messages for you to feel guilty or anxious about.

We have presented golf's twelve most frequent irrational beliefs. As you can see, they are fallacies which can be banished from your foursome. At the end of this chapter we will present an outline for modifying your irrational self-messages. Before we do that, however, it is appropriate to address the particular irrational concerns of the professional golfer whose livelihood may depend on his performance.

The rules of rational golf do not change because there is money to be made. The pro faces the same desire to play well and win as the rest of us do. It simply becomes *more* inconvenient to miss a three-foot putt for a championship. If there is $20,000 riding on it, a miss may even be very inconvenient but it is still not *awful, horrible,* or *terrible.* It is not a death sentence. All of the things that you enjoy in this world will not disappear. It may be unpleasant but you will have other lucrative three-foot putts to make and you will make your share of them.

Earlier we referred to the role that age seems to play in developing the yips. There are many differences between the veteran and the relative newcomer to the professional tour. Perhaps the most significant of these differences is that the older golfer has seen so many more "disasters" on the tour. He knows that even the truly skilled golfer cannot keep ahead of the game constantly. He is no longer able to maintain the naive self-confidence born of youth. The older golfer stops believing that he can win the next tournament. He begins to doubt how many more times he will be in contention. Once he has done that he adds pressure to himself by saying that he *must* shoot well, because this could be his last chance. Yet even if he never wins another tournament, his worth as a human being is not diminished. The next day he can still enjoy his family, his favorite meal, and the beauty of the night sky, whether or not he made the $25,000 putt at the Westchester Classic.

The professional golfer can find the pressure and his reaction to it fun and interesting, as Dave Stockton does, or he can turn it into a morbid soliloquy on all the wonderful things he missed out on when he missed those putts. If he is smart enough to realize that missing is not a catastrophe he will probably continue to make many of those putts. On the other hand, if he turns $10,000 into the difference between life and death, he will produce the kind of anxiety that will eventually drive him off the tour. Once you start to tell yourself that you can stand the negative outcome, that it is not horrible to miss a short putt, and that you are not less of a human being if you do not win, there is nothing to be afraid of. You are on your way to playing calmly no matter what the financial stakes may be, how many people are watching on television, or whom you are playing.

For most golfers winter is a slow time. Unless you live in a very warm climate you cannot play, and indoor practice has obvious limitations. It is, however, an excellent time for mental housecleaning. It is a season when you can examine your beliefs about golf and rigorously practice discarding those that are irrational, emotion arousing, and self-defeating. The outline presented below for disputing your irrational golf ideas is based on the work of Albert Ellis and his associates Robert Harper, Maxie Maultsby, Howard Kassinove, Bill Knauss, and Ray DiGiuseppe. If you use this outline to practice disputing your irrational ideas over the winter you may be able to significantly alter your psychological perception of the sport by throwing out much of the mental garbage that adds to your handicap.

Start by thinking of a golf event in your life that leads to negative emotions such as anxiety, guilt, or anger. Find ten minutes to relax in an easy chair and think back to the last time you experienced this event in actual play. Try to imagine it so vividly that you can feel the negative emotion that you felt at that time. Now start to notice what you are telling yourself about the situation or event and see if your thoughts are rational.

Let's try a rather common example. Many golfers will be anxious if they believe:

"In match play when my partner hits a bad shot it means that I really *have to* put my shot on the pin."

Begin by asking yourself why you *think* you have to make a good shot in this situation. Make a list of your reasons:

1. Because if I don't make the shot we will lose the hole.

2. Because if I don't make a good shot here I'll have to scramble like hell on the next shot.

3. Because we are running out of time in this match.

4. Because after we lose this hole we will be one down and it is harder to come back and win once you are down a hole.

5. Because I'm the better player of the team and I'm supposed to take up the slack when my partner is out of the hole (or), because my partner has been carrying us for this round and now I have to come through for him.

6. We have to halve this hole at worst because all of my bugaboo holes are coming up soon and I know we won't do well on those.

7. Because if I hit a bad shot too we will just hand the other team the hole. It is terrible to play so badly that the opponents don't even have to work to win.

The self- messages on this list are all irrational. All of these unpleasant outcomes from a bad shot do not amount to even a minor disaster. They are really a list of preferences. They suggest why you would *like, wish,* or *want* to sink the shot. There is *no reason* why you *have to!* It may not be desirable to lose a hole but it is not mortifying. It is inconvenient, not horrible, to be one down. It is unpleasant but not awful to lose a golf match. You can stand not bailing out your partner's poor shot. If he thinks that you *should* or *ought* to make up for his errors, you might suggest that he get a copy of this book to get rid of his irrational beliefs. Remember that each hole, in fact, each shot is an independent event. Because you had trouble with fourteen and fifteen last weekend is no reason to believe that you will play them poorly this time around. It is certainly unreasonable to tighten up on thirteen because you "know" that you will not do well on fourteen and fifteen.

Now make a second list of the positive things that could happen if you do not hit a good shot:

1. This gives me a chance to work on developing a more Hagen-like, rational philosophy of golf.

2. I could learn to find it challenging and enjoyable to be in a position where I would like to hit a good recovery shot.

3. It gives me the impetus to work on improving my short game (putting, chipping, pitching, sand shots, etc.) so that I will not overemphasize my driving and approach shots. If I do that I will stop feeling like I have to be on top of the pin with every approach.

4. I could realize that even losing a golf match or hitting some bad shots is better than being stuck at home doing housework or cutting the lawn.

5. I could recognize that if I continue to lose every match and play very poorly I will probably develop other interests. These other pursuits will give me a variety of satisfactions so that my entire self-esteem is not based on making certain golf shots.

Suppose that you do feel some pressure in a close match, you can learn to enjoy that pressure. You can observe it and find it interesting rather than threatening. One of the joys of golf is that you can recover from a bad shot. Given that you play a whole round, no one swing of the club ever puts you out of business for the day. Why not enjoy the challenge of recovering, that too is an interesting facet of the game. Even if you are a touring professional, golf is not your whole life. A poor round, a devastating year, or even the end of your golfing career is not the end of you! Your list of rational positive outcomes of a poor shot will help you keep the stress of the game in its proper perspective. If you never hit a bad shot and played only from tee, to fairway, to green, golf would get pretty dull for you. You can remind yourself that part of the fun is enjoying the novelty that course architects work so hard to put into the game. Finally, remember that there is no reason that you must hit good shots, play perfectly, or even improve. The only thing that you have to do is to enjoy the game because it is irrational to keep doing something that you do not find rewarding. If you continue to make unrealistic demands on yourself you cannot possibly have fun playing golf. If you stop making those demands you will relax, enjoy the game more, and play better. Unlike tennis or basketball, golf gives you plenty of time between shots. Use this time to dispute your irrational golf beliefs.

Perhaps it is best to end this chapter with an example of how even the stress of big money, professional golf can be controlled by banishing irrational, anxiety-producing ideas. Johnny Miller (*Golf Magazine,* 1977) describes the tension of a golfer on the professional tour through the analogy of a car's tachometer that approaches a red danger signal when the golfer becomes too emotional. He states that "the trick is to know . . . it is approaching the danger level when you are getting too excited to play well. There are . . . lots of players who come down to the wire and blow up. The key for me came at the U. S. Open at Oakmont. *I told myself that I couldn't care less what happened . . .* I birdied the first four holes but I couldn't putt after that for five holes. I was choking my guts out. Then I got it together again by saying to myself 'you've got no chance to win choking like this so just go ahead and play, and, if it works, fine, if it doesn't, forget it.' " He shot a 63!

Philosophically Miller has hit an ace. It is equally possible for you to learn how to leave your emotions at home when you take to the course.

13

Practice: How to Get Yourself to Do It

*"Nobody—but nobody—has ever be-
come really proficient at golf without
practice. . . ."*

JACK NICKLAUS

Perhaps there is no sport in which practice plays a larger role than golf. Golf is a game of precision. You cannot hope to play it well without practice. Compared to other major sports, it involves the most finesse and control, therefore it is the most responsive to the effects of drill. Good golfers come in a wide variety of physiques and statures with vast differences in natural ability. No sport has as many unlikely-looking champions. The range goes from the beautiful Jan Stephenson to the portly Bob Murphy. In fact, golf is one of the few sports in which the relatively small man or woman can overcome the power advantage of a larger opponent as Gary Player and Judy Rankin have proven. The number of proficient golfers who have conquered the loss of an arm is ample testimony to the benefits that practice can have in surmounting physical limitations. It is hard to imagine a player with a similar handicap succeeding in football, basketball, or baseball. It might be possible, say, for an outfielder to catch a ball, hook his glove under his chin, and grab the ball in his bare hand as it dropped. He could then throw the ball in with the same hand that caught it. Such a technique would require incredible timing and hours of repetition if it could be mastered at all. Yet, an outfielder named Pete Gray played seventy-seven games for the St. Louis Browns using exactly this method, batting left, catching left, and throwing left. In 1945, he hit .218 and struck out only eleven times in 234 at bats against Major League pitching. That's what practice can do for you! It is even more important in a game like golf where the ball stands still than it is in baseball where success is limited by speed and reaction time.

The greats of golf are virtually unanimous on the importance of practice (Nieporte and Sauers, 1968). While Hogan and Player may be the paragons of the practice area, no one disputes the value of practice for the serious golfer. There is also fairly general agreement on what should be practiced. The recommendations are usually to spend one's time on the scoring area: putting, chipping, and pitching. Patty Berg (1977) suggests working your way up through every club in the bag. Paul Runyan (1962) argues that you should begin with the putter and wend your way back to the longer shots. Gary Player (1962) very sensibly adds that one should also end a practice session on the green to regain the feel necessary for the scoring aspects of the game.

But how do you engage in such designed practice at a driving range? It isn't easy! As the great teaching pro, John Jacobs (Jacobs and Bowden, 1972), observed, what most golfers do at the driving range "may be exercise but it isn't practice." If you must practice at a driving range try to follow these simple rules:

1. Begin with the shorter clubs.

2. Hit most of your shots off the grass or at worst the mat.

3. Avoid rapid fire, aimless swinging.

4. Always play each shot as if it was the middle of a round. Plan it, aim for a target, and engage in your usual preshot routine just as you would on the course.

5. Spend your time on the clubs that give you the most trouble. Use the opportunity to hit your favorite club as a reward for hitting the clubs you hate.

6. Have a goal in mind for the practice session. If you are going out just to hit a few balls, stay home.

7. When you get tired, QUIT!! "You must hit every ball in the bucket" is not one of the ten commandments of golf.

8. Don't practice in the rain or wind unless you expect to be playing under these conditions.

Improper practice is worse than no practice at all. Remember that you are trying to build muscle memory. You are endeavoring to teach your muscles what a good shot feels like. As Patty Berg (1977) has observed, when a professional golfer has a particularly spectacular round he is likely to head for the practice area because he doesn't want his muscles to forget how it felt to hit those good shots. He wants to groove that swing.

When you just swat balls or fail to follow your normal preshot routine you are building sloppiness into your game. Every time you hit without aiming for a target you are practicing bad golf. When you practice in the rain or high winds you are likely to make adjustments in your swing that represent repeated rehearsals for your muscles. These adjustments are being grooved. They will follow you from the practice area to the course even if it isn't raining or windy when you play.

Perhaps the most pernicious habit a golfer can get into is practicing when he is tired. As Gary Player (1962) points out, fatigue leads to forcing your swing and destroys your timing. There is nothing wrong with not hitting the last five balls in a basket. Although you may believe that you aren't getting your money's worth, it really isn't wasteful to hand those few balls back in. The bad habits that you learn from hitting while bushed will cost you much more money on the course and at the lesson tee than you save by the pseudo-frugality of hitting every ball in the basket.

Leave your bucket of balls some distance behind you to avoid simply drilling balls without thinking between shots. Balls should not be so far away that you lose your concentration but they should be at a distance that provides a break to think about the target and evaluate the previous shot.

Drilling rapid-fire drives to the point of fatigue combines golf's two worst practice habits. As bad as either of these errors is singly, in combination they can really ruin your swing. A perfect example of these effects was provided by Tod Gittleson, one of the subjects in our research at Old Westbury Country Club in New York. In his early sixties, Mr. Gittleson is in exceptional physical condition. As founder of the Hofstra Health Center he is a superb model of the beneficial effects of cardiovascular exercise. Unfortunately he is such a devotee of fitness that he would invariably use his practice sessions as demonstrations of his physical prowess by pumping out drive after drive while denying any effects of fatigue. It is impossible to guess how much damage this forced practice was doing to his swing although it may have helped some people to recognize the value of aerobic exercise. We can only tell you that trying to hit the ball as far as you can, as quickly as you can, for as long as you can will end with your playing as badly as you can.

Does this mean that practice must be drudgery? If you can't machine-gun shots out of sight, are we taking all of the fun out of practice? No, we are not! It is quite possible to enjoy interesting, beneficial practice while remembering that it is where rather than how far you hit a golf ball that is important.

The best way to avoid aimlessly knocking balls out into a pasture is to keep a record of your practice shots. If you have to mark down the result of each shot you won't have to worry about becoming an automaton. In addition, record keeping will help you focus on the goal of the practice and serve as a cue to relax, take a couple of deep breaths and follow through on the rest of your preshot playing ritual.

Both Ben Hogan (Hogan and Wind, 1957) and Patty Berg (1977) keep a book of session-by-session records in order to measure the effects of practice. The best way to keep such records is to plot your shot-by-shot ledger on a graph just as you would for the data from your actual play (See Chapter 7). By charting your results in this way you can see the gains that you make in practice and identify the goals for your next outing. Practice has a significant natural advantage over actual match conditions in that you can choose what shot you wish to perfect. If you throw away this advantage by just hitting your favorite club or not bothering to set goals for improvement, you are wasting your practice time.

It is best to pick out a target and give yourself a goal for every practice shot. The *Golf Digest* Panel of Editors (1978) suggests that you can even use your practice time to pace off yardage on your shots and gain information for future club selection. While this might be time consuming, it has obvious benefits for your play. It also forces you to avoid thoughtless swinging, because it requires a target and implies establishing a goal for each practice session.

Most authorities feel that forty-five minutes to an hour is a good limit to set for any one session. For the average golfer it may be difficult to find the time for a lot of practice. As Doug Ford (1960) and many others have suggested, the best time for corrective practice is right after a round. Your errors are fresh in your mind so it is easy to set practice goals. Further, if you played a particular shot badly, that is not the muscle memory that you want to take home with you. If club conditions permit, you may even be able to play the exact shot that you botched in the day's match out on the course in order to get the feel of doing it correctly. On the other hand, if you can't seem to get that shot right don't keep practicing it incorrectly. You will just be grooving muscle memory for bad shots. Instead take a lesson or a series of lessons from your pro. Practice sessions that follow a lesson can be very productive. Any learning experience requires homework. Practice is the homework for your golf lessons (Chinnock, 1976), but it is only helpful if someone has taught you the correct action.

You should avoid practicing before you play. A full session of practice before a round is likely to leave you tired and may sap your confidence if your practice was devoted to curing the faults of your game. Obviously you need to warm up before a match. This is probably best accomplished by moving backward from the hole in an abbreviated mastery chain. Many of the game's top professionals recommend a warm-up to remind your muscles of how it feels to make the appropriate swing at various distances; therefore, you must attempt a variety of shots. However, this is not the time to try to make major changes in your swing. Such corrective practice belongs after the round, not before. Like your practice sessions, your warm-up should begin and end on the green so that you retain your feel for the short game.

What you should practice depends on the state of your game but for the average golfer we believe that practicing our mastery chain is the most effective way to use your practice time. If you listen to the practice programs espoused by the game's greats such as Snead, Nicklaus, Player, and Casper you will find that their suggestions are very similar to ours. Jack Nicklaus (Nicklaus and Bowden, 1974) reports that he practices to get a certain feel on every shot. He knows he has that feel when he can hit, for example, ten consecutive shots exactly the way he wants them. Like Billy Casper, Nicklaus believes that you should stop practicing once this is accomplished so that you gain the confidence that comes from ending with good shots. The professional often practices to overcome a minor flaw in his game or to refine his skills in a very specific way such as fading his three-wood. For general practice Billy Casper recommends starting two feet from the cup and moving back in one-foot intervals (Casper and Collett, 1961). For the

TABLE 8

Practice Chain and Mastery Criterion.

Step	Shot	Mastery Criterion
1	3-foot putt	4 putts consecutively holed from around the horn
2	10-foot putt	4 putts consecutively rolled to within 1 foot from around the horn
3	30-foot putt	4 putts consecutively rolled to within 2 feet from around the horn
4	35-foot chip 5 feet off green w/7-iron	3 out of 5 within 6 feet
5	35-foot chip 15 feet off green w/wedge	3 out of 5 within 6 feet
6	35-yard pitch shot	3 out of 5 within 15 feet
7	75-yard pitch shot	3 out of 5 within 30 feet
8	125-yard shot	3 out of 5 within 45 feet
9	175-yard shot	3 out of 6 within 66 feet
10	Optional for golfers capable of driving over 175 yards *without pressing*	3 out of 4 drives on the fairway (short grass)

amateur attempting to get his tempo, feel, and muscle memory down correctly, the abbreviated chain in Table 8 is the most appropriate way to distribute his practice time.

In the first chapter of this book we were rather critical of the way that golf has traditionally been taught. We have no such reservations about what the legends of the game have written about practice. For the low-handicap golfer the programs that they recommend are faultless methods for fine tuning a motor skill. It is not difficult to surmise the reason that most of the world's best players are so much more astute about practice than they are in their advice for learning the game. All of the game's class players practice. They have first-hand experience in the most profitable allocation of limited practice time. On the other hand, very few of golf's champions actually learned to play golf through the methods that they recommend for others. The great golfer has so much difficulty advising the twenty-year-old who is just taking up the game or the thirty-five-year-old, fifteen handicapper, because they have never been in the same position as their students. Almost all of the game's name professionals learned to play well before they were twenty and were certainly scratch players by the age of thirty-five. Thus, the most frequently espoused methods of teaching the game violate many of the rules of how people best learn, but much of the conventional wisdom on practice embodies sound learning theory. A good example of this expertise is Gary Player's (1962) writing on practice which seems particularly well thought out.

It is not enough to know what to practice. The real key is getting yourself to do it. Probably the easiest practice to fit into a busy schedule can be done on the bedroom rug, office carpet, or backyard grass. Fifteen minutes each day of swinging without the ball can protect your tempo and muscle memory. This is the procedure that Bobby Locke (1954) endorsed. He believed that tension comes from losing the feel of your game. This daily ritual is designed to keep that from happening. Although this requires only fifteen minutes a day, it is likely that as few as ten good, back-and-through movements would be enough to maintain a well-grooved swing.

The trick to getting yourself to actually engage in such practice is to make it convenient to do so. Bring a club to the office or leave one close at hand at home. Establish a habit of taking practice swings each day at the same time. Tie it into some sort of cue such as the eleven o'clock news, finishing dinner, or taking your daily shower. Pick a signal that occurs everyday so that your phantom swings become a ritual in the same sense as shaving or putting on your makeup. It will be helpful in the beginning to take a pocket calendar and cross out each day when you complete your practice swings. Once the habit is established this will no longer be necessary. We are in agreement with Locke that if you follow this program through the winter you will be a leg up on your game when spring comes.

Swinging without a ball is a beneficial technique for maintaining your game, but most golfers require knowledge of results in order to improve their game. Feedback on where the ball went with each swing adjustment can only be obtained at a practice area. But the practice area has not been nicknamed "Misery Hill" for nothing. Practice can be crushingly dull unless you take some steps to make it less tedious. The easiest solution to this problem is to find somebody who can regularly go to practice with you. The worth of this suggestion lies not in the misery-that-loves-company of two bored golfers but in the joys of competitive practice. There is really no substitute for this kind of drill. It facilitates transfer from the practice area to course play by making you practice under competitive conditions. As Mickey Wright (1962) has observed, the more you can relate practice to a playing round, the more you will benefit. In a one-page *Golf Digest* article that contained an abundance of good ideas, Paul Runyan (1975) outlined competitive practice games for every aspect of golf from putting to sand play. The most important facet of these practice matches is to set up a handicap system that makes the practice truly competitive. Who wins or loses is less important than maintaining both parties' interest in the routine. It is often a good idea to make some small wager on the outcome such as who pays for the bucket of balls or who buys the postpractice beers. For many players though, winning will be enough but if one player wins all the time he will no longer feel challenged and his partner will give up and lose interest. The mis-match will end with neither party practicing very often.

It is difficult to prescribe the exact number of strokes that should be allotted to each player based simply on comparing overall handicaps. As you well know, two seven-handicap golfers may have very different games. One might be able to sink ten consecutive six-footers quite easily while the other has a great fairway game but putts like a drunken lumberjack. The best way to set up your initial practice matches is to spend the first session going over the practice chain back-ward from the green. Keep a record of each player's success at every step. Then when you start to practice competitively you can set individualized standards to handicap the matches. For example, you might require the better chipper to land three out of four shots within a three-foot circle of tees around a practice hole as opposed to only two of four by his less proficient partner. Similarly, standards on the driving range might vary from five dead straight, two-hundred-plus yard drives to three out of five but none that were topped or sliced.

It is most important that as you continue to practice the rules for winning be-come more exacting. This is part of the idea of mastery-based instruction. The better you get, the more difficult the challenge should be until you become so proficient that a new challenge is called for. In the chipping example you might change from three out of four to seven out of eight, or you might decrease the target circle from three to two feet. You must avoid allowing your goals to be-come static. When practicing driving you should try to imagine increasingly nar-row fairways so that your driving will become more precise. To sum up, the practice games must get more demanding as you improve so that you can im-prove that much more.

You can even extend the criterion setting to include a task that you must ac-complish before you allow yourself to leave the practice area. Tom Watson (1977) suggests, for example, that sinking thirty consecutive two- and three-footers before allowing yourself to quit creates some real tension toward the end of the sequence. Watson believes that this represents good rehearsal for the stress of actual play. Preparation for course stress in this manner is unques-tionably advantageous, but there is the danger of practicing under conditions of fatigue inherent in this scheme. We believe that it is useful to finish any practice session with positive results but that the mastery criteria should not be so difficult as to extend your practice time beyond your endurance. Watson's ap-proach is a good one but it depends on you to use common sense in applying it.

The most difficult situation to set appropriate goals for is the short putt. In-side four feet most middle handicap golfers can quickly learn to sink ten flat, straight putts in a row, although it requires greater skill if you compete from various positions around the hole as Billy Casper recommends. To increase the difficulty of this all-important practice exercise, find holes that offer more break as you become more skilled. If you have practiced and mastered putting within three feet of the hole you have realized a major stroke-saving skill. If you can realistically expect to make these shots you will have overcome a significant source of golf anxiety.

Another device for making a competitive practice game out of short- and medium-range putting is to substitute a coin for the cup on the practice green (Watson, 1977). This smaller target requires that you be more precise in your aim but you must not allow yourself to stroke the ball harder since the coin gives you no feedback on whether the ball would have dropped or gone over the hole. When we began our teaching program we occasionally had subjects who could not master even the ten-inch putt at the beginning of the chain. For these individuals we enlarged the hole and used a more controllable, larger ball so that our novice could get the feel of a successful swing. For the veteran golfer who already has the basic skills, Watson's technique of narrowing the target to the size of a coin should definitely improve precision.

PRACTICE WITHOUT A PARTNER

In our busy lives scheduling problems often make it impossible to locate a practice mate. If you can't make practice a social occasion, it makes it that much more difficult to get yourself to do it. It can be a lonely grind unless you program in some rewards to make it less distasteful. It is best to begin by making a schedule of practice times. Block out time in your appointment book or mark off your kitchen calendar to indicate practice sessions. BE REALISTIC! The worst thing you can do at this point is to schedule more practice time than you can actually fit in. If you do that you are likely to give up the whole idea of practice using the excuse that you have missed so many sessions that there is no point in continuing. Don't give yourself that excuse! Make a schedule that you can live with! Frank Chinnock believes that as little as an hour a week of the right kind of practice can be very meaningful. We would add that one hour of actual practice is worth much more than five scheduled hours that never come off.

Try not to schedule your practice sessions so that they are in competition with something else that you find rewarding. If you leave yourself a choice between going to see your girlfriend and practicing pitching, it is likely that the only pitching you'll do will be at the girlfriend. Instead, use your practice time to get yourself out of nasty jobs. Rather than ironing shirts go out and practice your putting. On a day when making out sales reports seems particularly unpleasant let them go until tomorrow while you work on getting out of the sand.

Even though you have no one to practice with, your practice need not be completely asocial. You can make a date to phone another member of your foursome once a week to discuss golf in general and your practice sessions in particular. This gives you someone to share your feelings of improvement with, as well as giving you someone to bolster your motivation when you feel like chucking the whole idea of practice.

One of the simplest techniques to increase practice time is to write a contract with yourself. If you have some other activity that you would rather be doing set up a fixed amount of practice time to be completed before you allow yourself to engage in that other activity. Psychologists call this the Premack Principle or "Grandma's Rule." It is usually stated as "you must finish practicing your violin before you go out to play baseball," but you can substitute your five-iron for the violin and trying on a new dress or having a couple of beers for playing baseball.

Keep in mind that the rewarding activity should be something that you really enjoy. If you look lousy in the new dress or if beer makes you sick, you may have trouble getting yourself back to the practice area. This system works best if you are adding something new rather than just trying to slip in golf practice before something you always do. If you love going to the movies but only go once a week let yourself go a second time if you have done your golf practice.

It is worthwhile to actually write out the contract. This may sound silly, but it is helpful. It is just too tempting to ignore contracts that you keep in your head or to decide to postpone beginning the contract until next week. If it is there in black and white it forces you to face the thought of breaking your commitment. The written contract serves as a reminder, not as a signal to feel guilty. If you start to play guilt games with yourself you are likely to drop the whole notion of a practice program and that is not what we are trying to achieve.

The rewards that you design for yourself need not be limited to other activities. There is no reason to avoid setting up a contract that allows you to buy something or get out of something on the basis of your practice. The contract might be for a new album, a rich dessert, or an expensive cigar. You can, for example, set a goal of 120 points, one point per minute of practice time, for a given week. If you reach that goal you can buy yourself a lottery ticket. Unlike other rewards, lottery tickets rarely lose their reward value because they involve the possibility, albeit remote, of collecting a very large pay-off.

If you are not currently practicing at all you should begin by rewarding yourself for very limited increases in practice time. Schedule a half-hour of practice after your next round; if you actually complete the session, buy yourself imported rather than domestic beer at the nineteenth hole. Slowly increase the amount of practice time that you have to put in to collect your spoils. Include your practice sessions at home as well as those at the range but don't give the same amount of weight to swinging without the ball that you do to hitting the real thing. The contract that you conclude with yourself might read something like the one below:

DATE: Week of April 11

PRACTICE:

1. One hour at the practice area   60 points
2. Fifteen minutes per day at home   45 points
   @ ½ point per minute (six days)
   (Swinging without a ball)

REWARD:

1. One lottery ticket for every
   90 points

Note that this contract does not demand perfection. The key to improving your practice time is not to make demands on yourself that you can't fulfill. Yet, we are not suggesting that you should cheat on the contract. If you only get 89 points you don't get the reward! If you find that you are asking too much of yourself back off on next week's contract or choose a more potent reward. At no point is it legitimate to collect the prize if you haven't fulfilled the contract.

If you wanted to invest even more time in practice you might expand the requirements after a few weeks in which the system is working successfully. Do not rush this process! The contract limits should be raised slowly so that you succeed; they should not be hurried into an expansion to failure. The example below represents a well-timed modification.

DATE: Week of May 8

PRACTICE:

1. Seventy-five minutes at the practice area   75 points

2. Fifteen minutes per day at home @ ½ point per minute (six days)   45 points

REWARD:

1. One lottery ticket for every 100 points

BONUS:

1. If I hole out all but one green in two putts or less in Saturday's match I will buy a golf magazine this week.

These practice contracts are even more effective if you include a bonus clause relating to your actual play. This important step is exemplified in the second contract. It calls attention to the purpose for all this practice by linking the practice and the play. The bonus clause should specify progress on the skill that you have been practicing rather than your overall game. Your baseline data from Chapter 7 can be quite useful for this purpose. If you have been recording the specifics of your play you can graph, for example, the amount of time that you spend per week on putting practice as a separate line on the same graph with your number of putts per round. If your program of drills is having the appropriate effect you will see that as your practice line goes up your putts per round line will descend. Eventually we hope that you will practice without needing artificial rewards. The knowledge that your game actually does improve when you practice specific skills will be all that is necessary to maintain your practice regimen.

Even though you have to practice alone, you needn't give up competition. It is possible to extend your practice time by designing a program of games for solitary skill programming. In a truly superb *Golf Magazine* piece we made reference to earlier, Tom Watson (1977) put forth twenty different, fun practice games. While many of these contests are not new with Watson, he deserves credit for being one of the few people to address this issue and bring together some sophisticated alternatives to practice monotony. Watson, Runyan, and others have made the point that one never has to practice alone as long as one has an imagination. As we noted earlier, young athletes in all sports practice against imaginary stars. They stop Walter Payton cold, drive past Jerry West, score goals on Tony Esposito, and hit Grand Slams off Bruce Sutter. Such imaginary rehearsal hardens them against the tension of the real thing and keeps them interested in their practice. If your club allows you to play two balls at a time, play a round against Jack Nicklaus, Tom Watson, Jane Blalock, or Nancy Lopez and keep score! If you really want to increase your skill with this exercise play the second ball for a short hitter like Paul Runyan so that you develop some finesse by using more club than you normally require for each shot. On a shot where you would normally hit a seven-iron, hit Runyan's ball with a six and take something off it. If you can handle three balls and the course permits, you can make it even more interesting. Add Arnold Palmer to your group and play all of the gambling shots you can on his ball to see what effect that has on your score. If you have the time you can play whole tournaments in which you get the practice benefit of every shot. By switching off your normal club selection you can make your old familiar course into a brand new experience ameliorating any boredom that develops from repeated play. This kind of on-course practice is particularly helpful because it leads to playing shots out of the rough and from hazards not found on the driving range.

If your club frowns on individual play or is too busy to tolerate it, find a par-three course for your practice rounds. Par-threes provide a layout in which most of the shots are within the cone of contention which is exactly where most of your practice time should be spent.

Competition against imaginary rivals is also worthwhile on the practice green. Find ten golf balls that you can easily differentiate. Let one of the balls be yours and assign the other nine to master putters such as George Archer, Horton Smith, Kathy Whitworth, Nancy Lopez, Bobby Locke, Billy Casper, Bob Rosburg, Walter Hagen, and George Low. Now drop the balls in a circle two feet from the hole and sink them. Move back one foot at a time and do the same thing. Keep track of how each of your players does out to fifteen feet or more. You can keep score on this drill by just making a check mark next to the name of the player each time that you miss for them. Bear in mind that it is best to let yourself go last in any imaginary contest so that you get used to the "pressure" of wanting to match your opponent's shot.

Your confrontations with the legends of the game need not be limited to putting. You can match sand shots with Player and Blalock, chips with Hagen, and even skip shots off the water with Lon Hinkle if you feel like it. While the most profitable area for practice is that green oasis that surrounds the cup, imaginary competition can be extended all the way back to the driving range. You can play the eighteen holes of your home course against Carner or Snead in fantasy, hitting every shot but the putts. Just pick out a sign or other landmark to serve as the imaginary flag. Set up one-, two-, and three-putt distances from the improvised hole. Once you have marked off the putting ranges in your head you can play each hole just as you would on the course and simply add the appropriate number of putts based on where the approach shot landed. If you don't know any course well enough to play it in your mind, you're sure to find the lay-out of Augusta, Baltusrol, or Pebble Beach in one of the current golf periodicals. You can use a copy of one of these courses for your fantasy of the Masters or Open.

If you don't wish to dignify Nicklaus or Lopez by taking them on, you can always play against a perfectly matched and delightful opponent: yourself. Drills that involve trying to putt, chip, or drive the ball inside your last shot (i.e., closer to some target) are excellent training. Extending your practice session until you have bettered your best shot of early in the session is a good idea for emphasizing improvement. Of course, if you hit one stoney on the first try don't use this drill to try to better that shot by a half-inch. That would be wasting valuable practice time.

Watson (1977) and Toski (1978) recommend trying to estimate where a shot or putt has gone without following it visually. This exercise is designed to develop a "feel" for distance and direction. It is particularly useful when done in relative terms, that is by comparing the present shot to the one that you hit a few seconds before. This exercise is to help your muscles identify the necessary strength and orientation. It is likely to be of considerable benefit to the experienced golfer because it teaches the individual to notice how muscles feel on each shot.

MENTAL PRACTICE

Every golfer knows that a short warm-up is necessary to loosen the muscles and regain one's touch before playing a round. Unfortunately, few golfers engage in any mental preparation before they hit the first tee. Your psychological warm-up should begin in the car on the way to the club. This is the time to rehearse your coping statements, dismiss any irrational fears, and relax yourself for the match to come. While it is not advisable to do relaxation exercises while driving, you can rehearse the course and prepare controlled reactions to any emotional stress that you are likely to encounter. As you dress for the match set one personal goal for the day's play and acknowledge that you will be satisfied if, for example, your putting is good even if your score isn't. A physical warm-up that includes some putting and approach shots is essential to a good round. A mental preparation that clears the cobwebs and demons from your golf psychology is equally crucial for sound play.

The rules for getting yourself to practice the mental game differ little from those that foster progress in physical practice except that mental drill requires less of a special effort. You can practice rational thinking, relaxation, or coping statements almost anywhere and work in ten minutes of calming thoughts with

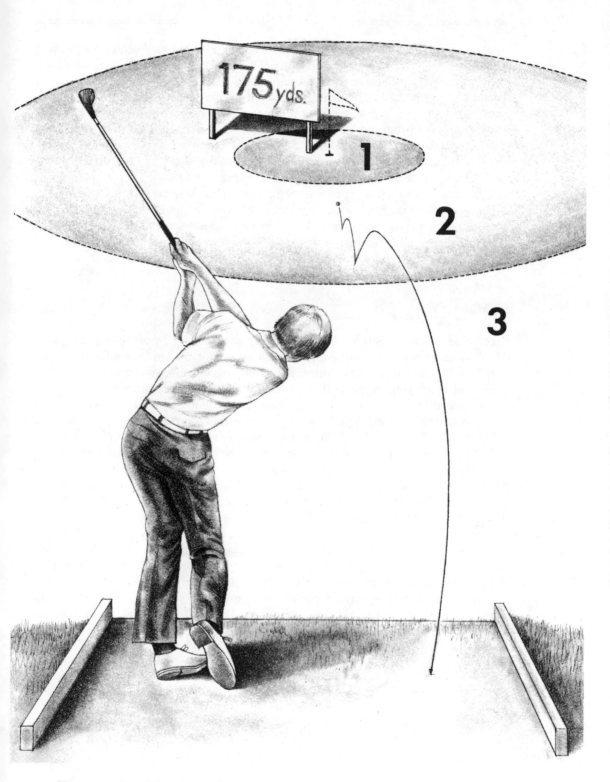

You can play the eighteen holes of your home course against Carner or Snead in fantasy, hitting every shot but the putts.

little inconvenience. Since you can profit from as little as two minutes of sound thinking about your game, you do not need large blocks of time for correcting your golf hang-ups. Nevertheless, you are likely to find the techniques of scheduling and rewarding yourself for mental rehearsal beneficial in keeping you going. Recording your practice is as indispensable for good mental habits as it is in your physical program. You will profit most if you know how much you tried to overpractice your anxiety on the course, how many sessions you spent disputing your irrational ideas, or what coping mechanism you used before a given shot. This record keeping serves as a cue to remind you to practice but, as in physical practice, it has a far more crucial function than just serving as a reminder. If you accurately measure your play you can compare the effects of your mental practice techniques as they are reflected in your actual scores. You can then see improvement or find out that your particular case of golf nerves responds better to a change in philosophy than it does to relaxation training or vice versa.

SUMMARY

Practice is serious business. It is absolutely essential to improving your game. There is no reason why your practice sessions cannot be fun and interesting, but they should never deteriorate into just horsing around unless you are simply not interested in playing better golf. Goalless practice is worse than no practice at all because it builds in a cavalier approach to the game. We would like to close this chapter with an example to help you remember to take your practice time seriously. In Chapter 7 we introduced you to the Brittain-Hurr system for collecting data on your game. Some years ago Dr. Bill Brittain, one of the developers of that system, bought himself a new set of graphite shafts and headed out for the practice range in the company of the then Lycoming College golf coach, Jim Waite. As Waite tells it Brittain was clowning around with his driver toward the end of the session. He took a running leap at the last of his striped balls sitting up on the range tee. His off-balance swing missed the ball completely but connected solidly with the head of his three-wood which was lying beside the mat. The impact left both clubs damaged and one golfer with a more serious attitude toward practice. You aren't likely to break your clubs if you fail to concentrate during your practice turns but you can surely bend your swing way out of shape. May we remind you again that if you teach yourself sloppy golf in practice, that is the golf that you will learn to play in competition.

14

Epilogue

*"Give the ball a good healthy whack—
and enjoy yourself."*

ARNOLD PALMER

It is traditional to end golf books by wishing the reader good luck on the course. We are not going to do that. If you do what we have described in this book you won't need the luck, and if you don't it won't help. So, get together with your favorite teaching pro to work your way back from the green to the tee. Remember that you must master every step along the way. If you learn the lessons of this book you will be a more relaxed and competent golfer.

Our research has demonstrated that the methods presented in this work offer an effective approach to better golf. But the evidence is far from complete. As we noted in Chapter 8, there have been relatively few scientific studies on golf. For the mental aspects of the game there is even a paucity of good first-person reports on the effects of various behavior change strategies. We would hope that as you try the various innovations outlined in this book, you will collect data (See Chapter 7) on your own performance. If you make a conscientious effort to employ these techniques and rigorously collect data on the changes in your game, we would be very interested in your results. Even a simple description of the program that you employed and its effects would be very helpful. It would be even better if you could send us a copy of your scores before and after your new program, or graphs similar to those in Chapter 7. Our research is continuing. If you have experiences that could contribute to improving our program, send it to us at the following address:

Dr. Richard M. O'Brien
Department of Psychology
Hofstra University
Hempstead, N.Y. 11550

FURTHER READING

No one golf book can teach you all there is to know about this complex sport. If you are really into the game we have probably just whetted your appetite for additional forays into the golf literature. There are a great many fine books to choose from. They vary in sophistication and approach from light, entertaining reading to advanced instruction. We believe that the books listed below are particularly valuable. To help the reader identify a book to fit his needs, we have divided the list into categories that reflect the goals of the authors.

1. ENTERTAINING GOLF BOOKS OF GENERAL INTEREST

For the golfer who is seeking only to satisfy his interest in the game rather than hoping to receive instruction, we would recommend any of the following books without hesitation:

1. *The World of Golf and the Game of Life,* by Charles Kemp, 1978.

2. *Teed Off,* by Dave Hill and Nick Seitz, 1977.

3. *The Guts to Win,* by Jane Blalock and Duane Netland, 1977.

4. *The Bogey Man,* by George Plimpton, 1967.

These works are entertaining as well as being well written. They read quickly, yet they offer an insightful picture of modern golf. Kemp's work, in particular, must be singled out for its psychological sophistication in addition to sound observations on the game. The golfer who decides to spend an evening with any of these books is in for an interesting and enlightening time.

2. SCIENTIFIC STUDIES OF GOLF

There are really only three books on golf that make any attempt to scientifically study the sport. You are holding one of them in your hand. The other two, listed below, also represent worthwhile reading for the serious golfer.

1. *The Search for the Perfect Swing,* by Alistair Cochran and John Stobbs, 1968.

2. *Mind Over Golf,* by Tom Nieporte and Donald Sauers, 1968.

The Search for the Perfect Swing is a must if you are interested in the mechanics of the game. *Mind Over Golf* represents the only controlled effort to solicit the opinions of the game's top professionals. It covers subjects varying from psychological techniques to the importance of various mechanical skills.

3. INSTRUCTIONAL BOOKS

There are many, many well-written books that offer instructional help for both the veteran and novice golfer. The list below represents those that seem to provide the greatest amount of information in the most easily learned form. The latter point is of particular importance in that knowledge of the game is not easily communicated on the printed page. In our view these books embody the most direct hope of further improving your skills through home study.

1. Any book by Tommy Armour, particularly, *How to Play Your Best Golf All the Time,* 1952.

2. *The Touch System for Better Golf,* by Bob Toski, 1971.

3. *Gary Player's Golf Secrets,* by Gary Player, 1962.

4. *Pure Golf,* by Johnny Miller and Dale Shankland, 1976.

5. *Inside Golf for Women,* by Patty Berg, 1977.

6. *How to Break 90—Consistently,* by Frank Chinnock, 1976.

7. *A New Way to Better Golf,* by Alex Morrison, 1946.

8. *How You Can Play Better Golf Using Self-Hypnosis,* by Jack Heise, 1961.

This is not meant to be an exhaustive list. There are some fine golf books that space limitations prevent us from mentioning. Yet, for the mechanical aspects of the game any golfer will probably benefit from reading Armour, Toski, Player, or Miller. While Patty Berg's book is oriented toward women, there is nothing sexist about good golf. The knowledge that it imparts is applicable to either sex. Frank Chinnock's book seems particularly well suited to helping the golfer with a high handicap because of its clear, concise teaching style. On the mental side, both Alex Morrison and Jack Heise supply some meaningful observations for the golfer who experiences psychological traps in his game. For the beginner Morrison's book may be preferable since it offers a more integrated approach to teaching both the physical and psychological aspects of the game.

4. SPORTS PSYCHOLOGY—GENERAL READINGS

The final book that we would like to recommend does not fit under any of the other classifications because it does not deal specifically with golf. Nonetheless, anyone sincerely interested in sports could profit from reading:

1. *The Inner Athlete: Mind Plus Muscle for Winning,* by Robert Nideffer, 1976.

Dr. Nideffer is an experienced sports psychologist and consultant to the NFL's Buffalo Bills. He suggests many ideas that can be used in conjunction with the programs that we have presented in this volume.

5. GOLF PERIODICALS

We would be remiss if we did not cite one other prominent source of golf wisdom, the magazines of the sport. As you can see from our reference list we have relied heavily on publications such as *Golf Magazine, Golf Digest,* and *Golf World* as sources of current information about the game. If you maintain a continuing interest in golf, you are likely to find these periodicals informative and interesting.

A FINAL WORD

Because we have done the research on this method of teaching golf we have no doubt that if you follow our program you will see improvement in your golf skills. The techniques that we provide for emotional control are the latest available. There is every reason to believe that they can help your head game if you work with them. But reading this book and sticking it on a shelf won't do much for your game. Use the programs described and be patient. Remember that the trip from 90 to 72 has to go through 88. Unless you are a beginner you have been working at mishitting shots and developing golf hang-ups for a long time. Nothing can correct those problems overnight. This book and some perseverance *can* help you lower your score and put the fun back in your golf.

APPENDIX 1

**Group mean from the hole for each golfer taking three shots
at fourteen distances**

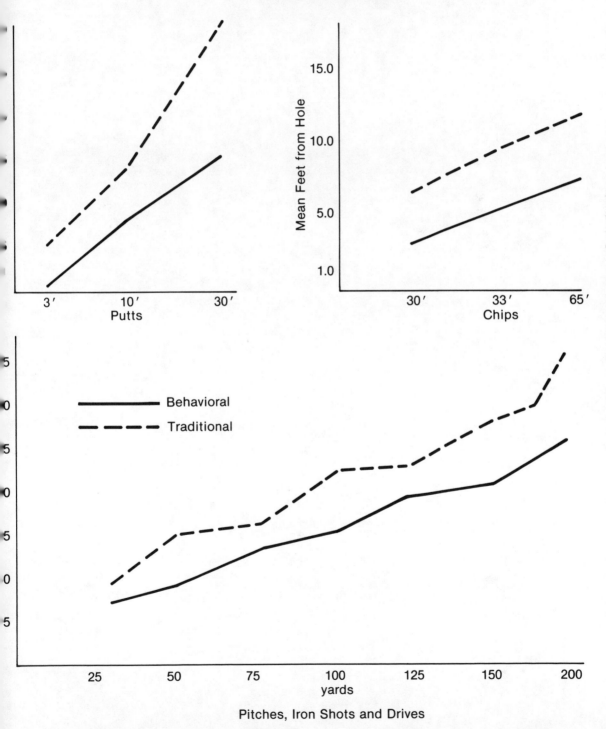

Pitches, Iron Shots and Drives

APPENDIX 2

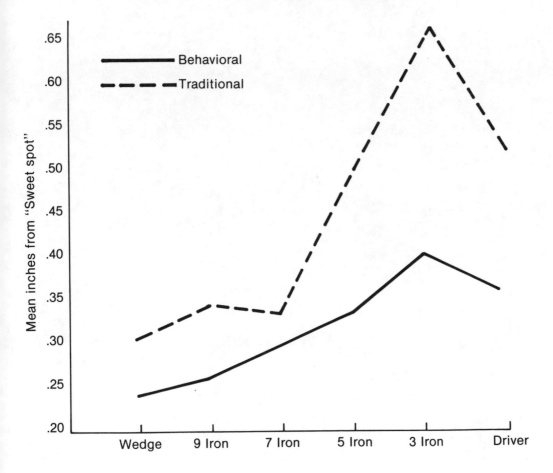

Mean Distance from the Clubface Sweet Spot
for Six Clubs by Group

REFERENCES

Ammons, R. B. "Effects of Knowledge of Performance: A Survey and Tentative Theoretical Formulation." *Journal of General Psychology,* 1956, 54, 279–99.

Armour, T. D. *How to Play Your Best Golf All the Time.* New York: Simon & Schuster, 1952.

Armour, T. D. *Tommy Armour's ABC's of Golf.* New York: Simon & Schuster, 1967.

Aultman, D. and The Editors of *Golf Digest. The Square to Square Golf Swing.* Norwalk, CT: *Golf Digest,* 1970.

Barber, T. X. "Suggested ('Hypnotic') Behavior; the Trance Paradigm versus an Alternative Paradigm." In E. Fromm and R. E. Shor (Eds.) *Hypnosis: Research Developments and Perspectives.* Chicago: Aldine, 1972.

Barber, T. X., Spanos, N. P., and Chaves, J. F. *Hypnotism, Imagination and Human Potentialities.* New York: Pergamon Press, 1974.

Barkow, A. "Tom Terrific Tells All about Terrible Tom." *Golf Magazine,* 1977, 19 (7), 39–41, 90–94.

Bartlett, M. "Nancy with the Laughing Face." *Golf Magazine,* 1978, 20 (6), 62–64.

Bennett, G. "Putting." In L. Robinson and J. Graham (Eds.) *Golfer's Digest,* Vol. 1. Chicago: Follett, 1966.

Benson, H. *The Relaxation Response.* New York: Morrow, 1975.

Berg, P. *Inside Golf for Women.* Chicago: Contemporary, 1977.

Bernstein, D. A. and Borkovec, T. D. *Progressive Relaxation Training.* Champaign, IL: Research Press, 1973.

Blalock, J. and Netland, D. *The Guts to Win.* New York: Simon & Schuster, 1977.

Bolt, T. and Griffith, W. C. *How to Keep Your Temper on the Golf Course.* New York: McKay, 1969.

Bolt, T. and Mann, J. *The Hole Truth.* Philadelphia: Lippincott, 1971.

Boros, J. "Relax and Play Better Golf." *Golf Magazine,* 1976, 18 (5), 46–48.

Bowers, K. S. *Hypnosis for the Seriously Curious.* Monterey, CA: Brooks-Cole, 1976.

Brewer, G. *Score Better than You Swing.* Norwalk, CT: *Golf Digest*/Rand McNally, 1968.

Brittain, W. P. and Hurr, L. F. *Plā-Par*. Williamsport, PA: Productive Learning Associates, 1974.

Brown, C. "Computer Backs Casper as Golf's Top Shotmaker." *Golf Digest,* 1969, 20 (1), 28–32.

Brown, P. P. "How to Keep Your Temper on the Course." *Golf Digest,* 1979, 30 (3), 80–84.

Burke, J., Jr. "Help Yourself Get the Most from Your Golf Lessons." In L. Robinson and J. Graham (Eds.) *Golfer's Digest,* Vol. 1. Chicago: Follett, 1966.

Case, H. W. "Theraputic Methods in Stuttering and Speech Blocking." In H. J. Eysenck (Ed.) *Behavior Therapy and the Neuroses*. New York: Macmillan, 1960.

Casper, B. *Golf Shotmaking with Billy Casper*. Norwalk, CT: *Golf Digest,* 1966.

Casper, B., Jr. and Collett, D. *Chipping and Putting*. New York: Ronald, 1961.

Chinnock, F. *How to Break 90—Consistently*. Philadelphia: Lippincott, 1976.

Cochran, A. and Stobbs, J. *The Search for the Perfect Swing*. Philadelphia: Lippincott, 1968.

Corbin, C. B. "Mental Practice." In W. P. Morgan (Ed.) *Erogenic Aids in Muscular Performance*. New York: Academic Press, 1972.

Craighead, L. W., O'Brien, R. M., and Stunkard, A. J. *Behavioral and Pharmacological Treatments of Obesity*. Paper presented at the meeting of the American Psychological Association, Toronto, August–September, 1978.

Dennis, L. "Johnny Miller's Key Swing Thoughts." *Golf Digest,* 1974, 24 (10).

Dennis, L. "A New View of the Takeaway: Setting the Angle Early." *Golf Digest,* 1974a, 25 (3), 40–46.

Desiderato, O. and Miller, I. B. "Improving Tennis Performance by Cognitive Behavior Modification." *The Behavior Therapist,* 1979, 2 (4), 19.

Dunlap, K. *Habits, Their Making and Unmaking*. New York: Liveright, 1932.

Dunlap, K. "Repetition in the Breaking of Habits." *Scientific Monographs,* 1930, 30, 66–70.

Dunn, S. *Golf Fundamentals*. 1922, reprinted New York: Arno Press, 1977.

Ellis, A. and Harper, R. A. *A New Guide to Rational Living*. No. Hollywood, CA: Wilshire, 1978.

Ford, D. *How I Play Inside Golf*. Englewood Cliffs, NJ: Prentice-Hall, 1960.

Fox, L. "Hypnotized Heroes." New York *Daily News,* July 15, 1979, 14–15.

Frankl, V. E. "Paradoxical Intention: A Logotherapeutic Technique." *American Journal of Psychiatry,* 1960, 14, 520–35.

Giacalone, A. V. *The Use of Hypnosis and Relaxation in Controlling Spastic and Athetoid Movements in Cerebral Palsy.* Unpublished doctoral dissertation, Hofstra University, 1979.

Golf Digest. "Golf Digest Computer Picks Golf's Top Shotmakers." *Golf Digest,* 1968, 19 (1), 28–32.

Golf Digest, Editors of. *All About Putting.* New York: Coward, McCann & Geoghegan, 1973.

Golf Digest, Editors of. "What's Ahead?" *Golf Digest,* 1979, 30 (2), 43–44.

Golf Digest, Panel of Editors. "How to Practice Like a Pro." *Golf Digest,* 1978, 29 (3), 50–58.

Golf Magazine. "Roundtable on Choking." *Golf Magazine,* 1977, 19 (8), 36–37, 73–74.

Grout, J. and Aultman, R. *Let Me Teach You Golf as I Taught Jack Nicklaus.* New York: Atheneum/SMI, 1975.

Gunderson, J. "As the Knees Go, So Goes Golf Power." In L. Robinson and J. Graham (Eds.) *Golfer's Digest,* Vol. 1. Chicago: Follett, 1966.

Harbert, C. "Intimidation." *Golf Magazine,* 1978, 20 (8), 68–90.

Harrison, W. and Mitchell, M. "Target Your Thoughts." *Golf Magazine,* 1978, 20 (6), 74–77.

Haynie, S. *Golf: A Natural Course for Women.* New York: Atheneum, 1975.

Heise, J. *How You Can Play Better Golf Using Self-Hypnosis.* Hollywood, CA: Wilshire, 1961.

Hilgard, E. R. *Hypnotic Susceptibility.* New York: Harcourt, Brace & World, 1965.

Hill, D. and Seitz, N. *Teed Off.* Englewood Cliffs, NJ: Prentice-Hall, 1977.

Hogan, B. *Power Golf.* New York: Barnes, 1948.

Hogan, B. and Wind, H. W. *Five Lessons the Modern Fundamentals of Golf.* New York: Cornerstone, 1957.

Holsopple, J. A. and Vanouse, I. "A Note on the Beta Hypothesis of Learning." *School & Society,* 1929, 29, 15–16.

Irwin, H. "Look Out for No. 1." *Golf Magazine,* 1978, 20 (6), 86–87.

Jacobs, J. and Bowden, K. *Practical Golf.* New York: Quadrangle, 1972.

Jacobson, E. *Progressive Relaxation.* Chicago: University of Chicago, 1938.

Johnson, K. R. and Ruskin, R. S. *Behavioral Instruction: An Evaluative Review.* Washington, D.C.: American Psychological Association, 1977.

Jones, R. T. *Bobby Jones on Golf.* Garden City, NY: Doubleday, 1966.

Jones, R. T. *Golf Is My Game.* Garden City, NY: Doubleday, 1960.

Keller, F. S. "Goodbye Teacher." *Journal of Applied Behavior Analysis,* 1968, 1, 78–79.

Kelliher, M. S. "A Scientific System for Improvement." In T. Michael (Ed.) *Golfer's Digest,* Vol. 4. Chicago: Follett, 1970.

Kemp, C. L. *The World of Golf and the Game of Life.* St. Louis: Bethany, 1978.

King, L. *The Master Key to Success at Golf.* New York: Harper & Row, 1962.

Komaki, J. and Barnett, F. T. "A Behavioral Approach to Coaching Football: Improving Play Execution of the Offensive Backfield on a Youth Football Team." *Journal of Applied Behavior Analysis,* 1977, 10, 657–64.

Lema, T. and Harvey, S. *Champagne Tony's Golf Tips.* New York: McGraw-Hill, 1966.

Lindsley, O. R. Unpublished and undated paper, University of Kansas.

Littler, G. and Collett, D. *How to Master the Irons.* New York: Ronald, 1962.

Locke, B. *Bobby Locke on Golf.* New York: Simon & Schuster, 1954.

Malott, R. W., et al. *Contingency Management.* Kalamazoo, MI: Behavioradelia, 1971.

May, J. P. "PGA Tour Talk." *Golf Digest,* 1979, 30 (8), 123.

McCormick, M. H. *The World of Professional Golf, 1968 Edition.* Cleveland: World Publishing, 1968.

Meichenbaum, D. *Cognitive Behavior Modification.* New York: Plenum, 1977.

Meichenbaum, D. and Turk, L. "The Cognitive-Behavioral Management of Anxiety, Anger and Pain." In P. Davidson (Ed.) *The Behavioral Management of Anxiety, Depression and Pain.* New York: Brunner Mazel, 1976.

Merklingar, A. "Golf Can Be as Simple as This." *Golf Magazine,* 1977, 19 (2), 76–79.

Merrins, E. "Rhythm, Timing and Tempo." *Golf Magazine,* 1979, 21 (4), 37.

Middlecoff, C. "Aim Before You Swing." In T. Michael (Ed.) *Golfer's Digest,* Vol. 3. Chicago: Follett, 1968.

Miller, J. and Shankland, D. *Pure Golf.* Garden City, NY: Doubleday, 1976.

Mills, M. "Playing the Wedge from Grass and Sand." In J. Coyne (Ed.) *The New Golf for Women.* Garden City, NY: Rutledge-Doubleday, 1973.

Moran, S. "Ladies, Daydream Your Way to Lower Scores." *Golf Digest,* 1978, 29 (4), 135–42.

Morrison, A. J. *A New Way to Better Golf.* New York: Simon & Schuster, 1946.

Morrison, A. J. *Better Golf Without Practice.* New York: Simon & Schuster, 1940.

Murphy, M. and White, R. A. *The Psychic Side of Sports.* Reading, MA: Addison-Wesley, 1978.

Nash, A. N., Muczyk, J. P., and Vettori, F. "The Relative Practical Effectiveness of Programmed Instruction." *Personnel Psychology,* 1971, 24, 397–418.

Nelson, B. "Controlling Your Long Irons." In L. Robinson and J. Graham (Eds.) *Golfer's Digest,* Vol. 1. Chicago: Follett, 1966.

Nicklaus, J. "Jack's Playing Lesson 12: Manufacturing Shots by Using Your Imagination." *Golf Digest,* 1978, 29 (5), 128–29.

Nicklaus, J. (In) "What Does a Good Swing Feel Like?" *Golf Magazine,* 1979, 21 (10), 50–53.

Nicklaus, J. and Bowden, K. *Golf My Way.* New York: Simon & Schuster, 1974.

Nicklaus, J. and Wind, H. W. *The Greatest Game of All.* New York: Simon & Schuster, 1969.

Nideffer, R. M. *The Inner Athlete: Mind Plus Muscle for Winning.* New York: Crowell, 1976.

Nieporte, T. and Sauers, D. *Mind Over Golf.* Garden City, NY: Doubleday, 1968.

Novaco, R. *Anger Control: The Development and Evaluation of an Experimental Treatment.* Lexington, MA: 1975.

O'Brien, R. M. "Negative Practice and Desensitization of Anxiety about Examinations." *Psychological Reports,* 1976, 38, 1147–53.

O'Brien, R. M., Cooley, L. E., Ciotti, J., and Henninger, K. M. "Augmentation of Systematic Desensitization of Snake Phobia Through Post-hypnotic Dream Suggestion." *American Journal of Clinical Hypnosis,* in press.

O'Brien, R. M. and Dickinson, A. M. "Contingency Factors in Negative Practice of Smoking." *Psychological Reports,* 1977, 40, 495–505.

O'Brien, R. M., Dickinson, A. M., and Rosow, M. (Eds.) *Industrial Behavior Modification: A Learning Based Approach to Business Management.* New York: Pergamon Press, 1981.

O'Brien, R. M., Kramer, C. E., Chiglinsky, M. A., Stevens, G. E., Nunan, L. J., and Fritzo, J. A. "Moral Development Examined Through Hypnotic and Task Motivated Age-regression." *American Journal of Clinical Hypnosis,* 1977, 19, 209–13.

O'Brien, R. M. and Rabuck, S. J. "A Failure to Hypnotically Produce Nocturnal Emissions." *American Journal of Clinical Hypnosis,* 1977, 19, 182–84.

O'Brien, R. M. and Simek, T. G. *A Comparison of Behavioral and Traditional Methods of Teaching Golf.* Paper presented at the meeting of the American Psychological Association, Toronto, August–September, 1978.

Palmer, A. *My Game and Yours.* New York: Simon & Schuster, 1963.

Parish, M., Lundy, R., and Leibowitz, H. W. "Hypnotic Age Regression and the Magnitudes of the Ponzo and Poggendorf Illusions." *Journal of Abnormal Psychology,* 1969, 74, 693–98.

Perls, F. *In and Out of the Garbage Pail.* Moab, UT: Real People Press, 1969.

Player, G. *Gary Player's Golf Secrets*. Englewood Cliffs, NJ: Prentice-Hall, 1962.

Plimpton, G. *The Bogey Man*. New York: Harper & Row, 1967.

Polin, A. T. "The Effect of Flooding and Physical Suppression as an Anxiety-motivated Avoidance Response." *Journal of Psychology*, 1959, 47, 253–55.

Price, C. "Golf's Fair Lady." *Golf Magazine*, 1977, 19 (7), 63–70.

Rathus, S. A. and Nevid, J. S. *BT/Behavior Therapy: Strategies for Solving Problems in Living*. Garden City, NY: Doubleday, 1977.

Reiff, R. and Scheerer, M. *Memory and Hypnotic Age Regression: Developmental Aspects of Cognitive Function Explored Through Hypnosis*. New York: International Universities Press, 1959.

Richardson, A. "Mental Practice: A Review and Discussion." *Research Quarterly*, 1967, 38, 95–107.

Rimm, D. C. and Masters, J. C. *Behavior Therapy, Techniques and Empirical Findings* (2nd Edition). New York: Academic Press, 1979.

Rodriguez, J. *Chi Chi's Secrets of Power Golf*. New York: Viking, 1967.

Rosburg, B. *The Putter Book*. S. Norwalk, CT: *Golf Digest*, 1963.

Runyan, P. "Make Your Practice Competitive." *Golf Digest*, 1975, 26 (9), 83.

Runyan, P. *Paul Runyan's Book for Senior Golfers*. New York: Dodd Mead, 1962.

Sachs, L. B. and Anderson, W. L. "Modification of Hypnotic Susceptibility." *International Journal of Clinical and Experimental Hypnosis*, 1967, 15, 172–80.

Schapp, D. (Ed.) *Pro, Frank Beard on the Golf Course*. New York: World, 1970.

Schultz, J. and Luthe, W. *Autogenic Training*. New York: Grune & Stratton, 1959.

Scott, T. and Cousins, G. *The Golf Immortals*. New York: Hart, 1969.

Seitz, N. "Harry Pressler, A Great Teacher of Women." *Golf Digest*, 1974, 25 (5).

Simek, T. C. and O'Brien, R. M. "Immediate Auditory Feedback to Improve Putting Quickly." *Perceptual and Motor Skills*, 1978, 47, 1133–34.

Simek, T. C. and O'Brien, R. M. *Feedback and Charting to Improve Golf Skills*. Paper presented at the meeting of the Association for Behavior Analysis. Dearborn, MI, May, 1980.

Simek, T. C., Miller, R., and O'Brien, R. M. *A Comparison of Visualization and Relaxation to Improve Golf Skills*. Paper presented at the meeting of the American Psychological Association, Montreal, September, 1980.

Skinner, B. F. *Science and Human Behavior*. New York: Macmillan, 1953.

Skinner, B. F. *The Technology of Teaching*. New York: Appleton-Century-Crofts, 1968.

Snead, S. "Don't Let the Years Dull Your Swing." *Golf Digest,* 1968, 19 (5), 50.

Snead, S. *Sam Snead on Golf.* Englewood Cliffs, NJ: Prentice-Hall, 1961.

Snead, S. "Sam Snead Talks to Seniors: How to Hit on All Cylinders." *Golf Digest,* 1979, 30 (8), 21.

Snead, S. and Stump, A. *The Education of a Golfer.* New York: Simon & Schuster, 1962.

Sports Illustrated Book of Golf. Philadelphia: Lippincott, 1970.

Stacy, H. "Hollis Stacy's Sand Method." *Golf Digest,* 1979, 30 (7), 110–13.

Staib, A. R. and Logan, D. R. "Hypnotic Stimulation of Breast Growth." *American Journal of Clinical Hypnosis,* 1977, 19, 201–8.

Stampfl, T. G. and Levis, D. J. "Phobic Patients: Treatment with the Learning Theory Approach of Implosive Therapy." *Voices: the Art and Science of Psychotherapy,* 1973, 41, 37–42.

Stephenson, J. "Short Game." *Golf Magazine,* 1979, 21 (1), 55.

Stockton, D. "How to Make Pressure Putts." *Golf Digest,* 1977, 28 (8), 39–43.

Streim, L. *A Comparison of the Relative Efficacies of Negative Practice and Anxiety Management Training in the Treatment of Math Anxiety.* Unpublished doctoral dissertation, Hofstra University, 1979.

Suggs, L. "It's All in Your Head." In F. R. Sammis (Ed.) *Golf for Women.* Garden City, NY: Rutledge-Doubleday, 1960.

Suggs, L. *Par Golf for Women.* New York: Prentice-Hall, 1953.

Suinn, R. M. "Behavioral Methods at the Winter Olympic Games." *Behavior Therapy,* 1977, 8, 283–84.

Suinn, R. M. "Removing Emotional Obstacles to Learning and Performance by Visuo-motor Rehearsal." *Behavior Therapy,* 1972, 3, 308–10.

Suinn, R. M. and Richardson, F. "Anxiety Management Training: A Nonspecific Behavior Therapy Program for Anxiety Control." *Behavior Therapy,* 1971, 4, 498–511.

Tolhurst, D. "A Complete Guide to the Mind." *Golf Magazine,* 1979, 21 (2), 223, 246.

Tolhurst, D. "Can Hypnosis Help Your Game?" *Golf Magazine,* 1978, 20 (12), 46–47, 90.

Toski, B. *Beginner's Guide to Golf.* New York: Grosset & Dunlap, 1955.

Toski, B. *The Touch System for Better Golf.* Norwalk, CT: *Golf Digest,* 1971.

Toski, B. "How You Should Teach Your Child to Play Golf." *Golf Digest,* 1974, 25 (5).

Toski, B. (In) "How to Practice Like a Pro." *Golf Digest,* 1978, 29 (3), 50–58.

Toski, B. and Flick, J. *How to Become a Complete Golfer.* Norwalk, CT: *Golf Digest,* 1978.

Udolf, R. *Handbook of Hypnosis for Professionals*. New York: Van Nostrand Rhinhold, 1980.

Vardon, H. *How to Play Golf*. Turbotville, PA: Macrae-Smith, 1912.

Wadkins, L. "Lanny Wadkins Talks to Juniors." *Golf Digest,* 1973, 24 (2).

Wakeman, G. A. "Query on 'A revision of the fundamental law of habit formation.' " *Science,* 1928, 68, 135–36.

Washburn, M. F. *Movement and Mental Imagery*. Boston: Houghton, 1916.

Watson, T. "Are You Still Afraid of the Long Irons?" *Golf Magazine,* 1975, 17 (5), 50–53.

Watson, T. "Painless Practice." *Golf Magazine,* 1977, 19 (4), 78–80.

Wehrman, L. "Start Kids Putting." *Golf Digest,* 1965, 16 (3), 42–45.

Weiskopf, T. "Tom Weiskopf Tells You How to Sting Your Long Irons." *Golf Digest,* 1973, 24 (9), 38–40.

Weitzenhoffer, E. M. and Hilgard, E. R. *Stanford Hypnotic Susceptibility Scale: Forms A and B*. Palo Alto, CA: Consulting Psychologists Press, 1959.

Wells, S. F. "Improve Your Swing Without Swinging." *Golf Digest,* 1962, 13 (12), 24–28.

Whitworth, K. "From Tee to Green." In J. Coyne (Ed.) *The New Golf for Women*. Garden City, NY: Rutledge-Doubleday, 1973.

Williams, E. and Sheehan, L. *How to Hit the Golf Ball Farther than You Ever Thought Possible*. Norwalk, CT: *Golf Digest,* 1979.

Williams, J. E. "Stimulation of Breast Growth by Hypnosis." *Journal of Sex Research,* 1974, 10, 316–26.

Wiren, G., Coop, R., and Sheehan, L. *The New Golf Mind*. Norwalk, CT: *Golf Digest,* 1978.

Wolpe, J. *Psychotherapy by Reciprocal Inhibition*. Stanford, CA: Stanford University, 1958.

Wolpe, J. *The Practice of Behavior Therapy*. New York: Pergamon Press, 1969.

Wood, S. "Hypnosis, a Cure for Your Golfing Yips?" *Golf Digest,* 1963, 14 (10), 50–54.

Wright, M. *Play Golf the Wright Way*. Garden City, NY: Doubleday, 1962.

Wright, M. "Who Says You Can't Get More Power Off the Tee." In L. Robinson and J. Graham (Eds.) *Golfer's Digest,* Vol. 1. Chicago: Follett, 1966.

Yates, A. J. "The Application of Learning Theory to the Treatment of Tics." *Journal of Abnormal and Social Psychology,* 1958, 56, 175–82.

Index